SAGE was founded in 1965 by Sara Miller McCune to support the dissemination of usable knowledge by publishing innovative and high-quality research and teaching content. Today, we publish over 900 journals, including those of more than 400 learned societies, more than 800 new books per year, and a growing range of library products including archives, data, case studies, reports, and video. SAGE remains majority-owned by our founder, and after Sara's lifetime will become owned by a charitable trust that secures our continued independence.

Los Angeles | London | New Delhi | Singapore | Washington DC | Melbourne

ALT-RIGHT MOVEMENT

ALT-RIGHT MOVEMENT

DISSECTING RACISM, PATRIARCHY AND ANTI-IMMIGRANT XENOPHOBIA

IPSITA CHATTERJEE

$\circledS$SAGE

Los Angeles | London | New Delhi
Singapore | Washington DC | Melbourne

First published in 2021 by

 SAGE Publications India Pvt Ltd
B1/I-1 Mohan Cooperative Industrial Area
Mathura Road, New Delhi 110 044, India
www.sagepub.in

SAGE Publications Inc
2455 Teller Road
Thousand Oaks, California 91320, USA

SAGE Publications Ltd
1 Oliver's Yard, 55 City Road
London EC1Y 1SP, United Kingdom

SAGE Publications Asia-Pacific Pte Ltd
18 Cross Street #10-10/11/12
China Square Central
Singapore 048423

Published by Vivek Mehra for SAGE Publications India Pvt Ltd, typeset in 10/12.5 pt ITC Stone Serif by AG Infographics, Delhi.

Library of Congress Control Number: 2021933398

ISBN: 978-93-5388-789-6 (HB)

SAGE Team: Rajesh Dey, Shipra Pant, Shivani A. Damle and Anupama Krishnan

In protest of George Floyd's murder (2020) and the oppression of marginalized people all over the world...

*For Nadia and Nesar,
who are living memories of Baba and Papa and here is hoping that they will fight for a just world in their own ways.*

Thank you for choosing a SAGE product!
If you have any comment, observation or feedback,
I would like to personally hear from you.

Please write to me at **contactceo@sagepub.in**

Vivek Mehra, Managing Director and CEO, SAGE India.

Contents

instance, it became clear to me that there were distinct clubs—philosopher-editor types, like Spencer, Bannon, Molyneux, Greg Johnson; misogynist/antifeminists like, Gavin McInnes and the Proud Boys club; the 'traditional wives' or as they are known within the Alt-right as 'trad wives' like Lana Lokteff and Ayla Stewart; the Islamophobes like Pamela Geller and the racists like all of them. All these groups use the electronic media extensively as the fora for their activism, outreach, recruitment of the middle-class White youth (both men and women), often through hyperbole, stylized videos, aggressive fear-mongering and incitement of nostalgia for a lost civilization. The rhetoric is colourful, openly hateful, sometimes drawing inspiration from the leftist high ideals of communism, often philosophically drawing from Evola, Nietzsche, Heidegger and de Benoist's European Identitarian movement. At other times, it involves ideo-entertainment, that is ideology fostered through talk shows and chat sessions. The surreal combination of theory and strategy, ideology and manifesto, and the production of what constitutes in the Alt-right's vision, 'the West' and 'the rest', the 'White man' and its 'other' is an insidiously creative recipe for movement building. Judging by the viewings, comments, following and number of people who pledge allegiance, and others who claim to be radicalized, the business of right-wing populism seem to be very successful. It is in that context, I decided to conceptualize this book as a sort of un-peeling of the layers that make the Alt-right. The purpose here is not to provide a temporal history of the Alt-right's emergence and its activities in time and space, but rather to explore who they are and how they crystalize into the 'who' and the 'they', how they coalesce into a nebulous identity category called 'Whiteness', who they draw inspiration from, and what aspect of these philosophies they find appealing and why. How then, after being inspired and hardened as the 'White men' of the 'West' do they then identify women, migrants and Muslims as their ideological other. Largest part of the book is an exploration of the 'other' through the Alt-right lens—a sort of a fascinating journey extrapolated from the 'right-wing' rabbit hole from cyber space, which we are unlikely to visit as liberals and leftists.

This book, therefore, forces us, that is, women and men who don't identify as Alt-right (the Alt-right refers to these men as 'unmanly men in skinny jeans') people of colour, migrants and Muslims to see ourselves as a kaleidoscopic template of the Alt-right's other. 'Reading' ourselves through Alt-right speak is an outer-body experience but a necessary one because it allows us to understand the ideo-epistemological terrains of a politics and movement that we often easily dismiss as crazy or fringe. But the fringe defines us by not only carving a niche in the cyber world but also defining electoral politics in power-ful parts of the world. It is imperative, therefore, that we study their world view and definition really well if we are to be an 'alt' to the Alt-right. The biggest and, I think, by far the most interesting claim this book makes is that while the Alt-right attacks liberal philosophy of multiculturalism and affirmation of diversity, yet it constructs an inverted form of multicultural-ism that is based on the affirmation of White majority identity and a fervent claim for recognition of 'Whiteness' as diverse in itself. Through the various chapters that follow, I hope to demonstrate that the failure to attempt a class analysis of neoliberalism-induced poverty, inequality and unemployment causes both liberal philosophy and the Alt-right to be stuck in a quagmire of identity affirmation—progressive affirmation for liberals and regressive affirmation for the Alt-right. And that is why liberal philosophy and Alt-right's ideo-epistemological praxis remain conjoined rather than becoming a probing critique of each other. This book makes a bold claim that what makes acceptable differences distinct from unacceptable differences (patriarchy, racism, elitism) is the gory history of exploitation, which produced the very inequalities that we contend with in the present. The hegemon that unleashed the violence of inequality cannot claim acceptability at any stage of history and at any site in geography; there is nothing fluid, porous or contingent about that. Liberal philosophy based on individual freedom fails to unequivocally make this distinction clear because, in essence, it does not want to disrupt the status quo (class, gender, racial). If happiness is contingent on the accumulation and preservation of private property, then such a society assumes that accumulation on class, racial and patriarchal lines is something that is inevitable. Liberalism, therefore, agrees that concentration of happiness (possessions, wealth, private property) is something the state should not police or disrupt; instead, the liberal state can affirm (multiculturalism) some unequal groups that have entered realms of acceptability. Individual freedom, therefore, provides solid ethical underpinnings to movements like Alt-right based on religious, racial and patriarchal hegemony because it never threatens to dismantle the history–geography of inequality produced by these hegemonic positions. Whether the Alt-right realizes it or not, it is the golden child of liberal individualism.

Acknowledgements

I started writing this book in a pre-COVID world, and as COVID swept over the world and shook from the very foundations, what individuals, communities, societies and institutions had assumed as normal, we all became aware that there will be, henceforth a different normal—a post-COVID normal. This book provided that continuous thread of normalcy for me as everything we knew as solid and firm slowly dissolved. Just about two days before the lockdown was declared over spring break and the University of North Texas suspended face-to-face teaching, my father (baba) passed away. He did not know that I had started writing another book. Books have always been an important part of his life. I grew up watching piles around him; he would read in every spare minute he had, and in some moments he would quote from memory a wonderful proverb, phrase or idiom that aptly described 'the situation'; those were life-defining moments for me. I often try to rethink and remember some of his oft-repeated sayings, or rather try to reconstruct and re-imagine how he would 'explain' or 'declare' the current situation. He wrote and published some fiction, and I know that in his heart he always wanted me to engage in writing, I felt his guiding hands as I ploughed through this book.

Post-COVID world and the humbling reality that unfolded, pushed me further—schools were closed, and kids were home, needing a lot of time and attention to keep up with their online schoolwork and other antics. There were moments when it felt like it would be impossible go write a paragraph, let alone a page or a book, but baba pushed me. The importance of family, community, school, teachers, day care workers, healthcare workers and working people in general, was reinforced in profound ways as social distancing was enforced. COVID held a mirror to our souls forcing us to reflect on how little time we spent together as family, how little patience do our kids get from us and how little attention we pay to the contributions of underpaid women like school teachers, day care workers, office staff and nurses. Millions of poor in India walked for thousands of miles to get back to their villages as lockdowns suddenly shut public transport—how unimportant was my book writing and my personal struggles compared to all this? And yet, it was important because struggles, however big or small, are important, they define us and how we see our reality, they help us grow if we are able to embrace them right and embrace them tight. The need for human contact and larger community was urgent in the midst of social distancing. Ideologies of hate and exclusion like the Alt-right fragment reality and create superficial communities, COVID and baba renewed my aspirations for struggle: my kind of struggle, the intellectual kind that critiques fragmentation, individualism, materialism and exclusionism, I felt renewed and ready. I plunged into this book project with vigour. Most mornings, I woke up well before the kids to finish this book bit by bit—once they were up, they would want me to play with them. Nadia (nine years old) and Nesar (four years) would wake up after, and Nesar would come running to the office, keen to understand what I was doing, or show me a toy; these distractions forced me to pause, but I had started looking forward to these pauses for they provided a renewed perspective. Nadia once saw books piled on my desk and asked with wonder, 'Have you read all of these?' Kids hardly read actual books these days! When I said that I had, she was alarmed and asked if I would want her to read so many books as well. It is important that kids understand the toils of intellectual struggles and their power to change the world, because kids already possess within them the ability to intellectualize and share love and coexistence in a way the grown-ups have long forgotten.

I could not visit my mother after my father's passing with all the airline closures and quarantines, I was amazed at the strength and composure with which Ma bore baba's death, her friend of over 50 years! Ma's strength, fortitude and constant encouragement for intellectual accomplishments live within me and I can't wait to see her smile as I surprise her with a copy of this book. I am grateful for my brother and sister-in-law, who are my dear friends, and my niece, who is becoming an accomplished writer herself, for being with Ma in her trying times, while I could only offer solace from a great distance.

I would probably never write anything if I did not share my life with Waquar; his social consciousness, his empathy for the oppressed, his strong sense of injustice give me a new perspective on everything, every day. As I wake up every morning, Waquar has already read in detail everything about the world and whatever is wrong within it—whatever exploitation, whatever injustice and whatever oppression that has materialized since the day before—Waquar has a perspective on it already. With great gusto every day, Waquar tells me everything that is wrong about the world and how we can make it right and asks my opinion about all these issues that he considers important. Even before I have had my morning coffee, I have the privilege to be inspired by the most compassionate intellectual in the world—it is like an adrenalin shot to my brain! I am thankful for this precious person, and I am grateful for my family—they are part of this book.

Dick Peet, my friend, mentor, and father figure is the brightest star in my intellectual firmament. He was in a medically induced coma in January of 2018 for over a week, and when he came back, he came back strong, took a couple of months only to recover (after an invasive heart surgery), and plunged into intellectual struggles, small and big—finding money to give grants to graduate students, trying to stretch the budget so more people could be helped. Dick's painstaking efforts for intellectual grunt work such as copyediting and editing the journal of *Human Geography* from noting and putting in intense labour through the night for many nights so that money could be saved and more students can be helped, is inspiring! Most intellectual heavyweights quit investing in the community once they become famous, not Dick, never Dick. Dick has always worked towards building an intellectual community, he inspires every intellectual struggle I undertake.

As I was polishing up this 'Acknowledgements', I received an email from Phil O'Keefe who is among the first tribe of radical geographers. He is Dick's friend from England, and therefore, our friend and mentor. His email said, 'I have been diagnosed with incurable cancer and it looks like a pretty swift end. I received the news last week. Don't worry. All is beautiful here as I prepare for my death.' Fond memories of the American Association of Geographers conference flooded me, some of the best moments in the conferences over the years would be sitting around chatting with Dick, Phil, Ed Soja, Neil Smith drinking beer and sharing meals—Phil insisted on ordering Indian food for us, he was 'an expert'. I emailed back: 'Dear Comrade O'Keefe, I just want to send you what we say in India, 'laal salaam' (red salute!). Comrades don't die! They never die because they represent hope and joy. And hope and joy never end in this world, that is why we stare at death and laugh at its face!' He said that he printed this in bold and put it up in his room and that it was like poetry. Dear Phil, thank you for the courage and laughter, inspiration and joy; you are the very spirit of what this book embodies—intellectual struggle that melts into hope. Phil O'Keefe passed away as I put finishing touches to this book.

My gratitude to Dr Butola, my mentor from India, and one of the most brilliant men I know. Dr Butola and I had many interesting discussions on 'individual liberalism' and 'possessive individualism' that forms the substance of Chapter 2. Dr Butola is a travelling library and can rattle off at least 20 references for any topic under the sun! He set me off in the right path with the right references at a time when this book was just an idea.

My students are my soul tribe, I merely echo what we seek together as a community, knowledge—thank you Richard Kirk, Samantha Espinoza, Hilary Anshah, Anna Baker, Sean Hickey and all undergraduate students, I love you! My friends bring me so much joy, positivity, sense of root and belonging that I would indeed be unstable, completely incapable of anything constructive if I did not see their smiling faces, hear their comforting voices, their encouragement and faith in me. Thank you Chetan, Aparna, Paul and Pinliang for being such supportive friends and colleagues, I always feel surrounded by your kindness and support. Michelle and Keshia, you rock! Thank you Jayson and Liliana, Deb and Amalia (and your kids), Steve, Daniel, Jude—the whole Clark-Castle street gang! Raju Das, Bikram, Ginu and Suvarna Reji, comrades, thank you for being in my life. Although many miles away, I always feel your presence in my heart. My school friends of many years have travelled a long road with me, they are my soul-family; I miss you Sumana, Raja, Abira, Sudipta, Sangita, Arpita, Meenakshi, Baisakhi, I love you and marvel at the small contexts of our coexistence that you still remember in such great detail.

My gratitude to the College of Liberal Arts and Social Sciences, University of North Texas for granting me a research leave in the fall of 2019 that helped jumpstart this book.

Introduction

Contemporary Alt-right movements combine Islamophobia, misogyny, racism, anti-migrant xenophobia into ideologies of 'othering', hatred and apartness that manifest in cyber-spheres and in everyday lives in cities and geographies in the USA. This book explores the Alt-right in the USA to understand how the Alt-right movement views its own identity, what kind of identity violations it claims to address? Who they identify as 'others'? And what are their strategies towards these 'others'? Richard Spencer, the most well-known among the White supremacist who coined the term 'Alt-right', draws inspiration from the left; he claims that the White American youth (mainly men) are stagnating under the hypnosis of Netflix, while White civilization crumbles around the weight of Hispanic and Muslim immigration. Spencer argues that the average White man needs a struggle, a high ideal, a motivating zeal that is larger than life. For Spencer, the left has an aspiration, a uto-pian desire for a communist society, which may or may not be achievable in one's lifetime but is important for consolidating a struggle for something more than the mundane desires for happiness. Mike Enoch, a White supremacist blogger, calls the Alt-right 'a right-wing worker's movement' (Mohdin 2018). Although, primarily, internet-based using stylized videos on YouTube, blogging internet-based channels and online journals

(*Occidental Observer, Counter Currents*) as their fora, the suave among the Alt-right leaders like Spencer and Yiannopoulos regularly give television and radio interviews and paid talks in university campuses across the globe. Although primarily internet-based, middle class and White male youth oriented, the outreach aspect of the Alt-right is prominent, and hence, the importance of provocative, colourful language and concepts that can shake the 'men' out of their comfort-induced stupor and extoll them out of man-caves for a 'greater cause'. Although the term 'Alt-right' was coined by Richard Spencer who started an internet-based magazine of the same name, the Alt-right has become an umbrella for loosely defined identity movements that coalesce around White identity, White supremacy and Western chauvinism. Spencer's version of the Alt-right puts out a philosophical flair frequently drawing from Nietzsche, Evola, de Benoist and European Identitarian politics to produce an ideology of Whiteness that has, according to him, a spiritual–material essence that is distinct. The spiritual essence of the White man is, according to Spencer, the passionate penchant for colonizing, conquering, voyaging and building civiliza-tions (like the European civilization) that is now buried in the couches and beers in the suburban homes of disgruntled youth who see no opportunity and nothing to aspire for. The mate-rial aspects of Alt-right's strategy are based on recreating that civilization into an exclusively White 'ethno-state', very much like Zionism and its realized aspiration in the state of Israel. Others like Yiannopoulos and David Duke of the Proud Boys club build up the Western male identity by concerting their attack on feminism as a false ideology and as a coping mecha-nism for fat, ugly women who want to hide their sexual failures. Irrespective of their interpersonal rivalries, fragmentation and dislike for each other and whether they self-identify within the banner of the Alt-right or not, they have in common a desire for formulating a White-male identity consciousness, they have a common desire to maintain the patriarchal status quo at home and beyond and, hence, virulently attack feminism, often blithely interchanging the term 'women' with 'feminists'. The Proud Boys club disclaims statistics on sexual assault of women in colleges and that women earn less than men for the same jobs. These groups also share in common a deep-seated hatred for Black and Brown people, non-White immigrants and Muslims, and an admiration for President Trump and Trump populism (Spencer 2015a; Yiannopoulos 2017). Trump era politics is seen as bolstering the White male consciousness with its unapologetically 'real' vocabulary in proudly differentiating between White civilizations and 'shit hole countries', between strong men and women and between meaningful conservatism that focuses on White national consciousness, rather than, neoliberal capitalism, and bringing democracy to the world (establishment conservatives and Bush era neoconservatives). As such, the geopolitics of anti-immigration, wall building and Muslim ban is seen by the Alt-right as an extension of the strong male patriarchal proclivities to save its women and civilization. Race is an important component of the Alt-right's identity coalescence; the Alt-right is openly racist, and has made racism fashionable by virulently attacking liberal politics of multiculturalism and diversity as 'White genocide' (Stern 2019). Spencer claimed this has contributed nothing to global history (*Guardian* 2017b). Greg Johnson (2017), the editor of *Counter Current*, commented that 'America would be a better place with no Blacks or Mexicans or Muslims' and 'White standards like walking on the sidewalk, not down the middle of the street, are oppressive to Blacks.' Stefan Molyneux (2019a), who runs a philosophy channel on YouTube—Freedomain—claims that there is no Shakespeare coming out of Sub-Saharan Africa, not because they 'are lazy, or bad, or lack moral qualities', it is their ethno-racial IQ (intelligence quotient) on average, implying that it is just an empirical fact that this average is lower than the Anglo-Saxon race. The Alt-right movement, therefore, has loosely combined anti-feminism, Islamophobia and anti-immigrant xenophobia into an overarching template of Western chauvinism that positions these 'others' (women, Muslims and migrants) as antithetical to the American way of life. With the Syrian refugee crisis and increase in volume of migrants and asylum seekers in different European countries, there has been a parallel rise of anti-Muslim hysteria and Muslim hate groups in Europe. Some of these groups have corresponding chapters across the Atlantic forging an American–European hate alliance. Similarly, feminism is viewed as a redundant ideology that attacks the traditional family structure.

In the backdrop of these identity contestations, it becomes imperative for academics interested in social justice to understand why and how hate is produced and nurtured. A systematic insight into the Alt-right way of life is urgent and timely as it can advance understandings on what coexistence would mean in a fast-globalizing world. The nurturing of hatred, I am arguing, is a conscious conceptual act that is fought on cyberspace but spills out into social life as the real and virtual spaces are almost seamless in today's world. The conceptual struggle crystalizes into certain conceptual fetishisms like 'White race', 'West', 'European civilization', 'ethno-space', 'White genocide', 'IQ tests' and conceptual aversions like 'feminists', 'Muslims', 'Mexicans', 'diversity' and 'multiculturalism'. While there are material dimensions to these concepts in terms of electoral politics, hate crimes, vitriol on social media and Charlottesville (BBC 2017) where one person was killed in skirmishes over Alt-right demonstrations, tracing the philosophical underpinnings and ideological attraction is equally important because acting and thinking, living and existing are imbricated. This book sets out to excavate that imbrication, that is, why they are what they are. In other words, it attempts to understand the philosophical–conceptual dimensions of how the Alt-right consciously identifies itself within Evola's 'spiritual man' (Hakl 2012), Nietzsche's (2018) 'powerful elite individuals', Heidegger's (1962) 'Being' that transcends the stupefying dullness of death at every moment and endorsing of de Benoist's (2012) 'right to European purity'. I also make an argument in this book that although the Alt-right identity is conceptually averse to liberal politics of individual freedom, multiculturalism and celebration of diversity (Tribute to Youth for Western Civilization 2009), unconsciously, it fits right into the liberal philosophy of individual freedom. Following Bentham, Mill, Smith, I argue that the central thesis of liberal morality is the self-interested rational man that pursues happiness within capitalism through competitive accumulation of stuff (objects, commodities, private property). Deep seated within the unequal history–geography of capitalism, the self-interested individual derives his identity as a productive, efficient being by negotiating the inequalities/disadvantages he has been placed within. Liberal society does not interrogate political–economic inequality, but claims that within universal concepts of freedom of opportunity, a hardworking individual can raise himself in life and identify with success/happiness and, hence gain affirmation. Any historical–geographical inequality based on race and ethnicity is 'recognized' (Fraser 1995) within the multiculturalist paradigm of diversity as strength—multiculturalism is the systemic affirmation for historical–geographical wrongs (slavery, genocide, colonization, displacement). Therefore, individual liberalism recognizes identity devaluation and creates a mosaic of 'acceptable' identities that need to be valourized, but beyond small diversity quotas, the society-system does not accept the onus of rectifying economic injustices that produce gaping inequalities of class, racial and gendered poverty. Therefore, class–communitarian injustices wreaked by a class–community of oppressors on another class–community of oppressed is not systemically addressed because this would mean setting systemic goals for emancipation rather than putting the onus of freedom on the individual. The Alt-right critiques the race–cultural affirmative aspects of individual liberalism, but plays an inverted multiculturalist identity politics that bases its existence on the affirmation of White identity. While liberal multiculturalism clamours for identity valourization of the identity minority, Alt-right proclaims identity marginality of the White majority; both seek cultural affirmation without addressing the economic conditions of oppression that produce marginalization. This is a dangerous mistake because without conceptual 'identification' of the oppressor as a class–community that steals, colonizes, displaces, enslaves and exploits, thus laying the template of inequality and oppression within which class–identity oppression manifests, the distinction between 'acceptable' differences and 'unacceptable' differences disappear. Therefore, the descendant of a White slave owner's identity tied to a confederal statue becomes as much an 'acceptable' quest for individual freedom as the descendant of a Black slave deprived of life and living. But the most important point that I want to make in this book is that while the Alt-right critiques the core principles of modern liberal philosophy, individual freedom based on self-interest, it is actually a product of the same. The Alt-right represents the virulent pursuit of individual self-interest, that is, the maximization of individual's freedom to pursue happiness through the establishment of the 'White male self' as the dominant race/gender that accumulates private property and profit. This conceptual excavation is the underlying thread of the book that then goes on to explicate how this White male self is juxtaposed against women expressed as anti-feminism (Chapter 4), against Muslims as Islamophobia (Chapter 5) and against migrants as anti-immigrant xenophobia (Chapter 6). The second chapter lays out the foundation on individual liberalism and indicates the philosophical umbilical cord that ties the Alt-right with liberalism. The third chapter explores the philosophical gurus of the Alt-right to demonstrate how contemporary hate groups, although reactionary, are often the results of intellectual sedimentation of a narcissistic ego-self expressed through the philosophy of man–patriarchy, individualism–selfishness, West–colonialism, and Christian–civilizing. In the next section, I briefly summarize the contents of the next few chapters.

In Chapter 2 titled 'Individual Freedom, Liberal Politics and the Production of Alt-right', I examine individualism, individualism's transition to liberalism, individualism's relation to family and society and individualism's intersection with the Alt-right. Following Bentham (1996), Mill (1966, 2010) and Smith (1999), I demonstrate that individual liberalism's central concept 'self-interest' is utilitarian where utility refers to the ability of an object to promote pleasure and happiness. Happiness is the experience of pleasure and the absence of pain. Therefore, pleasure and freedom from pain are the only things desirable as ends. All desirable things are desirable because there is pleasure inherent in them or they are a means to promote pleasure (Bentham 1996; Mill 1966; Mill 2010). To be an individual is to be an owner of one's own capacities and what one acquires through the use of those capacities. The stuff that is acquired is understood as private property, which are commodities that are inherently pleasurable. Much later, Ayn Rand (1964, 28) made a career out of individual liberalism that she based on the concept of 'rational self-interest'. Critiquing socialist, moralist, altruistic philosophies that call for the 'greater good', Rand proclaimed that rational selfishness embodied by objectivist-ethics do not require human sacrifices for individual good because rational interests do not clash. Rational self-interest not only applies to the acquisition, possession and consumption of goods that Macpherson (1962) calls 'possessive individualism', but also for love, friendship and respect, which are components of human good. Emotions like love, friendship and respect are, for Rand, 'spiritual payments' given for spiritual pleasure that one human derives from the virtues of another. As opposed to liberal individualism, I argue that Marx analyses society in communal terms understood as 'labour'. For Marx, a society based on private property is based on estrangement (not freedom) of labour from itself and from nature. Labour must sell or objectify her/his labour in order to acquire means of subsistence as she/he does not possess means of production (capital in capitalist societies) and in so doing, she must objectify nature as raw material—the essence of human experiences (species being) is then reduced to production–consumption (of private property). This reduction, according to Marx, is restrictive, alienating, causing estrangement and objectification, and is by no means emancipatory.

Emancipation or freedom for Marx would be emancipation of society from private property (from objectification, alienation and estrangement) and that would involve emancipation of labour. On the other hand, within liberal morality, the concept of freedom is negative, that is, it is 'freedom from' rather than 'freedom to'. Freedom is a state of being in which one is *not* restricted, *not* compelled, *not* interfered with (Arblaster 1984; Hobbes 1980). The state is seen as a primary institution of restriction, interreference and compulsion, therefore, the liberals have always obsessed about the freedom from control by the state. The repulsion towards the state is a characteristic that liberals share with Marxists, but Marxists critique the state as an ideological apparatus of class rule. Unlike Marxism, which is about explicating how theft of labour leads to the class accumulation of private property and a class-estrangement from the fruits of its own labour, liberal philosophy never questions the socio-economic structures that underlie merit/ingenuity/innovation like access to education, access to know-how, or access to cultural capital. The fact that the poor are poor not because merit is a biological condition that they do not possess but, rather, a direct result of entrapment in zip-codes with neglected schools, libraries, and computers is ignored by liberal philosophy.

In liberal capitalist societies, in the absence of conceptual and policy critique of inequality, difference (identity) becomes the site for grievance, recognition of grievance, affirmation of grievance and consolidation of social solidarity. Butler argues that not all difference is acceptable (Butler et al. 1997). There is, therefore, a need to ascertain the 'acceptable' differences from the 'unacceptable' differences and, also, along with it, unpack the concept of 'equality', because the acceptable differences must be valourized by a liberal democratic society or, in other words, the acceptable differences must be treated equally in order for the individual grounded within an acceptable lattice of identities to feel free to pursue happiness. Critiquing individual liberalism, I argue that multiculturalism has become a superficial and synthetic celebration of the 'cultural man' (the individual) while, simultaneously, dismissing the gory histories and geographies of inequality, poverty, colonialism produced by the pursuit of individualism. The hegemon that unleashed the violence of inequality cannot claim acceptability at any stage of history and at any site in geography, there is nothing fluid, porous or contingent about that. Culture and diversity without the historical–geographical context of their production is a meaningless abstraction. Liberal individualism wilfully abstracts cultural identity, so that it can become an unconfrontational container box for the lattice of exclusion hidden under identity politics.

The Alt-right movement reimagines the world as one where the identity of the West is supreme, but this 'identification' of the West is also based on a very particular imaginary of the 'West'. This particular imaginary is one that is not based on abstract principles of individual freedom but on a White, ethno-specific supremacy. In this way, the contemporary Alt-right movement shares an interesting tension with Western liberal capitalism. It is an interesting tension because, by self-proclamation, the Alt-right is a critique of liberalism and all that it stands for—multiculturalism, women's rights and pro-immigration. The Alt-right is, simultaneously, also against mainstream conservatism and what it represents—Cold War style anti-communism, anti-environmentalism and narrow focus on economics. The Alt-right criticizes what they view as 'meaningless abstractions' of liberal polity like freedom, liberty, spread of democracy, individual freedom and citizenship. The Alt-right's critique, however, is not positioned in alliance with the poor (class) who lack the freedom to pursue happiness in terms of access to education, healthcare and jobs. Instead, the Alt-right's critique emerges from an 'individual' that is emplaced in an identity lattice of Whiteness, maleness, Christianness, Americanness, Europeanness, or what they view as the specific ethno-racial compound that marks the 'West'. The Alt-right returns us to a model of ethno-nationalism and misogyny that the 'modern' concept of the 'secular nation' of the 19th and 20th century was supposed to eradicate (Anderson 1983; Gellner 1983; Hobsbawm 1990). In being antiquated in its situated identity politics, it is simultaneously suave having strong online presence and represented by articulate young men with college degrees and good jobs. Individual freedom, therefore, provides solid ethical underpinnings to movements like Alt-right based on religious, racial, patriarchal hegemony because it never threatens to dismantle the history–geography of inequality produced by these hegemonic positions. Whether the Alt-right realizes it or not, it is very much a product of liberal individualism.

In Chapter 3 titled 'Heidegger, Nietzsche and the Alt-right Philosophy', I argue that how we think about our actions and how our actions create thought are not easily separated. Therefore, philosophy and praxis are never separate. In other words, why we identify with something and not others, why and where we draw boundaries between us and the other are not arbitrary acts. In critically examining the Alt-right, it may seem that their ideological body politic is quite simple—identity surrounding White male chauvinism. Why does Alt-right's identification of maleness intersect with Whiteness though? What makes White male chauvinists distinguish themselves from, for example, Muslim men? Why is religion the boundary that separates White males from other males? How do White women enter the fold despite the fact that the movement is openly misogynistic? How is womanhood and gayness creatively negotiated within an overt masculinist ethics? How identities are coalesced, dissected, deconstructed, forged, perforated and represent the philosophical praxis or the ideological body politic. In this chapter, I explore Julius Evola, Alain de Benoist, Heidegger and Nietzsche's influence in Alt-right's philosophical praxis. These philosophers were picked because they were cited or quoted by the Alt-right movement in their blogs, speeches or videos.

Julius Evola, an Italian philosopher, aspired to revive the spiritual soul of the West. Evola called for a spiritual man that was evolved in body and mind. Evola was disenchanted by the mundanity and mechanization of modernity and wanted a spiritual nation that would contest modernity and the degeneration it brought. According to Evola, the attaining of enlightenment or spiritual consciousness by worthy individuals like elites and aristocrats within Western societies will rescue Italy and the West from the degeneration wreaked by modernity and place these societies in the higher path of Tradition. Physical and mental mastery can only be attained by 'superior' men who lead a 'superior' nation that must be protected from inferior men and women, is the kernel of the Evola-influenced Alt-right's body politic. In essence, for Evola, democracy, egalitarianism and materialism are the baser instincts that must be replaced in a spiritual West by the values of Tradition. The Alt-right inspired by Evola believes that the White men of American and European descent are already *higher* and *supreme* beings, and as an elite race they should be allowed to protect their purity. Ethno-purity of the West becomes the higher path of tradition, and hence, the Alt-right demonstrates little interest in the geopolitics of American exceptionalism, spread of democracy or neoliberal capitalism. From Alain de Benoist, the Alt-right borrows the concept of 'ethnopluralism', which is the idea that all ethnic groups have the right to preserve differences/boundaries including the 'strong' ethnicities/identities. Ethnopluralism became the inspiration for the European Identitarian movement, which became a kind of inverted multiculturalism involving the affirmation of dominant identities that are perceived to be under attack, and, therefore, possessing right to remain separate but equal. The Alt-right has ideologically converted Benoist's ethnopluralism into its material manifestation—the demand for a White ethno-state.

The Alt-right's enchantment with Nietzsche (1920, 47) as the 'red-pill' moment (radicalizing moment drawn from Nietzsche's radical call to action against stupefaction by religion (Nietzsche's attack on Christianity). The Alt-right enjoys the fact that Nietzsche claims that humanity has been weakened ('domestic animal') and seduced by the ideologies of modernity that render existence inauthentic. They draw from Nietzsche's idea that happiness rests on the claim to power through terror, the most terrifying being is the most powerful being. Heidegger's claim that, in liberal modernity, we lead an inauthentic existence (*Dasien*) focusing our energies in executing the mediocre, banal, stupefying nothingness of everyday existence has deeply impacted Richard Spencer, who frequently comments on the hypnosis by Netflix and the need to struggle towards a motivating zeal. More contemporary works like Huntington's *Who are We?* enables the Alt-right to create ideological legitimacy for their West-versus-rest paradigm. Huntington's conceptualization of the difference between settlers and immigrants is a keystone aspect of the Alt-right's agenda. America, according to Huntington, is a Judea-Christian-Anglo civilization because the Judea-Christian-Anglo settler *found* America. 'Before immigrants could come to America, settlers had to found America' (Huntington 2004, 40). 'Founding', as opposed to integrating, assimilating and blending, is an act of establishing supremacy by killing and conquering that, ultimately, leads to 'settling'.

Chapter 3 teases out the philosophical underpinnings of the Alt-right's praxis. The words (West, White, higher, civilized, stronger, settler) that the Alt-right choose to frame their ideological body politic (biological racism, cultural racism, White nationalism, Western chauvinism) heavily depends on available templates or distorted world views produced by racist, White men. The Alt-right, following its philosophical gurus, have successfully transmuted 'racism' as a respectable and spiritual ideology. This chapter attempts to demonstrate that this intellectual legitimization is not a chaotic act of a few crazy White men, it is a philosophical praxis or a well-defined strategy.

For the women in the Alt-right movement there are essential socio-biological categories that set women apart from men. Chapter 4 titled 'Alt-right Women and the Reconstruction of Patriarchy and Feminism' discusses how the women of the Alt-right are playing an important role in affirming White male supremacy and self-tiering themselves as soft, emotional, beautiful, family-oriented, homemakers and husband seekers as opposed to men as builders, leaders, providers and protectors (Mattheis 2018). Lana Lokteff who runs Red Ice, an Alt-right media company, posits 'femininity' as an *essential* category that is becoming of women but unbecoming of men. The implication is that 'feminine' men are weak (because women are the weaker sex), and therefore, they pander to weak geopolitics of pro-migration and border porosity. Similarly, endorsement of progressive sexual politics or environmental politics is also seen as left's emasculation bordering on perversion. The Alt-right claims that progressive women are 'loose', devoid of beauty and femininity (ugly and fat) and, hence family values, and, therefore, are compelled by the need to prove their left-oriented sexual politics. Not only is there an attempt to 'fix' gender, where womanhood is equated with traits of beauty, thinness and traditionally familial, but also a sexual narcissism that, simultaneously, disparages women when they don't meet the warped standards of femininity but powerfully 'castrates' masculinity if they happen to be against homophobia. The devotion with which Alt-right women pedestalize phallocentric versions of sexuality in a socially programmed way is the Stockholm syndrome where women wilfully align with her exploiter, the left is seen not as a liberator from oppressive fixed categories like impossible standards of beauty and nurture, but a destabilizing force that distorts womanhood and distorts manhood—ugliness begets ugliness.

Chapter 4 discusses how Lokteff and other women of the Alt-right have self-styled themselves as 'trad wives', short for 'traditional wife', who embody feminine and wifely qualities like submissiveness, chastity, willingness to do household chores and want many children. The trad wives carefully manage their blogs and websites with photos that display themselves in comfortable homes engaged in wifely duties like baking while looking picture-perfect in dresses or skirts. The very essence of feminism, which is about critiquing socially normalized gender roles and expectations like men as rational, women as emotional, men as protectors, bread winners and providers, and women as receivers of provisions and protection, is used and misused in confused yet strategic ways. In Alt-right women's self-directed misogyny, the 'lioness' is strongest when it is sensuously compliant, gracefully non-aggressive and homely. However, what Alt-right's YouTube activism achieves is a selective propagation of the master narratives of White supremacy and patriarchy using Black men and White women as anchors who, by virtue of their racial and gender marginality, turn upside down the very notions of racism and patriarchy. Their endorsement of the structures of oppression create an oppressor–oppressed toxic bond where the latter legitimizes the former even when the former disparages and oppresses the latter. Feminism, viewed through the Alt-right's lens, is an absurd, false ideology, unnatural, entitled and born out of patriarchal graciousness; it is a celebration of ugliness, fatness, political correctness and disruption of the natural biological division of labour that does not respect the power and innovative genius of man. The manosphere (Ging 2019), that is, the spaces of blogs, YouTube, Twitter and Instagram, has become the site for neo-masculinist/White-supremacist assertion. The manosphere serves as an apt site as it requires very little organizing, leg work, intellectual analysis and instead involves a seamless transition from computer games in mancaves and White boy's clubs to the world of perceived emasculation, thus, fuelling misogynistic vitriol against feminist takeover. Academics have indicated correlations between absence of college degree and economic vulnerability, and strong correlations between economic vulnerability and exclusionary politics based on misogyny and anti-immigrant xenophobia (Cohen, Luttig and Rogowski 2016).

In this chapter, I argue that two things make an identity oppressive and, hence, 'unacceptable'—its inability to recognize its own complicity in producing historical–geographical deval-ourization of 'others' (women, people of colour, indigenous groups, colonial subjects) and the arrogant self-valourization based on the devalourization of 'other'. Liberal multicultural-ism is complicit with the first, creating fertile conditions for liberal misogyny to flourish under 'cultural' movements like the Alt-right. While multiculturalism as a progressive praxis may openly critique far-right neo-masculinist movements like the Alt-right as unacceptable, and while the Alt-right itself may denounce 'minority-appeasing' pretentions of multiculturalism, yet it is in the liminality of these contradictions that unaccep-table Identitarian movements like Alt-right find comfortable breeding grounds. The Alt-right's anti-women/anti-feminist stance find comfortable breeding conditions rooted in clas-sical liberal ideas such as man as the rational, competitive individual, man as the individual and women as the familial. In these spaces of contradictions, the Alt-right views feminism as an antithesis to liberal capitalism where feminists revert the acceptable identity of capitalist geography by leaving home (sphere of the familial) and treading into work/politics/governance (sphere of the individual). It is ironic that liberal feminist agenda is exactly just so, dissolving women from their communitarian ethic and producing the workfare woman individual that populates the masculine sphere of work—this may seem contradictory to what the Alt-right wants, yet both Alt-right and liberal feminism (as well as liberal multiculturalism) believe in the production of the efficient individual that realizes its life-potential through workforce competition within capitalism. The difference being liberal feminists want more women to become individuals and Alt-right wants to keep workspaces intact for men. And, therefore, while they push against each other, there remains a narrow space where the core of one's personhood is similarly aligned for neo-masculinist movements, liberal feminists and multiculturalists, and this core is the self-valourization as individuals.

Chapter 5 ('Alt-right and Islamophobia as Disembodiment') demonstrates that Islamophobia presents a multifaceted opportunity for the Alt-right. The fear of Sharia Law, the veil, the immigrant status of Muslims combine to produce a cultural construction of the exotic other. The Muslim is embodied as outside the pale of Western civilization, antithetical to Western values, violent, sexist and homophobic. This construction of the Muslim other runs parallel to the feminist other constructed as fat, ugly, aggressive, abusive, incapable of raising children or having families. In producing (embodying) the Muslim, the Alt-right simultaneously unproduced (disembodies) her/him as an entire culture that must be 'located', 'opposed' and 'cast outside' (Gregory 2003) Western liberal democracy.

Blaut (1992), in his critique of Eurocentricity, has argued how biological racism of the past (measuring skulls to correlate with intelligence, and later on, genetics with IQ testing) transitions to religious racism, that is, biology being equal, some religions are more civilized (better) than others and then, more contemporarily (in a more secular world), into cultural racism, which is the world view that certain cultures are able to promote a modern and better way of life than certain others. Said (1979), Gregory (2003), Mamdani (2004), Abu-Lugodh (2002, 2013) and Bilge (2010), in their deconstruction of orientalism, indicate that the cultural construction of the racial other is more than just an aversion to a certain race, it is a mixture of aversion, confusion, ignorance and exotification of the entire life world of the racial other to create 'imagined geographies' (Said, Gregory), 'culture talk', 'cultural framing' (Abu-Lugodh) and 'feminist orientalism' (Bilge) through an assemblage of racist tropes and missionary zeal where the other's body, mind, private and public worlds are produced and unproduced as an unmodern, unequal, profane, and veiled outside to the 'West'.

Pamela Geller, founder of Stop Islamization of America (SIOA) and co-founder of American Freedom Defense Initiative (AFDI), in her speech reinforces this civilized versus savage narrative: 'In any war between the civilized man and the savage, support the civilized man. Support Israel, defeat Jihad!' (Geller 2012). The AFDI (http://afdi.us) website is replete with mugs, postcards, and T-shirts depicting the cartoonized figure of Mohammad as an angry, turbaned and bearded man saying 'You can't Draw me' to be sold for $50 apiece. A poster depicting Mohammed drawing a self-portrait calls for 'Mohammad art exhibit and cartoon contest.' The same website uses out-of-context and selective verses from the Koran to cast Mohammad as a sexually promiscuous misogynist, a paedophile, a violent man deploying draconian punishments. Gatestone Institute that calls itself a non-partisan think tank and declares its objective to educate the public on what the mainstream media does not report, they document articles on topics such as 'Islamization of France' or 'Muslim persecution of Christians'. Articles quote statistics on how churches are being closed down in Muslim majority countries, or how the Christian population is shrinking in 'Western' nations, and how Muslim fundamentalist clerics are rabble rousing and lynching poor Christian boys (Ibrahim 2018). These news items are listed with dates and places, but with no reference to any source or news organization, which makes it impossible to confirm their credibility.

Using similar examples as discussed before, Chapter 5 explores how the Alt-right's orientalist gaze confers a desirable essence for Western culture where its values embody emancipation and freedom as against Islam's savage essence and its expression—the Sharia. In the paradigm of Alt-right orientalism, Islamophobia does not displace the immigrant's culture, Islamophobia's 'culture talk' disembodies the Muslim but absorbs her culture within the paradigm of multicultural affirmation because everybody likes a bit of kebab, calligraphy and ethnic music. Restricting citizenship, denying asylum, cutting welfare to immigrants (E. H. 2017) disembodies the immigrant, puts her in place, separates her from the 'settler' and creates the Muslim. For the Alt-right and associated groups, the Muslim, very much like the feminists, only exists in reverse templates of villainy that disrupts the stable order of Western liberalism. According to the Alt-right, liberal media pampers multiculturalism to blatantly disregard universalist principles of Western civilization by unduly favouring the Muslim other. What the supreme settler culture avoids deconstructing is that universalism is actually Judea–Christian particularism, multiculturalism is superficial tokenism avoiding systemic overhaul of racism, civilization is a mental construct and the 'West' is an imagination depending on who gets to define what is supreme.

Chapter 6 titled 'White Fetishism, Ethno-space, and Anti-immigrant Xenophobia' explores how the Alt-right frames the migrant-other as opposed to White America. Discourse and policy attitude towards the migrant/racial 'other' is, what Winant (2001) argues, the link between structure and signification, that is, what race means within a set of discursive formation such as immigration policy (this discursive expression is the signification) and its relation to how social structures are organized, for example, access to jobs, nature of education and textbooks, and access to healthcare. I would argue that this link between structure and signification is a problematic and contradictory one. While the structures of free market capitalism, individual liberalism and democracy recognize the profit-seeking modern man that can be labour, an innovator, an investor, a capitalist, racialized imaginations, on the other hand, define a set of discursive formations like immigration policy that casts this very individual as premodern, barbaric, uncivilized, exotic and alien. In the Alt-right imaginary, White nationalism as an identity movement would aim to establish a 'White Nationalist society' based on racial separation, however, demanding racial separation would be a form of 'timid civic nationalism', which will work temporarily. In the long run, racial apartness within the same nation state carries with it the possibilities of 'repeating all the mistakes' such as mixed schools, mixed public spaces, interracial marriages, affirmative action resulting in complacency and profligacy among the White race. Therefore, the timidness of civic nationalism must be overcome to ultimately launch a virulent form of White identity based national movement that restores White settler's status quo by creating a White nation devoid of 'offending' immigrants such as Mexicans and Muslims.

For Richard Spencer, this restoration of White nationalist status quo finds pragmatic expression in the 'ethno-state' as a space carved out of Europe, from Portugal to Vladivostok. The nostalgia for the 'old world', the need to reclaim and preserve 'the White man's history and architecture' is evident when Spencer clarifies that the ethno-state cannot be in the USA, it has to be 'post-USA'. Other possibilities for actualizing the ethno-state includes conquest of spaces within the Western hemisphere and investment in the Third World countries to which immigrants in the USA who have not struck deep roots could go back. Spencer asserts that just like the creation of the ethno-state of Israel as a safe haven for Jewish identity movement was accomplished by the Zionist movement, the aspiration for reviving the spirit of West through a territorial manifestation of Whiteness is a possibility and necessity. The nostalgia for an 'authentic' White, Christian urban/suburban landscape with rows of nice homes, White picket fences, backyard barbecues, Sunday schools is what Spencer's Alt-right evokes as the cultural geography of the ethno-state. What Spencer's Alt-right ideology would not acknowledge is that 'trailer trash', 'mobile home colonies', 'hippie communes', 'redneck hick towns' and 'Hillbilly's honkytonk country side' are as much emblematic of the geography of White America's cultural sensibilities as White, middle-class neighbourhoods with picket fences. Greg Johnson, the editor of Alt-right magazine *Counter-Currents*, similarly, laments that the White man's actions are always dubbed as 'colonialism', 'imperialism', 'genocide' and 'gentrification'. What Johnson omits is the fact that the superimposition of 'nice White neighbourhoods' on Brown civilizations are blind spots on White memory that conveniently forgets that what looks White was never really White. Therefore, the 'timeless Whiteness' of Houston, Dallas and El Paso, for the Alt-right, is tainted by the brownness of the Mexican migrants, but the fact is, under the White patina of conquest, they were always Brown.

The history of the White race contained within nation states that Spencer selectively wishes to construct as the European culture represented in nostalgic White neighbourhoods is a pseudo-analysis of life that wishes to glorify certain class struggles while diminishing and erasing others. Therefore, White European conquest of the Brown and the Black world is supreme and aesthetic, but the Mexican or Latin American migrant's struggle to enter the USA or Syrian refugee's struggle to escape war induced by the 'West' by coming to a safe space in Europe and America is inferior and akin to culture of poverty, garish and exotic. Spencer and Johnson, therefore, represent outdated notions of biological racism updated with a heavy dose of White 'spirit' to create an internet-based ideology in support of a 'new-world', old-style colonialism not based on corporate profit, neoliberalism and World Bank control through structural adjustment, but through the construction of White geographies where spoils of racism can be relished and consumed through the White male pursuit of happiness.

Chapter 6 argues that class analysis of oppression cannot be avoided because if being human means emancipation from oppression, economic as well as cultural, then class eventuates dialectically in contexts of oppression and is not tied to skin colour or cephalic indices. Class analysis would mean that right-wing populism must reconceptualize value (as not racial/ bio-social) and liberal multiculturalism must reconceptualize value (as not profit accumulation), and both must critique systemic contexts that devalue humans as *classes of oppressed*. Anti-immigrant fetish does for the Alt-right what 'diversity' fetish does for liberal multiculturalism; they accord value to the surface of group identities such as Whiteness for the Alt-right and American pluralism for the multiculturalist, while both fail to excavate that value cannot be added unless one takes stock of what we value as a society, who produces this value? How value is accorded in society? How it is distributed? If life's value is lost because of the Hispanicization of Houston and El Paso and the Mexicanization of White, middle-class neighbourhoods and *kebaabification* of backyard barbecues, then the Alt-right must ask itself how it can capture, consolidate and preserve Whiteness in a globalizing world where production and con-sumption, or in other words, the market place that accords justice through demand, supply and price, has gone global? How to depend on Mexican nannies and the El Salvadorian day-caregivers, Honduran maids and Hispanic construction workers while keeping 'Brown culture' out of the ethno-state? If White life is not about the day-to-day mundanity of economic inter-class dependence (on migrant nannies and informal workers) and it is a 'higher' from of cultural ideal based on European cultural consciousness and if culture is White, Western phi-losophy, architecture, literature and cityscapes, how does this cultural artefact, this antiquated crucible, a European revival to be actualized and maintained without a class that must upkeep and maintain it? In concluding Chapter 6, I argue that conceptual fetish (of Whiteness, anti-immigrant xenophobia) has the same allure as Marx's commodity fetish; it commodi-fies Whiteness, Americanness and Europeanness into mythical products of 'metaphysical subtilities' that never existed in the first place. Affirming White identity becomes a system of sig-nification that does not eventuate from material struggles of everyday existence, but has to be artificially evoked through stylized YouTube videos that harnesses the nothingness of Netflix satiation.

In Conclusion, I argue that a social justice praxis grounded in a thorough understanding of the Alt-right movement must demystify the fact that the Alt-right's rationality for a White ethno-state is as much based on unjust identity politics as is individual liberalism's penchant for equal opportunity for unequal groups (classes). Both valourize templates of difference that accept pre-exiting discrimination (race for the Alt-right and class for individual liberalism) as a rational order of life. A radical critique of right populism in general, and Alt-right movement is particular, must intellectually dismantle the very paradigm of rationality that breeds both Alt-right's 'other' and individual liberalism's 'other'.

2

Individual Freedom, Liberal Politics and the Production of Alt-right

Introduction

I want to begin at the very beginning, or at least what many would consider the heart and soul of Western liberal democracy—individual freedom and self-interest. It can be safely said that at least in the American context, irrespective of our politics towards migrants, border porosity, women's reproductive rights, international relations, war, the Middle East—we are unwaveringly entrenched in our deep commitment to individual freedom. The self-labelling of the USA as the leader of the 'free world' crystallized a concept of freedom that has endured since the Cold War days. The Western Bloc ideologically adopted the 'free world' concept to separate themselves from the communist countries, thus starting our love affair with 'freedom' as a concept (Tierney 2017). In 2003, President Bush defended his pre-emptive attack on Iraq as 'operation Iraqi freedom', 'helping Iraqis achieve a united, stable and free country will require our sustained commitment,' and since then we know how the gift of freedom manifested as a lust for occupation (Glass 2017). It is as if Western capitalist societies in general, and the USA, in particular, derive their identity from this core characteristic of individual freedom. For most, individual freedom is co-terminus with democratic form of government—the right of every individual to vote, freedom of self-expression and the right to own private property. Therefore, any analysis of political–economic identity that is embedded in Western capitalism requires a deep exploration into the philosophical DNA of individual freedom.

Individualism, Happiness and Worth

Much of the philosophy of Western liberalism grounds the foundation of society on the individual. Hobbes, for instance, rejects Aristotle's idea that man is a social animal. Instead, Hobbes argues that communal institutions such as government and society are mechanisms established by individuals to represent their self-interest (1980, 1990, 2013). According to Bentham (Bentham 1996; Macpherson 1962), the individual–community contractual relation can be understood as a relationship where the individual is the real entity and the community is simply fictitious existing only to mirror the individual's self-interest.

> The community is a fictitious body, composed of the individual persons who are considered as constituting as it were its members. The interest of the community then is, what?—the sum of the interests of several members who compose it...It is in vain to talk of the interest of the community, without understanding what is the interest of the individual.

> It is in vain to talk of the interest of the community, without understanding what is the interest of the individual. A thing is said to promote the interest, or to be *for* the interest, of an individual, when it tends to add to the sum total of his pleasures: or, what come to the same thing, to diminish the sum total of his pains. (Parekh 2016, 68)

Therefore, self-interest is the only motivation behind individuals entering into social contract to form complex institutions like state or government. The theory of life based on individual self-interest is utilitarian where utility refers to the ability of an object to promote pleasure and happiness. Happiness is the experience of pleasure and the absence of pain. Therefore, pleasure and freedom from pain are the only things desirable as ends. All desirable things are desirable because there is pleasure inherent in them, or they are a means to promote pleasure (Bentham 1996; Mill 1966; Mill 2010). To be an individual is to be an owner of one's own capacities and what one acquires through the use of those capacities. The stuff that is acquired is understood as private property, which are commodities that are inherently pleasurable. Ownership is the essence of individuality and freedom means independence from others, and one is considered to be 'free' from others when she/he is allowed to own and use her/his private property. In other words, there is no freedom, and hence, no individuality to be gained from communal ownership or non-ownership. Therefore, public transport would be an example of restriction of individual freedom as it is a communal ownership of property mediated by other (government)—one is regimented by schedules, speed and routs set by others, and one's use of the modes of transport is not independent of others with whom one must share the seats, aisle and restrooms. A young student that is yet to acquire a home or a car and a homeless person that has neither are lacking individual freedom as their individual capacities are yet un-utilized or are squandered away from the ultimate pursuit of private property. Therefore, the student is yet to 'succeed in life'(student), and the homeless has 'failed to succeed' (homeless). The student must continue to use one's capacities in the individual pursuit of grades and grade point average (GPAs) that is an indicator in liberal capitalism of the promise of success, which means the promise of future ownership of private properties independent of the 'control' of others (neighbours, communities, governments, society). In this view of individual freedom, free time that a homeless person has at his/her disposal or leisure to gaze at the sky or paint a graffiti is not a measure of 'freedom'. Although time is an extremely important element of capitalism, simply put, time is money. David Harvey (1989) claims that capitalism strives for annihilation of space by time. The impediments and friction that space imposes on capital need to be overcome by ever-faster (reduced time) movement of capital (international credit cards, speculation). Yet, 'free' time does not equal to 'freedom' unless invested in the pursuit of private property. Similarly, a student's life is free from the shackles of mortgage payments and car payments, and hence, the ability to 'go nomad' (hiking, camping, international exchange programs) is not 'freedom' because this life represents the absence of private property. Ownership of private property is inherently freeing, even though it means being neck-deep in debt. Of course, the student life in the USA fettered by college loans constitute the irony of 'unfreedom'—the fact that public universities and federal programs alleviate, or promise to alleviate, or can be potentially used to alleviate such unfreedom is not seen as the power of communal ownership to increase freedom and individuality. Rather, it is seen as government reducing the freedom of the rich through higher taxes that would in turn be used to finance student loan subsidies. For example, the Bernie Sanders and Elizabeth Warren presidential campaign promises free college and debt forgiveness of $1.6 trillion in exiting student loan (Sanders) and a tiered loan forgiveness based on income category, that is, $50,000 in loan forgiveness for anyone making less than $100,000 per year (Warren) and no forgiveness for those making more than $250,000 a year (Golshan 2019a; Hazelrigg 2019). Marx (1844) has argued in his critique of capitalism, and Macpherson (Carens 1993) argued in his critique of possessive individualism that a system based on private property inevitably leads to concentration of ownership of means of production that leaves the larger class of society deprived of private property ('means of production' for Marx) and individual freedom (for Macpherson). For Marx, a society based on private property is based on estrangement (not freedom) of labour from itself and from nature. Labour must sell or objectify her/his labour in order to acquire means of subsistence as she/he does not possess means of production (capital in capitalist societies), and in so doing, she/he must objectify nature as raw material—the essence of human experiences (species being) is then reduced to production and consumption (of private property). This reduction, according to Marx, is restrictive, alienating, causing estrangement and objectification, and is by no means emancipatory. Emancipation or freedom, for Marx, would be emancipation of society from private property (from objectification, alienation and estrangement), and that would involve emancipation of workers. The cunning of private property is illustrated by Marx as,

> The 'secret' (that private property was the product of alienated labour) was only revealed at 'the culmination of the development of private property'. It could only be uncovered when private property had completed its domain over Man and became a 'world historical power',…Once private property became a 'world-historical power', every new product meant 'a new potential for mutual swindling and mutual plundering'. The need for money became the only need produced by the economic system and the neediness grew as the power of money increased. Everything was reduced to 'quantitative being.' (Marx and Engels 2002, 133–134)

Freedom contingent on possession and ownership version of liberal democracy obfuscates the objectified, alienated and commodity fetish-based characteristic of liberal society. Liberal capitalist society thrives on class oppression and class exploitation inherent in societies based on private but unequal ownership of property. This version of human nature and society, Macpherson calls, is 'possessive individualism' (1962, 3)—an individualism based on acquisition, possession and consumption, and therefore, a limited and one-dimensional view of human nature and life itself. This impoverished view is captured by Carens (1993) as,

> The possessive view of life distorts the democratic ideal, which Macpherson described as a commitment to 'provide the conditions for the full and free development of

the essential human capacities of all members of society. According to Macpherson, possessive individualism reduces lofty goal to the maximization of utilities.

On the other hand, Ayn Rand (1964, 8) proposes an 'Objectivist ethics' that is based on 'rational selfishness' as opposed to the 'brotherhood of men'. Rational selfishness directly contradicts Marx's emancipation of workers and Macpherson's commitment for full and free development of *all* members of society. This commitment to universal or societal upliftment is, according to Rand, based on irrational whims. For Rand (1964, 27), altruism is 'moral cannibalism' based on the premise that happiness of one member of society is predicated on the injury/sacrifice of another. In the previous context, taxing the rich and subsidizing college loans involves punishing the rich, hence irrational morality imposed by a government will cannibalize rational and productive members of society. Critiquing socialist, moralist, altruistic philosophies that call for the 'greater good', Rand proclaims that rational selfishness embodied by objectivist ethics do not require human sacrifices for individual good because rational interests do not clash. Rational self-interest not only applies to the acquisition, possession and consumption of goods that Macpherson calls 'possessive individualism' but also for love, friendship and respect, which are components of human good. Emotions like love, friendship and respect are, for Rand, 'spiritual payments' given for spiritual pleasure that one human derives from the virtues of another. Therefore, for Rand (1964, 29–30),

> To love is to value. Only a rationally selfish man, a man of *self-esteem*, is capable of love—

> Because he is the only man capable of holding firm, consistent, uncompromising, unbetrayed values. The man who does not value himself, cannot value anything or anyone.

> It is only on the basis of rational selfishness—on the basis of justice—that men can be fit to live together in a free, peaceful, prosperous, benevolent, *rational* society. (emphasis in the original)

Rand's *The Virtue of Selfishness* (1964) from which the afore-mentioned excerpt is drawn and, in general, her body of work constructs selfishness as the basis of individual identity and freedom. Selfishness implies rationality and is the source of all happiness, and hence freedom, peace and prosperity in a benevolent and civilized society. This happiness which is the foundation of human good includes consumptive functions and also emotional functions, both of which can be acquired through the exchange of value. Of course, all this is inspired by the guru of self-love, Adam Smith, who argued that it will be hard to depend on benevolence of each other, rather, one must appeal to self-love of others and demonstrate to them that it is in their self-interest to help others, therefore, Smith (1999, 63) contends:

> He will be more likely to prevail if he can interest their self-love in his favour, and show them that it is for their own advantage to do for him what he requires of them. Whoever offers to another a bargain of any kind, proposes to do this. Give me that which I want, and you shall have this which you want, is the meaning of every such offer; and it is in this manner that we obtain from one another the far greater part of those good offices which we stand in need of. It is not from the benevolence of the butcher, the brewer, or the baker, that we expect our dinner, but from their regard to their own interest. We address ourselves, not to their humanity but to their self-love, and never talk to them of our own necessities but of their advantages....

Therefore, exchange of value, and hence happiness is acquired not by appealing to the humanity in human souls but their self-interest. Value for goods is easily transferred at the marketplace; value for emotions, on the other hand, can only be given by an individual who values himself/herself. Only when an individual is aware of her/his self-worth, can she/he be capable of holding rational values. An individual that does not value herself/himself is incapable of emotional functions. The implication, therefore, is that societies that are based on socialist or more communal relationships are irrational because they are based on the 'moral cannibalization' and devaluation of the individual. A devalued individual is unhappy and unfree as in 'Nazi Germany and Soviet Russia' (Rand 1964, 33–34). In such societies, the individual is 'selfless, voiceless, rightless slave of any need, claim or demand asserted by others'. Therefore, objectivist ethics should be the ethical foundation of 'the original American system, *Capitalism*' (Rand 1964, 31). On the other hand, for Marx, dissolution of the individual as community is the recovery of the true essence of being human engaged in authentic (not production and consumption, private property based) relationships with each other, in organic relationship with nature (not as raw material), and hence equals humanism. Communism is, therefore, the recovery of the human *species being* as community (not individual). For Marx, living as an individual is going against oneself, going against one's species and going against nature; that is why communism is the only way to resolve conflicts (Marx 1844, 135), these are the essential conflicts that communism resolves:

> Communism is the 'resolution of conflict between man and nature and between man and man—the true resolution of the strife between existence and essence, between objectification and self-confirmation, between freedom and necessity, between individual and the species. Communism is the riddle of history solved, and it knows itself to be this solution.

In Western capitalist societies and, more generally, all over the world, however, communism is presented as the 'reduced' ideology, ideology that reduced freedom and increased authoritarianism. But viewed from Marx's perspective, capitalism based on individualism is the reduced version of freedom. The individualist logic is for obvious reasons favoured by the class and cultural elites who then undertake the work of rendering individual freedom common-sensical through textbooks, religion, family, clubs, associations, friendships and marriage relationships. However, it is not as if Rand conducted a world-wide survey to empirically substantiate rational selfishness, therefore, her claims are as ideological as some claim Marxism to be. Although, interestingly, Marx's work is actually well-substantiated by ethnographic and quantitative data, Rand's work is not. If I peel through the layers of the ideology of individual freedom, it is possible to come towards entirely different 'rational' conclusions. The entire premise of the rational self-interest as the basis of individual freedom starts with the axiom that 'greater good' and 'societal upliftment' involves the *sacrifice* of one individual for another, and hence, it jeopardizes the pursuit of happiness. Sacrifice is also an arbitrary or whimsical act of altruism, and hence cannot be a solid foundation of society unless mediated by a government. The government, as the medium of disbursement of happiness, takes away individual's ability to pursue happiness, hence, it takes away individual freedom. The government must restrict itself to the maintenance of law, order and the protection of private property. However, what if we attack the very DNA of this argument and contend that individuals are imbricated in society, they are not atomically self-contained and cut-off from the communal. Every individual permeates into society (as Marx indicated through the concept of *species being*) and the society's upliftment and greater good permeates into the 'individual' (if there is ever such a thing as an individual). It would be impossible to pursue self-interest and, hence, utilitarian and emotional consumption if other individuals were unhappy, unfree and suffering from the lack of happiness. Every individual meld into groups such as class, ethnicity, gender, sexuality, religion and indigeneity. Identity is never completely individual, unless one lives as a cast-away in an isolated island or is a sociopath. For example, a woman driven by self-interest and economic emancipation will be severely limited if her *group* is *identified* by society as weak, irrational and incapable of economic decision-making. It would be impossible for the self-interested individual woman to acquire individual freedom on account of the existing gender bias in society, therefore, investment (material and emotional) in upliftment of gender identity (greater good) is not a sacrifice for that individual, it is a necessity. Such an investment is neither irrational, nor enslavement, nor an infringement of rights, nor an indicator of the lack of individual self-worth. Worth, I argue, is an ideological concept—depending on how we evaluate it (from the individualist perspective or the communal perspective), we can argue that there is an existential crisis, or at the same time, argue that there is an existential upliftment. Similarly, post-depression (1930s) capitalism (of the Keynesian variety) quickly learned that capitalist as a class cannot survive without the upliftment of labour that constitutes the mass of society that generates demand and fuels profit maximization. If labour is exploited through the rabid pursuit of self-interest by individual capitalists, then capitalism would self-destruct from the crisis of unemployment, inequality and lack of demand.

Peet (2007) deconstructs Ricardo's 'comparative advantage' theory as imperialist ideology. Peet points out that Ricardo's argument, that each nation should produce goods and services in which they have the highest comparative advantage or least comparative disadvantage compared to a trading-partner nation, is actually economic mumbo jumbo to accord Britain the exclusive right to control manufacturing, and hence accumulate geopolitical and geo-economic power. In other words, free trade theory (like Ricardo's comparative advantage) based on self-interest of the rational individual (Smith 1999, 2010) translating into national self-interest is an ideological act of according economic 'worth' to nations that have geopolitical clout, thereby devaluing nations that are agricultural, not because the agricultural nations were incapable of developing manufacturing, but because free trade theory is a crafty scientific way of putting a positive spin to 'unfreedom' of powerless nations. Unlike Rands's claim that selfishness is rational for all, selfishness is actually not rational for all but only for those that have the geopolitical power to be selfish. In the geo-economics of selfishness (free trade imperialism), nations that did not have economic power were deprived of happiness, freedom, peace and prosperity either through unfair terms of trade sucking away their worth or through direct colonization disrupting peace and progress in countries of Asia, Middle East, Africa and Latin America. Therefore, the New Deal in the American context and democratic socialism in the case of Western Europe were fervent attempts by governments to provide relief and redistribution to labour. In the American context, it was particularly geared towards the creation of a middle-class that would boost consumption, and hence extend the longevity of capitalism (Peet 2009). The various socialist principles incorporated with democratic socialism (paid holidays for workers, free healthcare, free education) and New Deal variety in the liberal democracy of the USA (social security, Medicare, Medicaid, unemployment compensation, subsidized housing) are not examples of 'sacrifice' but examples of 'necessity'—necessity that individuals in class–society must invest for their upliftment. Therefore, depending on how we measure existential worth, greater good and societal upliftment can be understood as either sacrifice (by individualist ethics) or necessary conditions for the pursuit of happiness. If existential worth is measured in terms of short term, immediate consumption in an atomic abstraction of a world, then greater good is an evil. If, on the other hand, existential worth is measured in terms of long-term happiness and assured survival of the so-called individual in a larger society, then greater good is the fundamental DNA of individual freedom and happiness.

Sen, in his article 'Rational Fools' (1990, 37), critiques the self-interest obsession of neoclassical economic theory, arguing that such a limited view of human nature casts humanity in rather simplistic terms. 'The *purely* economic man is indeed close to being a social moron. Economic theory has been much preoccupied with this rational fool decked in the glory of his *one* all-purpose preference ordering.' Duty, love and self-interest casts the multidimensional human in such a way that it is often impossible to isolate and analyse them (Mansbridge 1990). Held (1990) argues that mothering and caregiving cannot be philosophized within limited conceptualizations of rational self-interest. This is not to essentialize mothering as a supreme moral activity outside the purview of trading instinct, but rather to emphasize the absurdity of considering babies as little, rational individuals contracting with their mothers for care. Therefore, if the core of individuality is the ownership and acquisition of private property (possessive individualism), and the independence of an individual from another (objectivist ethics), motherhood involves moral-cannibalism (of the caregiver), especially if the society accords no worth to caregiving either in economic or emotional terms. Rand would claim that mothering is the spiritual payment that the caregiver pays in return for the pleasure of 'acquiring' a new human, however, any caregiver that has changed multiple diapers through a sleepless night knows that caregiving has many moments that are neither pleasurable or contractual or spiritual, it involves repetitive and mundane acts similar to what a bank teller does or what a worker does in an assembly line. Sen, Mansbridge and Held's arguments can be used to critique rational self-interest, possessive individualism, objectivist ethics not so much from the perspective that ascribing worth is an ideological act (as I have argued above following Marx in the context of public subsidies, women's rights, and free trade), but rather from the perspective that human society consists of complex multidimensional relations like family, friendship, kinship, sisterhood, motherhood and brotherhood, which when subjected to isolation and analysis, lose their complexity. Therefore, economic theory in order to be a robust representation of societal reality must transcend the image of the one-dimensional 'rational fool' so that humans are not cast as 'social morons' in the pages of textbooks.

Individualism to Liberalism

'The liberal concept of moral life is individualistic' (Arblaster 1984, 17), which means morality cannot be dictated by the government or other religious and secular institutions. This was indeed emancipatory allowing for secularization from religious dogmas and whims of emperors and kings that were seen as God's representation on earth. This liberation from the shackles of divine law and the establishment of a theoretical foundation that allowed humans to question earthly and celestial powers was profoundly democratic. But this conception of democracy is essentially based on the individualistic and atomistic conception of society. The enlightenment and secularization of society allowed for the first time, a clear-cut separation between facts and morals. An individual should be free to choose her/his value based on a rational and objective assessment of facts. But these facts will not dictate what an individual should or should not do (moral obligation). The individual must conceptualize her/his own morality, therefore, Arblaster contends (1984, 17):

> Between the facts and moral evaluation of facts there lies a gulf which no logic can bridge. A starving child crying for food, a wounded man screaming in agony—these are facts. But to say that they are bad facts, as most people would, is not to describe them, but to evaluate the. To say that someone is starving is to say nothing about whether that is a good thing or a bad thing. That is a matter for moral judgement of the individual, and in such matters disagreement is always in principle possible.

Liberal theorists also believe that this individualistic liberal morality can be made more empirical and scientific if utilitarianism is adopted as its core premise, that is, accepting that humans are governed by desires and appetites. 'Good' is what humans desire and 'bad' is what they are averse towards. The 'good' and 'bad' can then be empirically computed in terms of pleasure and pain, and then, after successful calculation, what remains is the adjustment of each individual's satisfaction to those of all others in the society. Utilitarianism allows for liberty of taste and pursuits, of doing as we like as long as what we do does not harmfully impact others even though others may perceive our acts as wrong, foolish, amoral and perverse (Arblaster 1984; Mill 2010).

Within liberal morality, the concept of freedom is essentially negative, that is, it is usually seen as 'freedom from' rather than 'freedom to'. Freedom is a state of being in which one is *not* restricted, *not* compelled, *not* interfered with. (Arblaster 1984; Hobbes 1980). The state is seen as a primary institution of restriction, interreference and compulsion, therefore, the liberals have always obsessed about the freedom from control by the state. The repulsion towards the state is a characteristic that liberals share with Marxists. Liberals attack the restriction of individual freedom by the state, and the Marxists critique the state as the instrument of class oppression. The difference between the liberal and Marxist stance towards the state is that while for the former the state represents an abstract, bureaucratic institution thriving by leeching individual freedom through taxation and interference of self-expression, for Marxists, the state is an ideological apparatus representing the interest of the bourgeoisie geared towards the exploitation of labour. Marxists do not view society as comprised by individuals, but rather, society is inherently birthed through production relations that are group based (class, kin-ordered, gendered) (Marx 1844; Marx and Engels 2002; Marx 2005). Therefore, for liberals, liberation from the state represents heightened individual freedom and self-expression, but for the Marxists, disappearance of the state means the dismantling of the concentration of ownership of means of production from the unproductive class (bourgeoise), and hence the end of exploitation of the proletariat.

Collective emancipation of the masses of society represents an ideal theory of life for Marxism, not the furtherance of individual freedom. Individual freedom for a Marxist is an illusion, a limited view of society because accumulation of objects of pleasure (through consumption and private property) does not set humanity free, it burdens the larger masses of society into a continuous chain of work/labouring in the pursuit of 'happiness', and work and labouring objectifies humans, estranges them from the fruits of their own labour, from each other and from nature. Also, those classes in society that have unfair advantage (capital) will invariably accumulate more than those that have no capital; therefore, the liberal view of society that ignores class, promotes class-inequality, and hence the absence of emancipation (freedom) for most members of society. Liberal philosophy, a product of enlightenment, has always attacked feudal order, divine origin, royal lineage and 'blue blood', in fact, proclamation of individual freedom is the claim that all individuals are equal irrespective of class, creed or colour, and therefore should have equal civil and political rights and equality of opportunity. However, while liberal philosophy does not support class order, it also does nothing to oppose class inequality and prefer to pretend that class is non-existent or subsumed within a large nebulous category—the middle class (as in the American context).

This liberal ambiguity of class inequality sits well with capitalism as the economic way of life. Liberalism flourished with capitalism producing liberal democracies. Free market capitalism, therefore, shares with liberalism the need to extract maximum freedom by limiting the power of the state to maintain law and order and military, an idea promoted to the fullest by Hayek and Friedman that informed the rejuvenation of classical liberal political economy through the contemporary neoliberal economics of Ragean and Thatcher in the 1980s and 1990s (Arblaster 1984; Friedman 2009; Hayek 2014; Peet 2009). The market runs on its own through the invisible hand of price (Smith 1999, 2010), and all rational individuals benefit from it provided that rationality is the one-dimensional pursuit of profit—an idea critiqued by Sen (1990), Held (1990) and Mansbridge (1990) (discussed previously). Post-1930s depression, the foundational premise of classical liberal economics was challenged by Keynes who argued that pursuit of self-interest does not always operate in public interest. In fact, if capitalism is to avert the fallacies of booms and busts (trade cycles) that lead to depression, stagnation and unemployment, then it must find a way to ensure that 'rational' individual acts at the market place are not leading to low-employment due to low-investment and low trickle down. Although not a socialist economist, Keynes argued that the government can play an important role in mitigating the volatility of the free market that can be a threat to the stability of capitalism. The state can perform certain economic functions that are not being covered through individual self-interest—this by no means, according to Keynes, harms individual enterprise, innovation and initiative. While capitalism has evolved temporally and also spatially, it has assumed various admixtures of state intervention and market freedom, nonetheless, overt hostility to state socialism remains a fashionable principle of liberalism (Arblaster 1984). This hostility has been challenged head-on by the Bernie Sanders presidential campaign. Sanders contends that democratic socialism (not state socialism) is essential for the furtherance of economic rights, which are also human rights, and that a political revolution is necessary to challenge the power of millionaires and billionaires, and fight for public healthcare and free college education (Golshan 2019b). What does this mean for liberal philosophy's stance towards economic inequality?

If individuals must follow self-interest to pursue profit, then it must mean that the liberals are arguing for a society where the individuals have the right to keep and enjoy their profit (in terms of wealth and private property). This implicitly means that not all individuals will accumulate the same amount of wealth and the same amount of economic freedom—millionaires and billionaires by virtue of their legacies are likely to accumulate and enjoy more wealth than often the remaining 80 per cent of the national population. Economic inequality, as Marxists have demonstrated, is social injustice, therefore, liberal philosophy is once again faced with a contradiction between individual self-interest and happiness. If liberal democratic capitalist societies become extremely unequal, it means that most individuals, despite their best efforts, are unhappy (facing social injustice) and, hence, unequal—what would this mean in the context of equal rights of all individuals (irrespective of colour, creed and class)? Because class is ignored in liberal philosophy, because liberal philosophy has to remain ambiguous about state intervention in the market to the point of being hostile to it, and if inequality and social injustice are concepts that must be subsumed under nebulous categories like 'happiness', what does it do to one of the fundamental principles of liberal philosophy and equality? Liberal philosophy unsatisfactorily addresses this contradiction by dealing with equality as equal opportunity for all. Hereditary inequality based on name, family position and status is to be rejected when opportunities are presented to individuals, however, individuals based on their merit, ingenuity and innovation may end up unequal— inequality based on merit is acceptable and rewarded. Liberal philosophy never questions the socio-economic structures that underlie merit/ingenuity/innovation such as access to education, access to know-how or access to cultural capital. The fact that the poor are poor not because merit is a biological condition that they do not possess, but rather a direct result of entrapment in zip-codes with neglected schools, libraries and computers is ignored by liberal philosophy. Lack of merit is a reflection of systemic neglect producing families and communities that suffer from a vicious cycle of lack (of infrastructure, training, emotional investment, parental supervision and economic opportunity). Lack of merit is also an expression of temporal and spatial concentration of crime, gentrification, homelessness and substance abuse that the society has failed to mitigate.

Individualism, Family and Society

As discussed before, individual freedom that forms the essential core of liberal political philosophy understands the society/community/public sphere as the sum of all individual self-interests. The society is a mechanism setup by individuals to represent their self-interest. This brings us to an interesting contradiction, that is, how would liberalism negotiate the private (home/family) in juxtaposition with the public (society)? Is the private a sum of individual self-interest of the various members of the family? Is the family adjusted to a calculus of pleasure and pain of different members to produce maximum satisfaction? If so, how does the concept of individual freedom deal with inequality within the family, for example, systemic inequality fostered by patriarchal gender roles? If, in the public sphere, liberalism presupposes equal opportunities for all, but does not take accountability for resultant inequalities based on systemic injustice, how then is injustice negotiated within the family? Feminist theory has provided a sophisticated analysis of society indicating that the private and the public are intricately connected and no societal inequality or injustice (economic or otherwise) can be appropriately overturned unless the exploitative gender roles within the family are addressed (Elshtain 1993; Foucault 1990; Gavison 1992; Mouffe 2013). The question of individual freedom directly confronts caregiving if caregiving is gendered and unpaid. In other words, if cleaning, cooking and child-rearing is perceived as a natural extension of women's personality (as has been perceived in most societies), and these roles are unpaid, does caregiving truly represent expression of women's self-interest? If women decide to swipe these roles for public roles like 'work' that has been traditionally accorded economic remuneration, then who should be self-interested in providing caregiving? Feminists have indicated that the spatial separation of the public (work/society) and the private (home/family) spheres have curbed individual freedom (Foucault 1990; Mouffe 2013). For example, in agricultural or hunting and gathering societies, the 'work' sphere (agricultural field, wilderness) is often an extension of the home, therefore, despite being charged with caregiving roles, it is/was possible for women to step out and participate in these economic activities, and therefore have some freedom in the economic/sustenance decisions of the family. With industrial capitalism and the separation of the factory from the home, the traditional gender roles were solidified by capitalist patriarchy leaving women to the 'emotional' sphere of the home (Eisenstein 2005; Foucault 1990), when women did step out in the pursuit of individual freedom, they experienced ghettoization within low-paying 'feminine jobs', for example, cutting–stitching jobs in factories, cleaning and janitorial work or teaching and nursing (Fernandez-Kelly1983; Safa 1981; Standing 1989; Ward 1990).

Ghettoization of women in certain line of work that are low paying or wage discrepancy between men and women for the same work, feminists argue, are a result of normalized gendered roles within the family based on exploitative patriarchal norms (Eisenstein 2005; Freeman 2000; Mies 2007). What is normalized in the private is extended into the public, and unless the private is disrupted, there would be no disruption in the public, and women will face unfreedoms in both spheres. How can liberal individualism based on self-interest (objectivist ethics, possessive individualism) maximize individual freedom for women if patriarchy produces opposition between men and women's self-interest? Liberal feminists have addressed this issue by demanding that 'work' be made more gender-inclusive (both in terms of nature of work and pay), pushing for valourization of caregiving (maternity leave, family wage) and rendering caregiving as gender porous (Evans 2003; MacLean 2002). Therefore, adjusting pleasure and pain between different members of the family by financially compensating care giving and re-distributing it to male members would adjust women's satisfaction with respect to others in the family and society. Promotion of equal opportunity at the workplace and equal contribution at home enhances individual freedom. Socialist feminists, however, argue that liberal feminism does not fundamentally change patriarchal structures within society because work can never be the site for emancipation as long as it is being done under capitalism (Eisenstein 2005). Labour is never fairly valourized within capitalism as the existence of inequality is a necessary condition for the survival of capitalism (between labour and capital). Therefore, working (labouring) involves co-optation by capital by means of wage exploitation, which is even more acute in late-capitalism through sweat-shop, industrial home works, precaritization—all of which tend to be female 'dominated'. Thus, individual women gain the 'individual freedom' to buy, consume and possess objects (objectivist ethics, possessive individualism), but this does not represent emancipation of women either within the private or public—the 'glitter of globalization' masquerades as freedom while women as a group and poor women as a gendered class continue to be exploited (Eisenstein 2005; Rosen 2002; Ward 1990). Post-structural feminists contend that it is not just the dismantling of capitalism that can emancipate women, society must address colonization of women's body through representation, commodification and consumption (Benhabib 1999;

Butler 1988; Hooks 1992). In other words, women's individual freedom is not just contingent on replacing capitalism with another economic system where women enjoy class equality and own their social product, but the new order of society should be such that the public and private (family and society) are co-imbricated in feminist embodiment of identity assemblages that challenge phallocentric disembodiment. Both Marxist and post-Marxist feminists are critical of liberal feminism that hinges on the conception of individual freedom because it neither addresses class/economic/structural impediments nor cultural/visual/representative impediments, therefore, it fails in its mission to remove restrictions, compulsions and interference which happens to be the definition of freedom under liberalism.

Identity and Individual Self-love

I have discussed before how liberal formulations built around individual freedom avoid dealing with class as a social category and instead valourizing the 'individual' as the unilateral agent of economic mobility based on hard work and merit. I have also discussed how this individualist ethic sits uncomfortably with family and gender as a social category, often avoiding radical systemic upheavals that may be needed to dismantle exploitation and phallocentrism, which are essential ingredients of capitalist patriarchy. This brings us to the obvious question of identity. Identity (race, religion, skin colour, sexuality, gender, language, accent, places of origin and belonging) 'identifies' the individual; individuals self-select or are socially conditioned to select identifiers. In other words, the 'abstract individual' of liberalism that diligently pursues happiness is doing so in the context of a lattice framework that she/he automatically inherits at birth or accumulates in the journey of life. Therefore, the individual is not as abstract as liberalism would have us believe, she/he is woven into the tapestry of social groupings whether she/he likes it or not. In that context, liberalism must find a way to accommodate identity. As previously noted, liberalism (liberal capitalism) will avoid any category that threatens the subsummation of the individual (e.g., class), or find a way to fit it despite the violence caused (as in the case of women and work and women and body within capitalism). In this section, I will argue that unlike class, identity, however, provides an excellent solvent for the survival and realization of the individual.

According to Butler, Laclau and Laddaga (1997), identities constitute themselves through differentiation that are socio-spatially produced to create a hegemonic inside and an outside. Recognizing the space/place contingency of 'othering' acknowledges that identity differences result from situated practices prevalent in particular local scales. Local scales consist of different socio-geographic realms such as nations, cities and places. Narratives of 'othering' acquire meaning within the socio-geographic realms of their creation and can be resisted within these realms if one has a stake in that place. Othering, difference and fragmentation relies on a romanticized construction of personhood where the essence of the 'self' is always already affirmed while the essence of the other bears the burden of unnaturalness, queerness, Blackness and feminineness (Benhabib 1999; Fuss 1989; Gilman 1985; Hooks 1992; Kobayashi and Peake 1994). In extreme instances of negation, the 'other' becomes 'homo sacer'—a subject position established under Roman Law to identify those whose death had no sacrificial value (Agamben 1998; Gregory 2004). Destabilizing the 'other' will require disrupting binaries between the privileged-self and the dehumanized other. Destabilizing the dehumanized other is made possible by recognizing that 'othering' is place contingent (Dear et al. 1997; Kobayashi and Peak 1994; Pratt 2004; Rose 1993), that identity is specifically constituted through experiences of exploitation (Hooks 1992), that difference can unite through an interstitial and not assimilationist politics (Benhabib 1999), that difference is produced by discrimination and not the other way round (Ong 2000; Young 2000). Butler argues that difference has become the site for intellectual and social solidarity; however, not all differences are acceptable (Butler et al. 1997). There is, therefore, a need to ascertain the 'acceptable' differences from the 'unacceptable' differences, and also along with it, unpack the concept of 'equality' because the acceptable differences must be valourized by a liberal democratic society, or in other words, the acceptable differences must be treated equally in order for the individual grounded within an acceptable lattice of identities to feel free to pursue happiness. At the same time, it is important to remember that not all 'unacceptable' differences or exclusions are justified; after all, it is the post-structuralist contention that acceptability and unacceptability are fluid categories operating within norms whose hegemony are contingent to place and time. Therefore, an acceptable exclusion within liberal formulations may not be an acceptable exclusion under socialist/radical formulations, and an acceptable exclusion within liberal formulations in one place may not be acceptable within liberal formulations in another place. Therefore, for Butler et al. (1997, 5),

> The 'inclusion' of all excluded categories would lead to psychosis, to a radically unlivable life, and to the destruction of polity as we understand it. So if we accept…that there is no polity, no sociality, no field of the political, without certain kind of exclusions having already been made—constitutive exclusion that produce a constitutive outside to any ideal of inclusiveness—that does not mean that we accept all sorts of exclusions as legitimate. It would be unwarranted to conclude that just because some exclusions are inevitable all exclusions are justified (Butler's contention).

In reply to Butler's argument that total equality/inclusion is impossible, Laclau (Butler et al. 1997) contends,

> I would argue that a society without exclusion is an impossible for more basic reasons than being an empirically unreachable ideal: it is also logically impossible as far as social is constructed through decisions taken in an undecidable terrain. We can deal as democratically as possible with exclusion (for instance, through the principle of majority, or through the protection of minorities), but this cannot conceal the fact that politics is to a large extent, a series of negotiations around the principle of exclusion which is always there as an ineradicable terrain of the social.

As the dialogue between Butler and Laclau indicates, politics is often a politics of negotiation of what identities are to be 'recognized' (Fraser 1995) and what identities are to be excluded; this politics of negotiation is based on whatever principle of exclusion a society has adopted, therefore, the social and the political are imbricated in creating the acceptable lattice on which the individual must stand in a liberal polity. The realm of exclusion is often contested as Laclau indicates, and electoral politics is one way of contesting this exclusion. For example, in the American context, the right of a woman over her reproductive rights is that site of contestation over the identity of exclusion. Because the majority of republican politics push for strict laws against abortion, a Republican-party-controlled government becomes an instrument of exclusion declaring illegal women's individual choices over their reproductive decisions (Guest 2019). Such a politics of exclusion is based on a certain reading of religious scriptures, thus creating 'an ineradicable terrain of the social' that grounds this politics of exclusion. Liberalism based on individualism becomes a steady calibration of 'equality' between the individual's desire/need (maybe for abortion) and what the polity and society has decided as acceptable (pro-life stance). The individual self-interest of women is restricted, therefore, curbing individual freedom over her body, yet that individual has to be deftly convinced that this is not an unequal act, not a restriction of freedom, in other words, it does not go against the root principles of liberalism. Identity is tricky that way, not only does it challenge and contest the liberal ethic of self-interest by putting the individual head on against the lattice of identity that she craves—a conundrum liberal polity and society must solve—but it also often proves to be a useful solvent for the melting of liberal individualist ethic in the 'big bucket of multiculturalism' (Ghender 2016; Plaut et al. 2009; Stuart and Ward 2019).

McLaren (Steinberg 1992, 399) describes this interesting solvent—diversity within the melting pot of multiculturalism—as,

> Harmonious ensemble of benign cultural spheres is a conservative and liberal model of multiculturalism, that in my

mind, should be jettisoned because, when we try to make culture an undisturbed space of harmony and agreement where social relations exist within cultural forms of uninterrupted accord, we ascribe to a form of social amnesia in which we forget that all knowledge is forged in histories that are played out in the fields of social antagonism.

The argument is that identity/culture/recognition are violent sites of exclusion played out in historically and placially contingent conflicted terrain. Multiculturalism is a clever ploy of liberal individualism allowing it to celebrate the narcissistic appetite of the 'cultural man' (the individual), at the same time, obfuscating the gory histories and geographies that produced it. Culture and diversity without the historical–geographical context of their production is a meaningless abstraction. Liberal individualism requires cultural identity to be a meaningless abstraction so that it can become an unconfrontational container-box for the lattice of exclusion hidden under identity politics. Kamat and Matthew (2003) indicate how the celebration of Hindu cultural iconography as multiculturalism in the USA can often be the 'benign' face of fascistic expatriate politics that marginalizes Muslim minorities in India. The same Indian migrants in the USA who celebrate diversity under multiculturalism by distributing samosas (fried Indian dumplings) and lighting diyas (earthen lamps) send dollars back home that fund exclusionary, minority-bashing politics in India. Bourdieu and Wacquant (1999, 42) indicate that the contemporary 'wooly spongy debate around multiculturalism' in the USA is an attempt to hide the general rise in inequality, exclusion of Blacks and the failure of the American Dream. According to Bourdieu and Wacquant, the inequalities, exclusions and disappearance of the middle class has assumed crisis proportion in the USA, therefore they claim:

> This is the crisis the word 'multicultural' conceals by restricting it artificially just to the academic microcosm and by expressing it in an ostensibly 'ethnic' idiom when what is principally at stake is not the recognition of marginalized cultures by academic canons but access to the instruments of (re) production

of the middle and upper classes—and first, among them, to the university—in the face of massive state retrenchments.

In essence, therefore, particularistic (read individualist) identity politics keeps the hardworking individual 'alive' by celebrating her cultural existence as an ethnic value to society, while at the same time, doing nothing to alleviate the systemic mayhem and oppression that make her very existence precarious. Political liberalism celebrates the 'accepted' lattice of identity and difference, but also, at the same time, considers the individual responsible for her socio-economic well-being. The politics of equality is an academic polemic of celebration of cultural difference where the production of difference through systemic exploitation is never contested.

Identity, therefore, is a double-edged sword; it is inherently contra-individual because it is based on identifying with others outside oneself. The individual, therefore, must exist within a lattice of society and polity that she/he inherits and accumulates, liberalism founded on an individualist ethic must be ingenious in accommodating identity. Because identity can be particularistic (I, me, self-love) and narcissistic—I am different and that is why I am unique—and it can simultaneously also be general and universalistic, such as gender, White male, Spanish-speaking or Native American, it is amenable medium for liberalism. When it suits the individualist ethic, it conveniently convinces the individual to subsume self-interest and *identify* with the lattice because, really, the lattice is just an extension of the self and expression of self-love (e.g., conservative women giving up reproductive rights in the interest of religious identification). However, at other times, liberal individualism celebrates the acceptable lattice as diversity and multiculturalism according to its ethnic value, but at the same time, it devalues the individual by sending her to work for her own upliftment (arguing that this is self-love), and therefore, does nothing to alleviate the very conditions that culturally marginalized this individual in the first place. Identity is, simultaneously, the self-love and self-hate of individualist ethic.

Right, Left and the Alt-right

Individual freedom, objectivist ethics and possessive individualism has been the bedrock of Western liberal philosophy both in the USA and in Western Europe. The 'enlightenment' epoch with its emphasis in empiricism, scientific explanation and, therefore, scepticism with divine origin placed the onus of change on the rational individual. Science, philosophy and political movements (Italian renaissance) reoriented the focus from God to man as the agent of change, and therefore, individual action and the philosophy behind it (e.g., Descartes *Cogito ergo sum*—I think, therefore I am) became the basis for planetary progress rather than fate. The protestant ethic, Weber (2013) argued, was the motor force behind industrial revolution and industrial capitalism in Western Europe and then, subsequently, in the New World because it emphasized that the 'elect' (selected) would go to heaven if she/he concentrated on repetitious, conscientious labour (production) in her/his lifetime. Accumulation of profit was sanctified as long as it was reinvested in society. This moral code fits very well with the classical economic prescriptions of Adam Smith and David Ricardo, and defined the transition from mercantile capitalism to free market capitalism based on free market imperialism and colonization of the resource-rich parts of the world. The central tenant of human existence and progress (economic and political), and the philosophical imperatives behind this was individual self-interest often used interchangeably to mean individual freedom or the freedom of the individual to pursue happiness without the interference of the state. The individualist ethic as I have argued before was not free from obvious tensions such as class–individual contradictions, individual–family contradictions, individual-identity contradictions and individual–gender contradictions. These contradictions were patched up, cobbled together, swept under by various iterations and re-explanations of the post-enlightenment individualist ethic like Keynesian economic principles in the post-depression era and then neoliberalism in the post-1980s (reformulation of Adam Smith and David Ricardo's free market principles applied this time through 'globalization' rather than old-style imperialism). In popular literature, Ayn Rand (as discussed before) played an important role in giving a fresh lease of life to individualism re-titled as 'objectivist ethic', thus denouncing any communal order as tyrannical. Multiculturalism emerged as an important component of American liberalism allowing the tension between individual self-interest (self-love) and identity to coexist in a fragile coalition, and the 'celebration of diversity and inclusion' became the hyphenated link in the self-interest–identity coalition. While individualism is the universal solvent for Western capitalism, irrespective of the ideological 'leanings' of political parties (Republican or Democrat in the USA), Neil Smith (2005) goes a step further to demonstrate that the liberal–conservative difference in the political map of the USA is actually an American invention in the 20th century with very little currency before that. He argues that liberals at the end of the 20th century have actually been quite conservative in the USA, Western Europe and Britain supporting the first World War and opposing communism. The individual's interest (based on property rights and electoral democracy) trumps the collective interest (state) and is expressed and realized through production and consumption and accumulation of profit (objectivist ethic) at the free market place (Smith, Ricardo, Hobbes, Locke, Bentham Keynesian moderation, Hayek, Friedman, Rand), and the endurance of profit as private property, finance capital and cultural capital represent the 'pursuit of happiness'. This pursuit of happiness of the individual Western man represents ultimate freedom and the universal pursuit of happiness—what is good for Britain is good for the world. In explaining the messianic zeal of the USA and its coalition for 'liberating Iraq', Smith (2005, 5) indicates:

> What was good for the United States was good for the world. If such a brash assumption of an American globalism was not always explicitly expressed in the new republic, it came to the fore with the doctrine of 'Manifest Destiny' and later with Wilson's 'Global Monroe Doctrine.' George Bush is the true inheritor of this liberal tradition: for him, a 'nation

founded on the universal claim of human rights' is ideally suited to lead the messianic global crusade for freedom insofar as 'freedom is the design of humanity and freedom is the direction of history.' America is the unique beacon of freedom, but the 'desire for freedom is present in every human heart'.

This 'desire for freedom' present in every individual human heart defined a kind of Western exceptionalism that permeates 'liberals' and 'conservatives' alike.

It is this DNA of Western liberal ethic founded on the concept of individual freedom that the Alt-right movement claims to challenge, uproot and dismantle. In that context, they claim to critique the 'liberals' and 'conservatives' alike in their obsession with what they view are leftist concepts such as diversity, liberty, freedom, multiculturalism, spread of free market capitalism and democracy. The right (conservatives) has become left (liberals), and the Alt-right provides the singular true hope for the future of the right. Richard Spencer (2015a), the founder of the Alt-right movement and the founder of the web magazine *Alt-right* explains:

Alt Right was a reaction against the mainstream conservative movement, or conservatism in America, particularly as it has manifested in the George Bush presidency, but also before that...Anti-war conservatists would say that 'we are the true conservatives...we are the true heir of the best of the conservative movement, I thought it was a losing argument.' I never started out liking conservatism...I think conservatism is actually something quite specific...there are two important aspects of what came to be called conservatism, the first of these aspects is liberty and freedom, freemarket and capitalism, it was an ideological antipode to Stalinism and Marxism...but I find this emphasis on liberty, freedom, freemarket quite a negative ideal...freedom for what? Freedom from who?... Does the capitalist want freedom so that he can destroy the natural world?...what is freedom for? Otherwise freedom is meaningless, you are fetishizing an anti-ideal.

The excerpt from Spencer's YouTube video clearly positions the Alt-right against the core principles of Western liberal democracy, namely, liberty, freedom and free market capitalism arguing that freedom itself means nothing. The negative idea of freedom that I discussed earlier, that is, 'freedom from' rather than 'freedom to' where freedom is a state of being in which one is *not* restricted, *not* compelled, *not* interfered with (Arblaster 1984; Hobbes 1980) is for the Alt-right, a vacuous abstraction, meaningless jargon, an 'anti-ideal' that is useless and intangible.

Spencer goes on to contrast the Alt-right movement from mainstream conservatives and neoconservatives of the Bush era and instead aligns with Trump's populism:

> It is easy to the see necons as the terrible perversion of the conservative movement...I disagree with that...what is remarkable is the continuity between them all, it is very difficult to see the difference between conservatism and neocons particularly, during the Bush administration...necons probably had higher IQs and were more cultured, but that's it.

> We have to liberate ourselves from that stuff...and find a totally new staring point, and that is really what I meant by alternative right...you could say what is this? Alternative to what?...Alt-Right in its inception was a kind of big tent and it has taken a life of its own through #AltRight... these are people who have liberated themselves from the left-right dialectic...these are those people who realize how useless the tax-cutting republicans are... these are people [members of the Alt-Right movement] who have come from college campuses that are dominated by social justice warriors, these are people who have seen the Black Lives Matter movement, these are people who see the refugee crisis in Europe and the migrant crisis in the US, they see how useless the tax-cutting republicans are... Donald Trump ironically has an important impact on the Al-Right because he has attacked and humiliated what the Alt-right movement hates. Trump has humiliated three bad forces, conservatism, Fox news, and GOP, and this is quite inspiring ...Alt-Right has influenced the Trump phenomenon...there has been an Alt-Rigtification

of mainstream conservatism, this is not a widespread phenomenon, it is happening in certain spots. (Spencer 2015b)

The Alt-right is motivated towards distancing themselves from the 'tax-cutting republicans' (conservatives against the state) and pro-Iraq war neoconservatives represent a continuum of outdated ideals that were designed as an antipode to the Cold War era. In other parts of the video, Spencer criticizes the Iraq war as 'stupid' and also ridicules the conservative movement's anti-environmental stance. Implicit in his statement is the urgency of dealing with the existential angst that multiculturalism, diversity and affirmative action has created among the White American male. Tax-cutting as a policy no longer represents enough of an aspiration for a young, college-going conservative male who is the 'other', the 'outside' to everything and everywhere. The American male finds his identity position attacked and annihilated by social justice movements such as women's movement, pro-immigration movements and movements that affirm the Black minority. Difference has become the site for intellectual and social solidarity, but the White male has been declared as 'unacceptable' in this coalition of justice and, therefore, kept outside the realm of equality. If 'acceptable' and 'unacceptable' are fluid categories operating within norms whose hegemonies are contingent to place and time, then the Alt-right claims to use that contingency in recreating a radical right that is anti-hegemonic and radical in ways that Marxism or socialism is (Spencer's own comparison). The right, White male must fight back from the margins not only through economic struggles against the state (tax-cutting) or through futile global pursuits such as free market globalization and warmongering, but through an anti-hegemonic struggle for 'acceptability'. Thus, according to Spencer, Donald Trump has cracked open the hard shell of freedom that encased the mushy ideas of multiculturalism smashing it to smithereens. In attacking individual freedom and its rainbow variant, multiculturalism and celebration of diversity, Trump has taken down the Grand Old Party, brought Fox news to his door, and attacked the ossified conservative establishment.

Youth for Western Civilization (YWC) is registered as a non-profit student organization that is part of the Alt-right movement opposing multiculturalism. Its Founder-President Kevin DeAnna claims that the organization now has chapters across dozens of university campuses in the USA and abroad. In an interview video posted on YouTube, DeAnna claims that,

> Western civilization is a compound of Christian, classical, and then the folk traditions of Europe...we don't just define it as just democracy, rule of law, and these universal institutions, we say that it is a specific culture that comes from a specific historical experience. (2012)

The 'Western civilization' is a specific ethno-racial compound, not abstractions like universal principles of civil liberty. Abstractions like universal principles of democracy, rule of law, individual freedom, liberty tend to create vacuous embodiment of a 'citizen'. A citizen is not a very useful category for the Alt-right movement because it is a catch-all container that can accommodate Brown, Black, White, women, a migrant and a refugee. The Alt-right movement committed to building a unique identity that challenges both mainstream conservatives and liberals sets up its agenda to attack the core principles of Western liberal democracies and individual freedom. Individual freedom existing within a lattice of 'acceptable' identities such as multiple races, gender, sexuality and migrant status becomes an inconvenience. Minorities are individuals too, and therefore, they must have freedom to procure education, apply for jobs, pursue business, and accumulate private property and profit. Within the paradigm of the multicultural individual, the hegemony of the European-originated Christian tradition is seen as waning. Here, 'Western' of course is a code for 'White' and 'civilization' becomes a code for 'race'.

In another video, former congressmen and advisor to YWC, Tom Tancredo explains that, 'we are the product of a Judea Christian-Anglo culture...all cultures are not the same, all political systems are not the same, some are better than others' (Tribute to Youth for Western Civilization 2009). Therefore, the Alt-right stance is very clear; there is nothing inherently valuable about diversity because some cultures/ identities (i.e., White Christian) are better than others, therefore, political systems founded upon these better and superior cultures are likely to be better. The implication is that there is a need to agitate against the liberal multicultural state and reorient American political system around the core principles of 'Western civilization', which is not individual freedom, but rather, the inherent superiority of the White Christian race. In other words, the USA and European countries must tackle the onslaught of diversity (migration, refugee crisis, women's equality) by unapologetically synthesizing Whiteness with Westernness—if the individual is to be set free, the Alt-right clamours for the liberation of White man from the oppression of diversity. In a separate video, but from the same montage (Tribute to Youth for Western Civilization 2009), Black leaders and preachers are depicted as rabble rousing and calling for the demise of the 'White man'. And simultaneously, Muslims in turbans and beard are shown as burning the American and British flags. These video clips are punctuated with clips from Pat Buchanan's speech on blood and soil that binds a culture to a common heritage drawn from the same history, literature and language. The video montage ends with flags from countries in Western Europe, America, Britain and Australia, in case the viewer had any doubts about which blood was tied to which soil (Tribute to Youth for Western Civilization 2009). Milo Yiannopoulos, a British journalist, Breitbart News star, and the 'pretty face' of Alt-right, has proudly proclaimed that feminism is cancer and that it has run its course. Milo went on to tell a journalist who claimed to be a feminist, 'I am sure they will cure you of that' (Studio 10 2017). In an interview (*Guardian* 2017a), Richard Spencer claimed that Africans have benefitted from White supremacy because the average lifespan of an African American in the USA is higher than an African in Africa. In the same interview, Spencer claimed that the course of world history would be exactly the same if the Africans did not exist, because 'we are the geniuses [White race] that drives it'. Spencer also called for a White safe 'ethno-space,' a nation of Whites, just as the Jews needed a safe space.

The Alt-right movement, therefore, reimagines the world as one where the West is supreme, but it is also based on a very particular imaginary of the 'West', one that is not based on abstract principles of individual freedom but on a White ethno-specific supremacy. In this way, the contemporary Alt-right movement is an interesting insertion within the tapestry of Western liberal capitalism. When I say Western liberal capitalism, I am referring to socio-political systems in the Global North (particularly USA and Western Europe). It is an interesting insertion because, by self-proclamation, the Alt-right is a critique of liberalism and all that its stands for: multiculturalism, women's rights and pro-immigration. The Alt-right is simultaneously also against mainstream conservatism and what it represents: Cold War style anti-communism, anti-environmentalism and narrow focus on economics. The Alt-right criticizes what they view as 'meaningless abstractions' of liberal polity such as freedom, liberty, spread of democracy, individual freedom and citizenship—in essence, they critique the very DNA of liberal capitalism as discussed before. Yet, the Alt-right's critique does not emerge from the position of the poor (class) who lack the freedom and liberty to pursue happiness in terms of access to college, healthcare and good jobs. Instead, the Alt-right's critique emerges from an individual that is emplaced in an identity lattice of Whiteness, maleness, Christianess, Americanness, Europeanness, or what they view as the specific ethno-racial compound that marks the 'West'. Clearly, it is not a critique of individual self-interest from the point of view of the proletariat (Marxist approach), or a critique of individual rationality from the point of view of welfare economics (Held 1990; Mansbridge 1990; Sen 1990). Instead, it is a return to a pre-secular model of blood and soil racism and misogyny that the 'modern' concept of the 'secular nation' of the 19th and 20th century was supposed to eradicate (Anderson 1983; Gellner 1983; Hobsbawm 1990). In being antiquated in its situated identity politics, it is simultaneously suave having strong online presence and represented by articulate young men with college degrees and good jobs. These contradictions need fuller examination.

But the most important point that I want to make in this book is that while the Alt-right critiques the core principles of modern liberal philosophy and individual freedom based on self-interest, it is actually a product of the same. The Alt-right represents the virulent pursuit of individual self-interest, that is, the maximization of individual's freedom to pursue happiness through the establishment of the 'self' as the dominant race/gender that accumulates private property and profit. This pursuit of happiness presumes that no matter where the starting point is, every individual is to be equally treated in terms of available opportunities. Therefore, in the Alt-right's imaginary multiculturalism, celebration of difference and affirmative action for minorities is hypocrisy and violation of happiness of the White male-self. Multiculturalism and feminism are unnecessary forms of political correctness that create ugly and weak women (*Herald Report* 2018) and affirmation for non-White races who simply do not possess the genius to make Western civilization great. The Alt-right strikes at the very heart of the individual versus identity contradiction within liberalism by flipping multiculturalism on its head and arguing for a reverse-culturalism where they discursively and empirically create a category of the victimized, marginalized, oppressed minority— the White man who needs affirmation and celebration. They attempt to reorder the 'acceptable' differences by arguing that the White man's identity is born out of exploitative experiences resulting out of many marginalization and victimization produced by man-hating feminists, White-hating non-Whites and Christian-hating Muslim migrants. Culture and diversity without the historical–geographical context of their production is a meaningless abstraction. Critics of multiculturalism have argued that liberal individualism requires cultural identity to be a meaningless abstraction so that it can become an unconfrontational container box for the lattice of exclusion hidden under the politics of identity and celebration of difference. If, as identity theorists claim, not all 'unacceptable' differences are justified, then what/who decides why an 'unacceptable' difference like Whiteness/maleness cannot clamour for equality at a certain place and time? This is the fallacy of liberalism; there is nothing more unequal than treating equally the unequals. Therefore, my argument is that individual freedom within liberal politics allow identity movements like Alt-right to flourish by not emphatically explicating the violence of pre-existing inequalities (class, race, culture, gender). It is the spatiality and history of the violence of inequality that sets apart 'acceptable' difference from 'unacceptable' difference. Uncritical celebration of diversity that does not explicate that the violence of economic (class) and cultural (identity) inequality can lead us to the slippery slope of fluid categories, where the male-White identity easily inserts and blends itself into this fluid, arguing that the White man today is as marginalized as the Jewish man during the Second World War era. In exploring the Alt-right in the USA and Europe, I hope to bring out this juxtaposition between individual freedom and reactionary identity arguing that liberalism's blind eye to the violence of inequality makes equality a porous category available for usurpation by the master hegemon. Whether the Alt-right is aware or not, as it critiques freedom, it thrives on it. I will explore this angle further in the later chapters.

Alt-right and Self-love

As discussed before, the Alt-right, although a heterogenous collective, demonstrates certain strands of commonality, for instance, they critique liberals and conservatives alike arguing that the conservative movement is outdated and not in tune with today's needs, it emphasizes identity politics rather than class politics, and argues that the status quo has been unfairly reversed against the White Christian man. The Alt-right is virulent in its attack on multicultural politics, does not recognize that diversity and celebration of minority identity is inherently valuable, is staunchly opposed to migration and refugee accommodation of non-White and Muslim populations, believes that the White race and White men need protection, affirmation and validation on account of being the stronger and more intelligent sex and race. These specific strands, that is, how and why the Alt-right fixate on it, what are their ideological underpinnings, and how does it construct and imagine the other as 'unacceptable' will be dealt in detail in the subsequent chapters.

The conceptual arguments that I have developed in this chapter are twofold: First, that individual freedom or self-interest has been the core principle of Western liberal capitalism (I am concentrating on the USA and Europe), and the idea of individual freedom as argued by critics (both of Marxist and non-Marxist persuasion) are rather narrow. Individual freedom focuses on one-dimensional 'rationality', that is, the idea that freedom includes multiplication of pleasure and minimization of pain, and multiplication of pleasure or happiness is achieved when individuals in society can acquire, accumulate and expand consumption, profit and private property. The freedom factor here involves removal of all impediments towards the pursuit of this happiness. Individual self-interest could be empirically adjusted to create collective institutions that represent this individual interest and not the 'greater common good', which can represent the 'tyranny' of social justice and the irrationality of altruism. When individual freedom or self-interest contradicts family dynamics of gender, societal dynamics of class, race and ethnicity, liberal politics falls short in dealing with these contradictions. It turns a blind eye to class because recognizing class inequality would mean dismantling the exploitative control of private property and wealth by few (class rich) in a society. Since private property and enhancement of wealth is coterminous with individual freedom, there is no way that liberal politics can dismantle class inequality. It attempts to resolves these issue through a fuzzy idea of equal opportunity for all, in other words, it does not matter how unequal your starting point is, if you work hard and are given equal opportunity, then liberalism proclaims that you should be able to pursue happiness. However, not everyone will be equally happy and that is a desirable condition because pursuit of self-interest means competition among different individuals. The larger economic system, that is, capitalism, is based on this liberal ethic, thus the market must be rendered free from government controls to allow unfettered accumulation of wealth. Of course, pure free market has only been a philosophical truism as indicated by Keynesian New Deal policies in the USA and social democratic principles in Western European countries.

Gender dynamics based on capitalist patriarchy within the household contradicts individual freedom of women when they are relegated to unpaid caregiving with no access to economic decision-making within the household. Liberal feminism has unsatisfactorily attempted to deal with this contradiction by fighting for job opportunities for women and equal pay at the place of work. But socialist feminists have effectively argued that more work and pay cheques drawn for women do not obfuscate exploitation at work and alter reproductive roles within the household. In cases where women go out to work, reproductive work of caregiving and child rearing are passed on to nannies who are exploited marginal women working these jobs out of seer desperation. Post-structuralist feminists have further argued that economic emancipation does not alter the very act of inscribing patriarchy on the body through discourses, learned behaviour and stylized gestures (Abu-Lughod 2013; Beauvoir 1974; Butler 1988) that are gendered acts. True emancipation is not rooted in individual freedom of women to pay for plastic surgery and buy new handbags, but in dismantling the patriarchal gaze that disembody the women as a person. This gender disembodiment is linked with other identities of race, ethnicity and sexuality as well.

The intersection of the individual with a social matrix or lattice of identity (gender, race, ethnicity, sexuality, linguistics positions, place of origin, migrant-citizen status) creates challenges for liberal philosophy—how to recognize the individual without being subsumed within a group identity? Identity theorists indicate that identity positions emerge out of experiences of exploitation that are situated and particular (individual) but are inflected with the identity of other individuals as well. Therefore, identity politics must be interstitial (demonstrating the tapestry of various inflections) and not assimilationist (melting of uniqueness into a 'larger general'). This challenge of recognizing the individual and the group identity is achieved within liberalism by the creation of a range of 'acceptable' differences that are spatially and temporally contingent. These acceptable differences are then valourized by equal treatment and through policies of multiculturalism.

My second argument is that the previous elements of liberalism allow reactionary identity movements like the Alt-right to germinate and grow roots. I indicate that most Alt-right activists denounce core values of liberalism like individual freedom as vacuous and meaningless because they perceive these as being misused by 'weaker' races and the 'weaker' sex through the 'backdoor' of multiculturalism, affirmative action and political correctness. However, it is liberalism's fixation with the individual's self-interest without addressing pre-existing violent tropes of class and cultural oppression that allow reactionary hegemonic identities like White maleness to claim marginalized positions. Because the violent history of racial and patriarchal suppression is swept under the carpet, oppressive identities (Whiteness, maleness, Christian fundamentalism) go unidentified, and hence, they rear their heads in opportune moments (Trump election, refugee crisis, migration crisis) to claim marginalized positions when they have actually always been the master hegemon of White capitalist patriarchy. If the boundaries between acceptable and unacceptable differences are fluid, and if liberal society does not categorically 'identify' what is unacceptable, then the unacceptable can claim inclusion and equality by penetrating the porous boundaries of acceptability. What makes acceptable differences distinct from unacceptable differences (patriarchy, racism, elitism) is the gory history of exploitation, which produced the very tropes of inequality that we contend with in the present. The hegemon that unleashed the violence of inequality cannot claim acceptability at any stage of history and at any site in geography, there is nothing fluid, porous or contingent about that. Liberal philosophy based on individual freedom fails to unequivocally make this distinction clear because, in essence, it does not want to disrupt the status quo (class, gender, racial). If happiness is contingent on the accumulation and preservation of objects, then such a society assumes that accumulation on class, racial and patriarchal lines is something that is inevitable. Liberalism, therefore, agrees that concentration of happiness (possessions, wealth, private property) is something the state should not police or disrupt, instead, the liberal state can affirm (multiculturalism) some unequal groups that have entered realms of acceptability. Individual freedom, therefore, provides solid ethical underpinnings to movements like Alt-right based on religious, racial and patriarchal hegemony because it never threatens to dismantle the history–geography of inequality produced by these hegemonic positions. Whether the Alt-right realizes it or not, it is the golden child of liberal individualism.

3

Heidegger, Nietzsche and the Alt-right Philosophy

The Alt-right

The Alt-right, short for Alternative Right, is mainly an internet-based, internet-based movement that distances itself from the mainstream right founded on values of conservatism (fiscal, anti-reproductive right, anti-environmental protection, anti-lesbian, gay, bisexual, transgender and queer [LGBTQ]) and from mainstream liberalism (promotion of multiculturalism, celebration of diversity, pro-migration, pro-welfare programs). It claims to capture 'alternative' and 'youthful' perspectives on what they believe the political and cultural right of the future should look like. Richard Spencer (2015b) claims to have coined the term 'Alt-right' and named the movement which has a wide tent but basically criticizes liberalism, old-style conservatism, Bush-era neoconservatism, and is pro-environment and anti-war. Spencer quit Taki's magazine, a paleoconservative magazine, and started a webzine called the *Alt-right*. The *Alt-right*,

Taki's magazine, Occidental Observer and former Trump advisor Steve Bannon's Breitbart News are the fora for the Alt-right's ideological expression. Recently, Alt-right went to the 'field'— most prominent amongst its rallies was at Charlottesville in August 2017, an event that broke into mayhem with the death of Heather Heyer, who was protesting the Alt-right and White nationalist presence in Charlottesville (Atkinson 2018; *Guardian* 2017a). Richard Spencer, Milo Yiannopoulos, Gavin McInnes (Proud Boys club) and Michael Cernovich (social media personality) are important spokespersons of the movement, often making trips to college campuses and TV news channels to spread the mission far and wide. Although, there are subtle differences in ideology between these Alt-right personalities (McInnes and Cernovich recently distancing themselves from the Alt-right), yet the basic tenets of White male supremacy, Western chauvinism and Islamophobia are the common underlying characteristics (Atkinson 2018; Southern Poverty Law Center 2019b). Spencer projects himself as the suave intellectual thinker type activist often citing Heidegger, Nietzsche, Julius Evola (philosophy of Tradition), Alain de Benoist, the French Right and the European Identitarianism movement as inspirations (Atkinson 2018; Horowitz 2017; Spencer 2015b). Milo Yiannopoulos presents himself as the openly gay, feminist-hating and Islamophobic counterpart unleashing 'shock and awe' in social media. Yiannopoulos was permanently banned from Twitter in 2016 for racial slurs (Ohlheiser 2016).

The Alt-right is not interested in the Bush-era ideology of American exceptionalism—America as an exceptional nation must wage pre-emptive war against hostile dictators and bring 'freedom' and 'democracy' or spread free market capitalism through neoliberalism (Spencer 2015b). Instead, the Alt-right focuses inward towards a racial, ethnocultural and anti-feminist politics. This 'alternative' perspective is based on an unapologetic promotion of White ethno-nationalism based on the belief that the White race is superior and needs to protect its purity by carving out an ethno-space that is free from racial mixing brought about by migration and interracial marriages.

The Alt-right is, therefore, explicitly anti-immigration and anti-refugee rehabilitation (Spencer 2015a). The Alt-right prefers to build on the existential angst of a depleted White masculinity emasculated through a liberal history (also promoted by mainstream conservatives) of multiculturalism, affirmative action and diversity policies that according to them, benefit only women and people of colour. Feminism creates ugly and weak women by promoting the idea that all body types ('even obese') are beautiful and race-based affirmative action allows weak and unintelligent races to bring down the greatness of White civilization. Milo Yiannopoulos, the former writer of Alt-right affiliated to Breitbart and currently, a vocal spokesperson for the movement, claims:

> To change societies beauty standards, to tell over-weight people that they can be beautiful, any size, sexy, any size, and healthy, any size, but that's a total lie. Dear, obese PhD. applicants if you don't have the will power to stop eating carbs, you won't have the will power to do a dissertation. (Yiannopoulos 2018)

Apart from the offense directed at body size, this tirade is also intended as an attack on college-going women (read feminists), who according to the Alt-right, are unworthy of college education having entered the system through diversity quotas. The Alt-right complains that these women swiftly turn into feminists and destroy the 'natural order of things', like the patriarchal household, heterosexual family system and men as breadwinners. The 'sexual revolution' has unfairly led to the 'empowerment' of one sex (women) over another (men). College education distorts scientifically and empirically validated theories of male biological superiority through ideological and imagined construction of systemic patriarchal oppression.

> The original, straightforward name 'feminist studies' was soon cast aside in favor of the deceptively neutral-sounding 'women's studies' (and more recently by 'gender studies'). From the start, however, such programs avoided the

objective, scientific study of women or the sexes: women's studies professors teach their students nothing about sexual genetics, fetal hormonalization, or empirically observable behavioral differences between men and women. Indeed, they advocate the suppression of such research. As two dissident feminist professors have phrased it, 'Feminist research demands loyalty to an ideological agenda rather than empirical adequacy and logical consistency'. (Baskerville 2018)

Therefore, one of the objectives of the Alt-right is to reverse the feminist ideological agenda by putting in centre stage the 'plights' of young men, specifically, Christian–White men. The other objective being the reversal of ideologies of racial inclusion, and hence preserving the purity of White European-American descent. Spencer expresses the Alt-right's disdain for racial inclusion by characterizing the promotion of diversity as structural racism (against the White race).

Diversity is a magical word in our times, but groups differ therefore, equality will never happen, ...it is not some male conspiracy....Diversity can only be achieved through racism: discriminating against males, discriminating against Caucasians, and discriminating against Asians...systemic, structural racism goes into the diversity agenda...racism against white males to achieve diversity....Endgame of diversity will be that there will be no white people working in corporations. We should be attacking systemic racism, we should be attacking structural racism. (Spencer 2015a)

Disdain for diversity/multiculturalism expresses itself through activism and agitation against migrants. The ontological inversion of structural racism to mean 'White plight' is not a vacuous sleight of hand, it thrives on what I have argued in the previous chapter, the fallacy of liberal individualism. Because liberal individualism does not conclusively differentiate between acceptable and unacceptable difference by clearly delineating the boundary line where 'unacceptable' is the secretion of the gory history and geography of exploitation, all differences are potentially acceptable as long as real or imagined 'exclusions' can be established. The Alt-right gleefully turns the liberal agenda on its head by demonstrating that the contemporary paradigm of diversity is discriminatory as it does not celebrate (hence exclude) male White identity. They build a successful empirical case by demonstrating the Browning of America through migration, marginalization of 'White males' in universities and corporations and challenging data on rape and gender violence. If, as per liberal individualism, racism is the discrimination of a particular race, then the Alt-right has amassed enough ammunition to build a case for 'White replacement and destruction movement'. A recent article published in the Alt-right mouthpiece 'deconstructs' (reduces) diversity as 'browning of America' and the 'eventual destruction of its White population'.

> 'Browning of America' is being caused by more than just non-White immigration, that another cause is racial intermixture, the actual browning of the White population itself, the accelerating cause of not just White racial replacement, but of actual White racial destruction, as: 'A sixth of newly married whites are married to someone of another race.... [and] white-black marriages have been rising since the 1960s, by about 50% per decade.' Now we know what 'diversity' really means, what it has always meant to its proponents and those who have elevated it above the vision and values of the Founding Fathers. It means, and always meant, the 'browning' of America, the transformation of America from a White country to a brown country, the replacement of White America by a brown America, by the dispossession, replacement and eventual destruction of its White population. (McCulloh 2019a)

The White dispossession and anti-immigration agenda are blended with misogyny and Islamophobia to create an amalgam of hate that is exclusive of all identities except male and white. For example, Gavin McInnes of the Proud Boys club denies that women are sexually assaulted or earn less than men.

> Women inventing problems and lying to create a world where feminists are needed. Like saying one in four women

will be sexually assaulted or raped in college—or saying that women earn less than men and there's a wage gap. Like just blatant lies to justify their existence.

'Women tend to choose jobs that are less strenuous, less risky, they tend to want to go home for their daughter's piano recital rather than stay at the office all night, and that costs them promotions down the line,' he said. (Hall 2017)

Similarly, Muslims are disparaged and White colonization lauded. Muslims are seen as an assault on Western male chauvinism because Muslimness as an identity is inherently imagined as non-Western and violent. In their desperation to forge a mega-violent identity that supersedes the audacity of 'Islamic terrorism', the Alt-right constructs the Muslim 'other' as morally depraved. The Alt-right also constructs the postcolonial 'other' as culturally inferior, unable to 'carry forward' the gifts of colonization bestowed on their 'primitive culture'.

Muslims have a problem with inbreeding. They tend to marry their first cousins…and that is a major problem here because when you have mentally damaged inbreds—which not all Muslims are, but a disproportionate number are—and you have a hate book called the Koran…you end up with a perfect recipe for mass murder…We brought roads and infrastructure to India and they are still using them as toilets. Our criminals built nice roads in Australia but aboriginals keep using them as a bed. The next time someone bitches about colonization, the correct response is 'You're welcome.' (McInnes 2018)

The Alt-right, therefore, is alternative to the mainstream right in their explicit identity-based agenda that distances itself from American global geopolitical ambition, which they view as warmongering and spread of capitalism. The Alt-right disclaims these global geopolitical ideologies as abstract and not in tune with the world view of young Americans. Instead, the Alt-right proudly proclaims political incorrectness on race, gender and religion by attacking diversity. Diversity is not viewed as the strength of Western liberal democracy, but rather as a structural assault on White male, Anglo-American Christian culture. In the presentation of White ethno-nationalism, Whiteness, maleness and Christianness are depicted as victimized by Brownness (immigration), women (feminism) and Muslims (Sharia-ization).

Gurus of the Right—Philosophical Praxis and the Alt-right

Philosophy and praxis are never separate; in fact, having separate words for referencing the two is an intellectual violence, a non-dialectical act that reality does not support. I have indicated in the previous chapter how liberal individualism (philosophy) is inescapably manifested in doing family, doing gender, doing identity and then politically recognizing these through multiculturalism, affirmative action and promotion of diversity (praxis)—in other words, how we think about our actions and how our actions create thought are not easily separated. Added to this is the issue that individual acts or acts of parties and groups like the Alt-right are not 'enacted' as discreet events, they are secretions of actions of others in space and time. Similarly, thoughts are hardly singular, they are always a compound reflection of history and geography (past, present, local, regional, national, global). This dialectic or philosophical praxis, that is, the actors, actions, agendas, thoughts, speeches and discourses are the ideological body politic of any reality. In other words, why we identify with something, and not others, why and where we draw boundaries between us and the other are not arbitrary acts. In critically examining the Alt-right, it may seem that their ideological body politic is quite simple, which is the valourization of identity surrounding White male chauvinism. Why does maleness intersect with Whiteness though? As I will later demonstrate that the Alt-right envisions Islam as misogynistic, if indeed this is the imaginary, and if indeed Islam is viewed as violent, what prevents the gun-toting Alt-right misogynists from aligning with the 'Islamic misogynists'? Why is religion the boundary that separates White males from other males? How do White women enter the fold despite its testosterone-steeped misogyny? How is womanhood and gayness creatively negotiated within an overt masculinist ethics? How identities are coalesced, dissected, deconstructed, forged, perforated represent the philosophical praxis and, hence, the ideological body politic. In what follows, I will look at Julius Evola, Alain de Benoist, Heidegger and Nietzsche's influence in Alt-right's philosophical praxis.

Evola and the Spiritual Man

Julius Evola, an Italian philosopher was mentioned in his Vatican speech by Alt-right enthusiast and former White House advisor Steve Bannon (Horowitz 2017). 'Julius Evola is one of the most fascinating men of the 20th century,' said Alt-right founder Richard Spencer. Evola's philosophical praxis, therefore, must be examined in order to understand the Alt-right's body politic. Evola was a trenchant critic of modernity, French Revolution, political ideals of democracy, rampant obsession with consumerism, vacuous (economistic) nature of 'progress' and base desires (sexual habits) of the masses. Evola aspired for a spiritual individual, and hence a spiritual nation that contested modernity and the degeneration it brought. According to Evola, the attaining of enlightenment or spiritual consciousness by worthy individuals (elites, aristocrats) within society will rescue Italy and the West from the baser instincts of modernity and place it in the higher path of Tradition. In essence, democracy, egalitarianism and materialism are the baser instincts that must be replaced in a 'spiritual West' by the values of Tradition. Tradition in Evola's writing always begins with a capital 'T'. Tradition, here, is not a return to a mythic golden age in history but the aspiration for perfection of man, that is, the Absolute being existing in a higher spiritual realm, determining the lower material world in which men live as an imperfect representation of the Absolute. Tradition is, therefore, the ability of few men to increasingly achieve control over their being (physical and mental) and attain the perfection of the

Absolute through enhancement of wisdom (enlightenment). Spiritual enlightenment can be attained through strict, rigorous, physical discipline of the body and simultaneous mental control leading to a higher from of individualism (not the self-interested, capitalist man), a spiritual individualism (Hakl 2012). Paul Furlong (2011, 32) explains Evola's concept of Tradition so succinctly, that there is no need to improve upon it; for Furlong,

> History is the unfolding in time and space of the cyclical struggle between Tradition and the forces of disorder, disintegration, contingency, and lack of differentiation, that are inherent in the processes of becoming. Modernity is the culmination of the temporary success of the forces of disorder, the Age of Darkness, a prelude to the return to the Golden Age and the re-emergence of the forces of Tradition.

Not all individuals in society possessed the biological propensity and strong mind to lead the world in the true spirit of Tradition. Therefore, only the chosen few could be part of the 'spiritual race' that had the mental faculties and military strength to produce a spiritual civilization defined by this 'New Man' (Wolff 2016, 483). A super race that displayed the biological and mental faculties for spiritual tradition, according to Evola, was a combination of the Aryan–German and the Roman race (Cassata 1933). Mussolini was fascinated by Evola's concept of 'spiritual racism' and inspired the fascist's circles during the war. Evola's fascism did not mean the rule of individual self-interest stemming from Adam Smith and Ricardo (classical economists discussed in the previous chapter), or class rule, but rather creation of a right that is based on authority and command in a hierarchical, aristocratic and feudal tradition (Wolff 2016). Evola's deep elitism ran counter to the ideals of United States' pursuit of happiness (capitalism) and of Marxism, both of which Evola considered materialistic, and spiritually defunct. Therefore, from critiquing modernity, Evola focused on critiquing the materialist-Marxist tradition flooding universities. Capitalist modernity, according to Evola, was an ever-expanding entity, a tiger with humanity riding it. According to Evola, it would be too dangerous to dismount the tiger, but the rider can keep riding the tiger until it is rendered depleted.

If we juxtapose Evola's traditionalist spiritual man and the spiritual nation alongside the Alt-right's vision laid out before, it is not difficult to deconstruct why the Alt-right has no interest in the geopolitics of war or America-led neoliberal globalization. American exceptionalism that has been the hallmark of the Bush-era neoconservatism is inherently based on the USA's global role as a supreme nation bringing 'democracy', 'freedom' and free market capitalism to the 'lesser' nations, even if it means inducing regime-change and pre-emptive war on those nations. The Alt-right has no interest in America's exceptional status in the global map, it is more interested in the internal re-conceptualization of the USA as a nation state. In this re-conceptualization, America must become a safe container for the supreme ethno-race, Whites of Anglo-American descent. The concept of the White ethno-state was put into context by President Trump when he remarked: 'Why should the United States take in immigrants from 'shithole countries' in Africa over people from places like Norway?' (Yee 2018). There is a clear sense of entitlement about the White ethnic makeup of the USA as if its entire Native American history did not even transpire. The implication of the statement is that the USA is a White nation state and should only receive White people, preferably of Nordic descent. The Alt-right does not stake claim on spiritual enlightenment and the emergence of a 'higher man'. The traditionalism borrowed from Evola seems to be an a priori belief that the White men of American and European descent are already a *higher* and *supreme* being, and as an elite race, they should be allowed to protect their purity. It is within that context of a priori sense of entitlement that Richard Spencer makes his statement that the continent of Africa and its people have had no impact on global history, and that African Americans are far better-off having gone through slavery (*Guardian* 2017a). The adherence to Evola's traditionalism is also expressed in the

Alt-right's absolute disdain for 'modern' 'democratic' principles of equality, multiculturalism, inclusion and diversity, seeing these as degenerate and harmful for White supremacy.

National Policy Institute, an Alt-right think tank published a piece on Darwinian evolution; the following is an excerpt from that piece:

> Unfortunately the pervasive influence of Cultural Marxism and the tactics of its adherents have prevented evolutionary approaches from spreading widely in the human sciences. This is apparent in the persistent rejection of any discussion of the biological basis of human racial differences, nowhere more so than in issues relating to IQ. This rejection is unfazed by the fact that there are few, if any, constructs in the social sciences more powerful than IQ. It correlates with and predicts an extremely wide range of social phenomena including, but not limited to, school and economic performance, criminal behavior, differences in wealth between nations, and demographic groups within nations. Among research psychologists this is well known and not particularly controversial. Equally well-known is that, based on decades of research, IQ is, in large measure, genetically determined.

> It is obvious why the left would object to evolutionary theories of human behavior that explain national, racial, and class differences, since the rejection of the particularities of human beings have been a motivating force of the Left since the French Revolution. (Roth 2015)

National Policy Institute, in the above-given excerpt, and, as well as, in many other pieces is determined towards creating a body of 'research' (philosophical praxis) that academically/scientifically legitimizes the connection between biology and intelligence reflected in IQ scores. This is not Evola's spiritual enlightenment per se, but a distorted modern version of it, which is ironic since Evola was staunchly against the materiality/empiricism of 'modern' scientific approach. Just as Evola critiqued the French Revolution (liberty, equality, fraternity) and the Marxists for their degenerate materialism, which puts the onus of oppression on the elites, the Alt-right also attacked the egalitarian tradition of the French Revolution and the Marxist penchant for celebrating the 'masses'. Interestingly, unlike Evola, the Alt-right cleverly deploys science to legitimize the 'inherent' differences (superiority/inferiority) between groups of people. The fact that intelligence measured through IQ is highly culturally particular, disadvantageous to those that are not accultured to it, and that intelligence can be understood in multifarious ways, and that it is socially conditioned by historical accessibility to cultural and economic resources (education, libraries, know-how, acumen, skills, inherited knowledge and wealth) are conveniently overlooked by both Evola and the Alt-right. Physical and mental mastery can only be attained by 'superior' men who lead a 'superior' nation, that must be protected from inferior men and women, is the kernel of the Evola-influenced Alt-right's body politic. There is a clear intentionality in this philosophical praxis to create a hierarchical order of things, otherwise, why would it not recognize something so obvious that labouring women and men all over the world, irrespective of colour, have the highest physical and mental temperance? Why else would a woman carrying stacks of bricks on her head with a child strapped to her back in hundred degrees of heat in India, be able to attain perfect balance if it was not for her supreme strength and singular mental focus? What is the science that proves Evola's philosophy that physical mastery (e.g., through mountaineering) and external detachment attained by the elite, is superior to what the woman at the construction site is able to achieve? What is more transcendental and consciousness-altering than a mother's singular focus towards feeding her baby under extreme physical and mental stress?

French Right and Identitarian Politics

With the waning of intellectual Marxism and the rise of neoliberal economic policies, there was a parallel rise of the French Right led by Alain de Benoist in the 1960s reaching its peak in the 1970s. Richard Spencer has on multiple occasions acknowledged that the French Right and the Identitarian movement has been an important source of inspiration for the Alt-right. The French Nouvelle Droite (ND—New Right) (Bar-On 2014) claims to transcend the traditional left–right dichotomy, criticize what they called the religion of human rights and multiculturalism, critique global capitalism, and hopes to reimagine an alternative to liberal and socialist modernity through a deeply cultural Identitarian politics that is almost Gramscian in conceptualization. Benoist claimed that elites must control cultural capital, that is, values, attitudes, belief systems, moral codes and representation, and disseminate and propagate them so thoroughly among the masses that 'cultural hegemony' is attained (Steinmetz-Jenkins 2017). In his 60 years' writing career in which he wrote over a 100 books, Benoist started the European 'identity movement' which, according to him, needs urgent protection from immigration, multinational capital and multiculturalism (Benoist and Champetier 2012). In his book *Manifesto for a European Renaissance* (Benoist and Champetier 2012), Benoist argues for 'ethnopluralism', the idea that all ethnic groups have the right to preserve differences/boundaries including the once that are 'strong' ethnicities/identities. Ethnopluralism became the inspiration for the ND's Identitarian movement, which became a kind of inverted multiculturalism—affirmation of dominant identities that are perceived to be under attack, and therefore their right to remain separate but equal. Inspired by Gramsci's cultural hegemony and the importance of control of cultural/intellectual capital, Benoist and his followers started an intellectual think tank called the Group for Research and Study of European Civilization, or GRECE (Benoist and Champetier 2012). It is from the GRECE that the ND emerged. *Manifesto for a European Renaissance* has become the moral code for the right in the USA, Europe and Russia. The Russian far-right extremist philosopher Aleksandr Dugin was inspired by Benoist in proposing the ethnopluralist concept of Eurasianism—Dugin is a staunch follower of Benoist (Williams 2017).

In the *View from the Right* (1977), Benoist declared that he and other members of GRECE considered the gradual homogenization of the world realized through global capitalism, immigration and egalitarian ideology to be unwanted. The concept of a 'global citizen' is suspect, a misnomer and imperialistic for the ND. The diversity in 'ethnopluralism' is not the concept of melting pot or multiculturalism, it is the idea of European purity, that is, French identity for Frenchmen as distinguished and separate from Moroccan identity for Moroccans. Bannon and Spencer draw succour from Benoist's Identitarian movement, often rendering porous White ethnicity/nationality into White Christianity. When Bannon addressed a conference organized by a conservative Catholic group in the Vatican, he claimed:

> We're at the very beginning stages of a very brutal and bloody conflict, of which, if the people in this room, the people in the church, do not bind together and really form what I feel is an aspect of the church militant, to really be able to not just stand with our beliefs, but to fight for our beliefs against this new barbarity that's starting.

The 'new barbarity' according to Bannon is the 'crisis both of capitalism, but really of the underpinnings of the Judeo-Christian West in our beliefs', or, in other words, the 'spread' of Islam (Feder 2016; Poggioli 2017). Cultural hegemony in Bannon's imagination is also religious hegemony, one in which the 'Christian-White' world must defend its purity by separating itself from the Muslim–Brown world that taints the former's purity through migration and capitalism. Shortly after Trump's inauguration, Spencer was attacked at a public gathering, he clarified that he was not a Neo-Nazi, but rather an 'Identitarian' (Williams 2017), and that he first discovered the inspiring works of the ideological figures of the ND in *Teleos*, an American journal of political theory. Benoist was invited to Spencer's think tank, National Policy Institute for a lecture (Williams 2017). While Benoist's ND was originally created to fight a world view of sameness (globalization, capitalism, immigration), and the right of ethnicities to protect separateness and difference, in the post-1990s, the focus has been the presence of Arab and African people in Europe. It is around the nexus of 'othering' of the immigrant and the Muslim, and their 'heathen appetite to consume' and destroy the purity of Judea-Christian civilization that the American Alt-right and the European Right converge. Benoist has been a studious follower of Julius Evola, and his Traditionalist school, arguing that fascistic tendencies that arose out of Evola's ideas is really the Black sheep of his philosophy; instead, Evola should be understood as a right-wing version of Gramsci. According to Benoist, Evola's contribution to the ND and the right world view in general would be a cultural/spiritual revival of the West, rather than direct pursuit of power. At this juncture, it is important to keep in mind that philosophical praxis that manifests as ideological body politic of the Alt-right does not suddenly erupt in a discursive vacuum. Even the most blithe White supremacist that has not read any text in philosophy has to borrow Gramsci's phrase, an 'organic intellectual' (Fischman and McLaren 2005; Gramsci 1992)—someone who converts mundane material experiences into conscious thought process based on the conceptual lenses she/he has acquired through family, religion, school and other civil society institutions. The civil society that embeds right world view is a particular one, a material–discursive one where Evola, Benoist and French Right discourses spontaneously and continuously blend with material actions (immigration, diversity policies) in such intricate ways that it is impossible to separate the material from the discursive. That is why in order to understand material contexts of othering (misogyny, Islamophobia orientalism, anti-immigrant xenophobia), it is important to wade through Evola, Benoist and other ideological influences given next.

Nietzsche, Heidegger and the Nothingness of Modernity

Richard Spencer famously remarked that he was 'red-pilled' by Nietzsche (Illing 2018; The Conversation 2018)—'red pill' referring to the movie *Matrix*, where the main character was awakened to the truth of his life and existence after he made a conscious choice to take the red pill. Nietzsche and Heidegger, famous philosophers from the left, now feature frequently on far-right websites. Both philosophers critique the spiritlessness of modernity and reject liberal democracy, enlightenment and ideas of equality. In *Genealogy of Morality and Other Writings* (1994), Nietzsche criticizes Christianity for overturning the hallowed Roman values of strength, will and nobility of spirit, and its replacement with pity, charity and humility—in essence, for Nietzsche, Christianity weakened humanity. The Alt-right too has no interest in the teachings of Christ, but they view Christianity as an important structure that serves to define 'White civilization' (Illing 2018). In *Antichrist* (1920, 45–46), Nietzsche claims:

> What is happiness?—The feeling that power increases—that resistance is overcome.

> Not contentment, but war; *not* virtue, but efficiency...The weak and the botched shall perish: first principle of our charity. And one should help them to it.

> What is more harmful than vice?—Practical sympathy for the botched and the weak—Christianity...

> ...but what type of man must be bred, must be willed, as being the most valuable, the most worthy of life, the most secure guarantee of the future.

> This more valuable type has appeared often enough in the past: but always as a happy accident, as an exception, never as deliberately willed. Very often it has been precisely the most feared; hitherto it has been almost terror of terrors;--and out of that terror the contrary type has been willed, cultivated and attained: the domestic animal, the herd animal, the sick brute-man—the Christian.

Unlike Rand's 'possessive individualism' (1964, 28) discussed in the previous chapter where selfishness is rationality and the source of all individual happiness and freedom, for Nietzsche, happiness depends on the accumulation of power, it is the concentration of power that makes an individual 'valuable', not just the possession of property, wealth and emotional nourishment. Happiness is not just contentment or maximization of pleasure and reduction of pain as liberal ethics codifies, but it is the pursuit of war. The happiest individual is terrifying, 'terror of terrors', and he does not pursue the virtues of charity. In the last context, Nietzsche's ideas blend with Rand's (1964, 27) idea of altruism as 'moral cannibalism'; charity, according to Nietzsche, is inefficient and according to Rand, irrational. Nietzsche, however, is ruthless in his attack claiming that 'virtue' creates the 'weak and the blotched'. Virtues like sympathy propounded by Christianity is worse than vice because it breeds the weak man, the tame man, 'the domestic animal' and makes society inefficient. The Alt-right inspired by Nietzsche, therefore, views the modern White society as weak, ravaged by the onslaught of Black lives Matter, multiculturalism, feminism, Islamization and border porosity. The fierce White man, 'terror of terrors', is much weakened, his value diminished by women, racial minorities and migrants.

Therefore, according to Spencer, Europe is the common home of all White men and those of European descent must unite, separate and breed the powerful and feared White man. The Alt-right movement is a war against the products of liberal weakness (Muslim migrants, independent women, racial minorities) that must die (Sedgwick 2019). The White race must allow the 'natural' biopolitics of evolution to unfold. Following is an idea inspired by Nietzsche (1920, 47) himself:

> Christianity is called the religion of pity—Pity stands in opposition to all the toxic passions that augment the energy of the feeling of aliveness: it is a depressant…Pity thwarts the whole law of evolution, which is the law of natural selection. It preserves whatever is ripe for destruction.

The Alt-right is unapologetically White supremacist, Islamophobic and anti-feminist because these are the products of 'pity' produced by liberal morality arising from Christianity, and in the 'natural' order of evolution, these identities should be put in their places or be slated for destruction. Nietzsche's characterization of women substantiates the point that women cannot be as powerful and as valuable as men, and therefore legitimizes the Alt-right's anti-feminist stance. Nietzsche (2018, 116) laments about the modern women:

> They [women] want more, they make claims...the rivalry for rights...woman is losing modesty. And let us immediately add that woman is also losing taste. She is unlearning to *fear* man: but the woman who 'unlearns to fear' sacrifices her most womanly instincts.

This fuels Spencer's Alt-right to dream of a White-man led Zionism under which the dispossessed White can form their ethno-state like Israel (Middle East Monitor 2018; Sommer 2017). Beiner (2018, 25) summarizes the essence of Nietzsche's philosophy on life as 'life-affirming experience of existence'. Life in order to be lived must be meaningful enough to affirm itself and help transcend itself. In order to live such a life, cultures need definite boundaries so that it can define its purpose, that is, 'wither and wither for'. Wading through life without a sense of purpose is not existence. Cultures led by powerful/ genius/elite individuals determine whether one is able to inhabit life-affirming existence or life-negating existence (Nietzsche 2018). Hence, the Alt-right gobbles up Nietzsche's blessings and imagines a worthy existence to be one where civilizations are bounded, hierarchical and led by 'culturally superior' elites.

Like Nietzsche, Heidegger despised the 'nothingness', spiritlessness and banality of modernity, and was against the spirit of equality and freedom that liberal democracy is said to have ushered. In *Being and Time* (1962), Heidegger directs his philosophical enquiry on human existence or being (*Dasien*). According to Heidegger, in liberal modernity, we lead an inauthentic existence (*Dasien*) focusing our energies in executing the mediocre, banal, stupefying nothingness of everyday existence. Instead, 'Being' should be an onslaught against nothingness (Heidegger

2003) of existence. But modern liberal democracy helps numb us to the 'Beingness of Being' (Heidegger 1962, 242), and also dulls us from the life-altering implications of the creativity of nothingness (death). If we were able to penetrate this stupefying dullness and resurrect our Being and make it attuned to the possibility of death at every moment of existence, we would radically fight for a more meaningful, authentic existence. While Heidegger did not believe in biological racism, he was confident that Hitler's Nazi movement had the true potential for resurrecting a meaningful, authentic existence in a way that liberal democracies were unable to create (Beiner 2018). The prosaic, boring and inconsequential stupor of life is poignantly placed in constant juxtaposition with the certainty of death, therefore, for Heidegger, there is need for a cultural revolution against the bourgeoise banality of everyday existence.

Richard Spencer held a conference in 2016, a couple of blocks from the White House, in which he delivered a speech that started with 'Hail Trump!' Many in the audience stood-up and broke out into Nazi salute.

> Hail Trump! Hail our people! Hail victory! The mainstream media or perhaps we should refer to them in original German: *Lügenpresse*...it is not just that many are genuinely stupid, indeed, one wonders if they are people at all, or soulless Gollum...

> To be white is to be striver, a crusader, an explorer, and a conqueror. We build, we produce, we go upward, and we recognize the central lie of American race relation, we don't exploit other groups, we don't gain anything form their presence, they need us and not the other way around. Within the very blood in our veins as children of the sun lies the potential for greatness, that is the great struggle we are called to, we are not meant to live in shame, and weakness, and disgrace. We were not meant to beg for moral validation from some of the most despicable creatures to ever populate the planet, we were meant to overcome, overcome all of it, because that is natural and normal for us (Lombroso and Appelbaum 2016).

Heidegger and Nietzsche were both important influences in Hitler's Nazi party. The Alt-right has made no attempt to hide their admiration for these philosophers and their unapologetic stance towards liberal democracy, principles of equality and freedom. As demonstrated in the interview excerpt above, the Alt-right has no hesitation in likening itself to the Nazi political movement. It is unclear whether the Alt-right actually imbibes the central ontology of Nietzsche and Heidegger, that is, their critique of the spritlessness, materiality and utter banality of modernity. There is nothing in the Alt-right rallies, memoirs, manifestos or speeches that critique the evils of commodification, over-consumption, credit dependence and nihilism. Spencer does claim that Alt-right and its boys are not interested in the spread of capitalism, but it is more in the context that they envision 'grand' projects such as corporate capitalism, spread of democracy and warmongering as misadventures of American neoconservatism. Therefore, nowhere in their discourses or actions do they attempt to radically revolt against the 'spiritlessness' of modernity, or even begin to critique the mechanization of life, technological dominance or environmental implications of modernity. Their enchantment with Nietzsche and Heidegger as the 'red-pill' moment is more a selective and superficial reclamation of the cultural, class and identity dimensions of these philosophers and their philosophy. They read in these philosophers their radical call to action against stupefaction by religion (Nietzsche's attack on Christianity) and the penchant for political correctness (democracy, equality, multiculturalism, diversity). They like the fact that these philosophers claim that humanity has been weakened ('domestic animal') and seduced by the ideologies of modernity that render existence inauthentic. They draw from Nietzsche that happiness rests on the claim to power through terror; the most terrifying being is most powerful, hence 'Hail Trump!' and mimicking Nazi salutation is that unapologetic admiration of terror as powerful. They read Heidegger's fascination with the Nazi movement as a template for an Alt-right led cultural revolution for the preservation of the contemporary

White race. This revolution for an authentic existence pivots on the 'return' of White power and the celebration of Whiteness as superior to what Spencer calls the 'despicable creatures' (people of other races) that depend on the White race and not the other way round. This White-Western-male existence into which all others must fit (non-Western, people of colour, non-Christian religious groups, women) must be wrested through crusade, strife, conquest and exploration (Spencer's speech above) because the 'very blood in our veins as children of the sun lies the potential for greatness, that is, the great struggle we are called to, we are not meant to live in shame and weakness, and disgrace'. This supposed greatness is the reclamation of the White-Being (Whiteness as authentic human existence) as it stands in the precipice of nothingness, that is, ego death, cultural death and racial death that brings disgrace and shame. Reclamation of the White *Dasien* has become, for the Alt-right, a struggle for existence and restoration of the 'natural order of things' (the reign of the Whiteman). If the 'natural order' declines, a diverse world will be born, one where humans are equal (class less), where there is equality between the West and the rest, equality between different races and between gender groups—such an equal and diverse modern society is the abyss of White-male nothingness that must be avoided at all cost.

West, White and World Dominance

Youth for Western Civilization (YWC) is an Alt-right support group that is registered as a non-profit student organization opposing multiculturalism. Its founder president Kevin DeAnna claims that the organization now has chapters across dozens of university campuses in the USA and abroad. In an interview video posted on YouTube, DeAnna claims that 'Western civilization is a compound of Christian, classical, and then the folk traditions of Europe…we don't just define it as just democracy, rule of law, and these universal institutions, we say that it is a specific culture that comes from a specific historical experience' (DeAnna, 2012). DeAnna claims that he and his group were intellectually influenced by Sam Huntington's *Who Are We?* (2004). DeAnna believes that Huntington accurately defines what it means to be American. Huntington has developed a track record for culturally-laced racist theories putting forward explanations for global conflicts through his earlier and much critiqued book *Clash of Civilizations* (2000). For Huntington, cultural differences are mainly religious differences based on which the world can be divided into civilizational blocs. In his scheme of classification, the West (viewed as Judeo-Christian) is pitted against other blocs like Islam, Hindu, Confucianism and African. Huntington pitches the West against the rest in a 'war of the worlds' scenario because cultural/religious differences are immutable. In *Who Are We?* Huntington traces the cultural-ethnic-religious foundation of the USA as a nation by claiming that F. D. Roosevelt and Kennedy were wrong when they proclaimed America as the nation of immigrants. Instead,

> Their [FDR's and Kennedy's] ancestors were not immigrants but settlers, and in its origins America was not a nation of immigrants, it was a society, or societies of settlers who came to the New World in the seventeenth and eighteenth century…settlers came to America because it was a *tabula rasa*. Apart from the Indian tribes, which could be killed off or pushed westward, no society was there; and they came in order to create societies that embodied and would reinforce the culture and values they brought with them from their origin country. (Huntington 2004, 39–40)

Thus, within the Huntingtonian paradigm, there is a difference between settlers and immigrants— 'settlers' is the contemporary variant of the older term 'colonialists' or 'conquistadors' and the difference between the two is in the settler's view of the world, the place to be settled is a clean slate, because the indigenous inhabitants simply blend into the wild like an animal. A 'settler', unlike an 'immigrant', is imbued with that 'sense of collective purpose' (2004, 39) 'to create a new society' where nothing existed. And therefore, America is a Judea-Christian-Anglo civilization, because the Judea-Christian-Anglo settler *found* America. 'Before immigrants could come to America, settlers had to found America' (Huntington 2004, 40). 'Founding', as opposed to integrating, assimilating and blending, is an act of establishing supremacy by killing and conquering that ultimately leads to 'settling'. This closely matches what Spencer claimed in his 2016 speech near the White House, 'To be White is to be striver, a crusader, an explorer, and a conqueror' (Lombroso and Appelbaum 2016). Native Americans did not 'settle', they never existed outside the state of nature and the savage wilderness. The immigrants that came after, blended within the fold of White protestant America. They did not 'found' America, and hence did not 'settle' because America had already been claimed, founded and settled. Therefore, for Huntington, America has a cultural core:

> America' core culture has been and, at the moment, is still primarily the culture of the seventeenth-and eighteenth-century settlers who founded American society. The central elements of that culture can be defined in a variety of ways but include the Christian religion, Protestant values and moralism, a work ethic, the English language, British traditions of law, justice, and the limits of government power, and a legacy of European art, literature, philosophy, and music. (Huntington 2004)

This settler–immigrant difference according to Huntington is the fundamental component of the Alt-right's philosophical praxis. The White Christian protestant has all the necessary elements, morality, values, work ethic, political institutions, and art and literature, therefore, they are culturally 'chosen' to settle and occupy and the 'despicable creatures to ever populate the planet' (Spencer 2015a, Lombroso and Appelbaum 2016) are always immigrants who simply are not racially, culturally equipped to fundamentally create civilizations, they must fit-in at the mercy of the settlers.

While not explicitly connected to biological racism, Huntington's work that inspires the Alt-right is undoubtedly culturally racial (some cultures are superior to others). However, the Alt-right, while avidly embracing Huntington's cultural racism, does not shy away from biological racism. The *Occidental Observer*, which is an Alt-right mouth piece, spends a lot of time and space researching and publishing articles on phenotypes and racial difference, genetic distance and race in an attempt to scientifically substantiate that racial difference is rooted in biology and not merely culture (McCulloh 2019a, b, c). The biocultural racism that is the basis of Alt-right's core agenda is boosted by Huntington's penchant for White supremacy. Huntington himself draws from and cites Madison Grant and Lothrop Stoddard, who have much to say about the biological basis of cultural supremacy. The biological basis of cultural supremacy is emphatically established by Grant (1918, 16–17) when he claims:

> There exists to-day a widespread and fatuous belief in the power of the environment, as well as of education and opportunity to alter heredity, which arises from the dogma of the brotherhood of man, derived in turn from the loose thinkers of the French Revolution and their American mimics...Thus the view that the Negro slave was an unfortunate cousin of the white man, deeply tanned by the tropic sun and denied the blessings of Christianity and civilization played no small part with the sentimentalists of the Civil war period...It must be borne in mind that the specializations which characterize the higher races are of relatively recent development, are highly unstable and when mixed with generalized or primitive characters tend to disappear...The cross between a white man and an Indian is an Indian; the cross between a white man and a Negro is a Negro; the cross between white man and a Hindu is a Hindu, and the cross between any of the three European races and a Jew is a Jew.

Stoddard, in his *Rising Tide of Color against White World-supremacy* (1923), claims:

> The West has justified—perhaps with some reason—every aggression on weaker races by the doctrine of the Survival of the Fittest; on the ground that it is best for future humanity that the unfit should be eliminated and give place to the most able race.

Therefore, the penchant for establishing the biological basis of racial supremacy has a long lineage. While Huntington moves with the times and obfuscates his racism/Western chauvinism under layers of cultural determinism, which he vaguely refers to as civilizational blocs, his forefathers are clear that neither environment, nor social transformation, nor conversion to Christianity can racially uplift the 'lesser men' to the status of the higher races (White men). It is this throbbing heart of hard-core biological racism that fuels the more socially acceptable cultural racism of Huntington. The National Policy Institute and the *Occidental Observer* tap into this 'West is the greatest' bandwagon and attempt to academically establish that White Americans and Europeans are its true owners, the 'most able race'. The Alt-right's concept of 'ethno-space' (*Guardian* 2017b) is an idea of spatial separation from the 'primitive characters' that threaten to dilute the 'specializations which characterize the higher races'. And this penchant for retaining the leadership of the 'most able race' and saving the West from extinction or White genocide translates into paranoia about falling birth rates among the White population (Stern 2019). The paranoia is so grave that Pat Buchanan, the contemporary ideological guru of the Alt-right movement, comments in *The Death of the West* (2002, 13):

> If the present fertility rates hold, Europe's population will decline to 207 million by the end of the twenty-first century, less than 30 percent of the present rate. The cradle of Western civilization will have become its grave.

> Why is this happening? Socialism, the beatific vision of European intellectuals for generations, is one reason. 'If everyone has the promise of a state pension, children are no longer a vital insurance policy against want in old age,' argues Dr. John Wallace of Bologna's Johns Hopkins University: 'If women can earn more than enough to be financially independent, a husband is no longer essential…

> By freeing husbands, wives, and children of family responsibilities, European socialists have eliminated the need for

families. Consequently, families have begun to disappear. When they are gone Europe goes with them. But as Europe is dying, the Third World adds one hundred million people—one New Mexico—every fifteen months. Forty new Mexicos in the Third World by 2050.

The Alt-right interprets this as imminent White extinction, and therefore prescribes that the most pro-White thing to do is procreation—having many children would be the biological–cultural affirmative action for the White race. Until immigration ban, refugee ban, re-introduction of racial segregation can be pushed on a consistent basis, procreation is the only means to keep alive the 'higher race'.

The throbbing heart behind Alt-right's philosophical praxis of Western chauvinism and White supremacy is an unapologetic biological–cultural racism that essentializes humanity by colour and gender. White and man equals to higher grade, civilized, most-able settler pitted against the primitive, lesser, weaker men and migrants. Human history, in the Alt-right's imagination, is a doom's day scenario where history ends with a whimper (Buchanan 2002), where the West clashes with the rest (Huntington 2000) and where the West comes to an end (Buchanan 2002). In all these 'end of the West' scenarios, West is reduced to an ethno-specific entity, that is, White culture. Genetics, bordering on eugenics, is seamlessly mixed with cultural bias to produce an ideology that is blind to the genetic contribution of Africa as a continent and cultural contribution of the Middle East as the cradle of civilization, ignorant about global migration and peopling of the world, and of indigenous inhabitants and indentured labours that produced world history and geography, West, east, or the rest. The fact that the settler–migrant distinction, the White–Brown/Black distinction, the West–rest distinction depends on who draws up the map and who writes history, and what is cunningly lost in translation is wilfully ignored. Ideological praxis, or philosophy and action—how we act and how we think about our actions, are dialectically conjoined. In this dialectic, the words (West,

White, higher, civilized, stronger, settler) we choose to frame our ideological body politic (biological racism, cultural racism, White nationalism, Western chauvinism) heavily depends on available templates or distorted world views produced by racist White men. Unfortunately, however the Alt-right has successfully transmuted 'racism' as a respectable ideology— Huntingtons and Buchanans of the world have an important role to play in the intellectual legitimization of this new brand of biocultural domination. This intellectual legitimization is not a chaotic act of a few crazy White men, it is a philosophical praxis or a well-defined strategy. In his piece on the Browning of the world published in the *Occidental Observer*, McCulloh says as much.

> The concept of race is not set in stone. How we behave on the basis of this information is not at all determined by the genetic data. We Europeans must define ourselves in a way that makes strategic sense. And we have to make explicit assertions of racial identity and explicit assertions of our racial interests. No other strategy will succeed in staving off the dispossession of European America. (McCulloh 2019a)

Philosophy, Praxis and Why We Are What We Are

The Alt-right is a reactionary movement of predominantly White men that wish to reimagine history (and geography) in the form of an exclusionary identity politics that is arrogantly based on the celebration of White maleness. The Alt-right claims to vociferously challenge what they believe is a faulty, weak, liberal, political correctness expressed as multiculturalism, pro-immigration, pro-refugee settlement and pro-affirmative action. Their discourse, speeches and interviews demonstrate un-apologetic racism that draw sustenance from the firm belief that the White race is culturally–biologically superior and is the harbinger of development, civilization and all that is good in human history. The Alt-right criticizes racial mixing (through marriage and migration) as a process that will ultimately erode the greatness of White race resulting in White genocide. Whiteness is also associated with the West, which, in the Alt-right's vision, should only include people of European descent with Christianity as their religious foundation. The lattice of identity, which forms the ideological kernel, that ultimately becomes the body politic of the Alt-right comprises of race (Whiteness), culture (Westernness and Christianity) and gender (maleness). The Alt-right is trenchant in its hatred for Islam and feminism calling the Koran a 'hate book' (McInnes 2018), feminism a cancer and an ideology that produces weak women (Brennan 2018). Buchanan (2010) laments that feminism is leading to the decline of the traditional family structure, deferment of marriage and decline of White birth rate. The Alt-right's aspiration for a glorious White–Western civilization, therefore, includes some bold political polices such as the creation of a White ethno-state, strict immigration policies curtailing the immigration of non-White races and prevention of refugee resettlement.

In this chapter, I provide philosophical underpinnings to the above by looking at Julius Evola, Nietzsche and Heidegger, French Right and Identitarian politics, and a group of philosophers that have intellectualized biological–cultural racism. It is my contention that acting and thinking about actions are dialectically conjoined, therefore, philosophy and praxis cannot be synthetically separated. In other words, how we think about our actions and how our actions produce thoughts cannot be easily distilled. The stance that the Alt-right adopts, that is, how it frames its speeches, interviews, rallies and demands are political acts that are not discreet events in space and time. The racism, misogyny, Islamophobia, Western chauvinism and White supremacy are a carefully selected lattice of identities inspired by thoughts (philosophy) of the group (Alt-right), as well as, other groups in different times and spaces. In that context, McCulloh's (2019a) statement that 'we Europeans must define ourselves in a way that makes strategic sense. And we have to make explicit assertions of racial identity and explicit assertions of our racial interests' is quite poignant.

Which lattice of identity makes 'strategic sense,' and what constitutes 'racial interests' are somethings that will be different for different groups. Certainly, Black Lives Matter will have a completely different racial interest and a completely different lattice of identity that makes strategic sense. The reason for this difference in strategy and interest between the Alt-right and Black Lives Matter is their difference in ideological praxis (philosophy and action). While Black Lives Matter may be influenced by Martin Luther King and civil rights movement, and may fight for justice against police brutality towards Black people (philosophy and action), the Alt-right is influenced by Evola, French Right, Nietzsche and Heidegger, and the Huntingtonian school, and 'acts out' against racial equality of people of colour and women's equality. The philosophy that informs praxis and back again is the ideological basis behind why we identify with something and not others, why and where we draw boundaries between us and the other. Questions such as the following can only be fully answered if we probe the philosophical basis of the Alt-right's praxis: Why does maleness intersect with Whiteness though? What prevents the gun-toting Alt-right misogynists from aligning with the 'Islamic misogynists'? Why is religion the boundary that separates White males from other males? It is in probing the philosophical basis of political praxis, that we come into terms with what is 'strategic' for the Alt-right and what identity lattice must be 'explicitly asserted'.

Gramsci, the Italian Marxist (Evola is considered its right-wing variant), was foremost in considering the importance of identity, especially religious identity in the production of class consciousness or lack of it. Eyerman (1984) argues that due to the importance of the Catholic Church in Italy, Gramsci was interested in analysing how religious identity interplayed with class consciousness, or, in other words, how the subjective symbolic superstructure is dialectically connected with the base or deep structure (economy/class position) (Gramsci 1992). Through cultural and symbolic means, the state penetrated civil society institutions like the church, school and family.

The bourgeoisie thus owns the means of material production (machines, tools) and also controls the means of symbolic production (ideas, imaginations, narratives and discourses) and, therefore, was capable of convincing at least a section of the working class that the preservation of status quo was good for all (Conroy 1984; Jessop 1991). A condition of class hegemony was produced by cultural and economic means when the bourgeoisie successfully re-articulated their very 'particular' interest as the 'general' interest of society and co-opted a sizeable section of the working class to consent to the existing regime of exploitation. The working class did not revolt in spite of deepening exploitation because they were implicated in false consciousnesses, which is the false belief that a system although exploitative of the working class is generally good for all. The consciousness was false and mystified because the exploited failed to analyse the real mechanisms of exploitation, that is, control of cultural and economic means of production by the elites. Evola did not use the term 'hegemony'; however, in critiquing modernity/democracy/equality, he laid out the foundations of a class-based feudal society extolling the role of the elite in attaining higher/spiritual status and thus ruling a society of lesser men for their own good. In other words, unlike Gramsci's angst that the prevalence of cultural hegemony stymied working class revolution, and hence progress towards emancipation from exploitation, Evola actually endorsed a kind of cultural/spiritual/racial hegemony of the elites and saw it as a panacea from the evils of modernity. Evola's disciples like Benoist and the French Right actually believed that the White French elite must control values, attributes and belief systems and create a 'cultural hegemony' that will propagate a certain identity, that is, purity of France—France for French men. Hence, ethnopluralism is the cultural–spatial expression of the 'right' kind of cultural hegemony where dominant identities like French Whiteness are allowed to protect their purity through boundary building. Nietzsche too endorsed the importance of boundaries so that cultures can define their purpose 'wither and wither for', and this purpose, according to Nietzsche, would be fulfilled by powerful genius elites who could contribute a life-affirming destiny to the masses. For Heidegger too, the banality and consumptive mundanity of modernity created an inauthentic existence, which only a biologically and culturally superior group (like the Nazi party) could overturn to create a meaningful *Dasien*. The cultural supremacy/elite supremacy is a dominant theme that ran through other biological/cultural determinist theories of Stoddard, Grant and Maddison. The moot point being the celebration of an essential cultural/racial/biological core (Whiteness/Westernness/maleness) which is superior/separate/distinct and, therefore, possessing the inherent right to preserve itself through boundary making (Benoist and Champetier 2012), conquest, strife, crusade, conquer (Grant 1918; Stoddard 1923; Spencer 2015a, Lombroso and Appelbaum 2016) and West's dominance of the rest (Huntington 2000).

Although it might seem that the Alt-right and its philosophical praxis defined by Evola, Benoist, French Identitarian movement, Nietzsche, Heidegger, Huntington et al is exclusionary, fringe and reactionary, I argue that the philosophical praxis fits very well within the gamut of liberal individualism. At first, this might seem contradictory because almost all the Alt-right gurus denounce the spirit of enlightenment, as in democracy, equality, multiculturalism and modernity. Yet, as I have illustrated in the previous chapter, when culture is interpreted and understood as decontextualized from the geography/history of its making, it becomes meaningless. In the realm of this decontextualized meaninglessness, it is then possible to create any kind of trauma as the basis for crystallization of identity lattice. Liberal individualism celebrates the freedom to realize oneself as a self-sufficient, competitive individual pursuing happiness through the possessions of property and material good. This notion of a liberal individual is an abstraction, an empty container that does not exist in reality. In the real world, the individual coexists in the context of family, identity and class groups so much so that it is impossible to delineate where the individual ends and the group begins. How to resolve this abstractionist individualism in the context of group existence (identity, class), which is a reality? Multiculturalism becomes an effective solution, the individual lives on to individually create her/his economic success, but in doing so, she/he is allowed to be juxtaposed within diverse identity groups that further her/his individual cultural interests (gender, racial, linguistic groups). The cunning of this philosophical praxis is razor sharp—class interest is ignored because economic gratification must be earned through the rationality of self-interested competing individuals, but cultural interest is celebrated through the identity lattices validated by multiculturalism. Why is culture celebrated in liberal individualism and not class? Because class interest may lead to group bargaining and socio-economic redistribution which goes against the interest of the elite class; the elite class must protect its economic hegemony by throwing class out and replacing it with the philosophical abstraction: 'the all-powerful, rational, happy individual', whose happiness or sadness is directly proportional to their own hard work and has nothing to do with systemic (historical/geographical) violation. But cultural interests, if decontextualized from their violent history of colonization, genocide and ghettoization, can be rendered benign and affirmed easily through multicultural projects such as multilingual schools, ethnic food, celebration of Kwanzaa and creation of the promotion of diversity committees in colleges. The economic elite readily partakes in the celebration of these identity affirmations as it does not directly threaten its economic and cultural hegemony. Elite class interest is protected as long as minority cultural affirmation is officially pursued.

The Alt-right, however, argues that liberal multiculturalism is threatening dominant cultural hegemony (White, male, Christian), and hence the need for ethno-space, ethnopluralism and destruction of liberal multiculturalism. What goes unnoticed behind the supposed war of philosophical praxes (Alt-right versus liberal multiculturalism) is the fact, that Whiteness/maleness/Christianness as an identity praxis is tightly imbricated in a sheath of violent cultural–biological philosophy (Evola, Benoist, Nietzsche, Heidegger, Huntington et al.), that has, in periods of history, supported domination/ exploitation of humans by man through colonization, genocide, bigotry and racial marginalization. And it is this history of domination that has contributed to the contemporary economic–cultural hegemony of White, male and Western chauvinism. While there is nothing inherently violent or racist about White identity, or being Western, or male, but the creative use of these identifiers in essentialist ways can obfuscate the violent history of domination and othering, and hence successfully co-opt multiculturalism by promoting the victimhood of White male Western identity. If liberal multiculturalism is about giving voice to, and protecting minority culture, why should it not protect White male Christian identity if it can be proved that such an identity is a fast-growing minority and is under threat of being violently eradicated by black people, Muslims and Mexicans? The Alt-right is out there proving just that and demanding affirmation, nation state, partition and protection. Unless liberal politics contextualizes culture within the gory history of colonization, slavery and genocide of indigenous populations all over the world, it cannot philosophically distinguish between acceptable difference that needs to be affirmed and the unacceptable identifiers that need to be critiqued. The unacceptable identifiers are not a priori essentialized containers of Whiteness, maleness, Westernness and Christianness—an identity lattice is unacceptable because it *emerges as unacceptable* through its contextual history of dominance and othering of those that are different from them. The reason why the philosophical gurus of the Alt-right can get away with a philosophical praxis that backs biological cultural superiority is because they never consider the historical/geographical injustices created by these 'superior' culture. Othering, slavery and colonization are injustices because the cultural–biological arrogance that labels a culture as 'superior' and possessing the right to colonize/enslave/convert 'inferior' cultures is a philosophical praxis that draws nourishment from a skewed vision that equates civilization/superiority exclusively with Euro-Anglo centric Western modernity—a modernity that most of these philosophers so emphatically dismissed. There is no sound philosophical–scientific basis to prove what constitutes 'superiority' of a culture beyond the fact that these philosophers were themselves White, male, Western and therefore ideologically induced to say so. Therefore, what truly separates acceptable identifiers from unacceptable identifiers is whether they were perpetrators of injustice or victims of injustice. An identity lattice that has an established history of perpetrating injustice (colonizing, lynching, apartheid) cannot claim affirmation, especially if it openly vocalizes its ambition to continue perpetrating those kinds of injustice.

Liberal multiculturalism as a philosophy does not engage in depth with the historicity of injustice because, doing so, may have economic ramifications like wealth redistribution for the violated groups, and therefore topple the whole band-wagon of liberal individualism and its belief that inequality is not an impediment for economic success. Class affirmation is the antithesis of liberal philosophy, and therefore, to avoid economic questions of redistribution/reparation/economic equality, liberal multiculturalism provides a safe and superficial breeding ground for identify affirmation only. Culture without economy and culture without history is a suitable container box for all kinds of differences that do not have to reveal their unjust history of domination and control as they seek affirmation. Therefore, while the Alt-right critiques liberal multiculturalism, and although Alt-right's praxis goes against the politics of liberal democracy, philosophically, the Alt-right fits very well within this decontextualized container box of multiculturalism. As Trumpism and Alt-right gain momentum, it will be very hard for liberal politics to philosophically exclude unacceptable difference. While liberal philosophy preserves the economic status quo, Alt-right's philosophical underpinnings preserve the cultural status quo. It will become very hard for liberal philosophical praxis to 'rationalize' why the self-interested man can keep his wealth despite the fact that it has been accrued through generational plunder and protected by tax policies that impoverish the greatest number, but it is wrong for the White man to affirm his 'superior' identity even though it has been accrued through cultural–biological plunder of people of colour and women. In essence, the philosophy underpinning liberalism and Alt-rightism is very similar, their praxis is superficially different: liberal politics practices progressive multiculturalism, Alt-right practices regressive multiculturalism—not only is the dialectics between philosophy and praxis conjoined, liberalism and Alt-right are dialectically conjoined as well!

4

Alt-right Women and the Reconstruction of Patriarchy and Feminism

The Patriarchal Gaze

In the previous chapters, I have drawn a parallel between liberalism as a political philosophy ingrained in individualist ethic and the Alt-right's philosophy arguing that both emphasize identity affirmations. Liberal philosophical praxis encourages superficial identity affirmation through myriad strategies of multiculturalism (for e.g., affirmative action and promotion of diversity in schools and colleges) in order to escape deep analyses of historical and geographical inequalities in distribution of capital (cultural and economic), wealth and property that underlie identity differences. Acknowledging class position as conjoined with identity discrimination (that racial minorities are also overwhelmingly poor) would require the capitalist state to enact policies of recognition and redistribution (Fraser 1995; Fraser and Honneth 2003). Redistribution if pursued robustly could mean land reforms, for example, reforms that overhaul the historical–geographical inequalities enacted by the pioneering plunder of Native American nations (Fershee 2004) in the USA and reparation to Third World nations for decades of imperial plunder by colonial nations. In other words, going beyond promotion of diversity along colour/linguistic lines (and actually enforcing socio-economic redistribution) could threaten the political economic core of capitalist-individualism, that is, accumulation of capital by some at the cost of others based on self-interest and competition. The Alt-right too, as I have demonstrated in the previous chapter, is heavily 'red-pilled' by Identitarian philosophies that invest in a reverse multiculturalism (reversal of the liberal model), that is, the affirmation of Whiteness and maleness as the basis of national consciousness of Western nation. The argument here is that with migration and racial mixing, the White race is swiftly becoming marginal in the USA and Europe (Almada 2017), and with the rising tide of feminism, able White men are marginalized in education and employment (Bergman 2018; May and Feldman 2019). Therefore, if marginality is the site of multicultural affirmation, then male identity and White identity are swiftly becoming minority positions, and hence, subjugated by the onslaught of misplaced Western liberalism, White males need immediate affirmation and redressal. Being an internet-based movement of middle-class White youth comfortably ensconced within college campuses, the Alt-right does not see the need to upset stable economic class divisions. Expanding Medicaid or Section 8 housing for the White poor does not capture Alt-right's imagination. Although not invested in the global spread of corporate capitalism, Alt-right is, at the same time, not geared to overhaul capitalism-driven wage and wealth inequalities—herein also lies Alt-right's similarity with liberal philosophy. Alt-right is, therefore, the mirror image of liberal individualism—equal and flipped. The flipping is a clever optical illusion where the multiculturalist ethic of preserving historically marginalized groups (racial, linguistic, ethnic, gender) is reproduced through a facsimile argument that Whiteness and maleness are on the verge of extinction—the illusion pivots around 'marginalization' being constructed as reduced number and reduced representation. Racism and patriarchy are oppressive identities that do not rely on numerical strength to exploit—a handful of White plantation owners and slave-drivers historically exploited large number of Black people, and it requires only one patriarch to regulate women's life in a household. Number derives exploitative power in the context of identity-valourization—a large number of people can be marginalized by few, a small number of people can be marginalized by many, one person can marginalize another. Whether an identity is 'acceptable' candidate for systemic affirmation depends on how numerical strength has been used and to what end. When an identity, irrespective of numerical strength, acquires systemic power, it has been valourized. If this systemic power is then used to exploit 'other' groups, then devalourization and marginalization has taken place irrespective of the numerical strength or weakness of the exploited group. The fact that Whiteness and maleness are identities that have been systemically valourized in the USA and Europe and all over the world is a claim that no longer requires substantiation. Racism, sexism and imperialism are realities that all systems grudgingly recognize. In that context, the Alt-right's claim to marginality rests on the clever manufacturing of a mirror image of identity devalourization, a leaf taken out of the liberal philosophy to demonstrate that migrants, Muslims and women today out-number White men in predominantly 'White Christian nations', male-dominated universities and jobs. Reduced numerical strength equates with reduced systemic power; therefore, the White man needs valourization, protection and safe ethno-space. Much ado about decline in White birth rates is made by the Alt-right (McCulloh 2019a) but nothing about President Trump's 'Pussy-grabbing' comment (ABC news 2017), or the sexual assault allegations directed at him by multiple women (Pearson, Gray and Vagianos 2019), or his comments about Mexicans as rapists (Reilly 2016), and migrants from 'shit-hole' countries in Africa (Yee 2018), all of which prove that despite decline in White birth rate, White men can easily project patriarchal and racist devalourization because they claim systemic power—numerical strength and systemic power may or may not be correlated, but there is an absolute correlation between oppressive identities, consolidation of systemic power and injustice. Two things make an identity oppressive and, hence, 'unacceptable': its inability to recognize its own complicity in producing historical–geographical devalourization of 'others' (women, people of colour, indigenous groups, colonial subjects), and the arrogant self-valourization based on devalourization of 'other'—for the 'pussy grabbing White man' no historical injustice was done to Black people and women because Black people deserved to be enslaved as they were inferior, and women deserved to be controlled and commodified because they were irrational objects. Since no oppression happened then, no oppression is happening now as the superior White man trample upon Brown people, Muslims and women. For the patriarchal White gaze, Blackness, Brownness, being Muslim and being women carries within them inherent inferior attributes; therefore, the White patriarchal identity that claims superiority does not produce oppression, only a justified tier system of identity, where the inferior must fall into place and celebrate the superior. When the 'inferior' does not fall into place, then they must be made to through the violence of intimidation, anti-immigration and anti-feminism.

Nothing Motivates Men than a Beautiful Woman in Need

The women of the Alt-right are playing an important role in affirming White male supremacy and self-tiering themselves as soft, emotional, beautiful, family-oriented, homemakers and husband seekers as opposed to men as builders, leaders, providers and protectors (Mattheis 2018). For the Alt-right women, this is not tiering but simply essential socio-biological categories that set women apart from men. Lana Lokteff, a Russian American from Oregon, co-runs Red Ice, an Alt-right media company, with her Swedish husband, Henrik Palmgren. At an Alt-right conference in 2017, Lokteff was the star speaker. With a self-assured calmness and a carefully cultivated non-aggressive, demure stance, Lokteff critiqued the perversion of gender roles unleashed by the left.

> The left is losing more women to us because the left offers feminized men in skinny jeans holding signs saying immigrants welcome, they push fat ugly women as the beauty ideal and claim that their husband must have sex with a man once in a while to prove that they are not homophobic, the white picket fence has been traded for a carbon neutral apartment in a diverse neighborhood enriched by third world immigrants... there are three important things important for women and they are engrained in her psyche...:beauty, family, home, women want to be beautiful, attract the best mate possible, and be protected and provided for until death, any woman who says differently is lying to herself...beauty, family, and home, are exactly what nationalism gives to women. We value the beauty of western civilization and the refined human form. European men build civilization and facilitated beauty in all its form, it's the ultimate romantic gesture to all European women. They build our civilization to enable our home, and the family, and protect the women, a nation is an extended family, your support system... left provides ugliness and violence, and that is why they are losing.... I meet women who say to me, I want a husband, I am 29, I need to have kids, I say 'come to a right wing conference,' and the good news is I have been seeing matches made left and right of the most beautiful couples, it is eugenics, we have an eugenic process that we find ourselves here...nothing motivates men than a beautiful women in need, a soft woman saying hard things can create repercussions throughout society, since we are not physically intimidating we can get away with saying hard things—lionesses yet sensual as silk. (Lokteff 2019)

The phallocentricity is palpable in the above speech; patriarchy combines with race in schizophrenic ways to reaffirm status quo. The preservation of racist and patriarchal status quo is celebrated through a psychotic Stockholm syndrome. The claim that 'the left offers feminized men in skinny jeans holding signs welcoming immigrants' is aimed towards the creation of a discursive template where left politics is an emasculating process of stripping men off their virility and creating 'feminized' or in other words, less than/unmanly/woman-like men. The choice of phrases explicates the very heart of Alt-right identity movement—in deliberately going against established feminist discourses that argue gender to be a social construct (not a biological essence), that is, masculinity and femininity are norms of existence socially produced and not biologically produced (Beauvoir 1974; Butler 1988). Lokteff herself posits 'femininity' as an *essential* category that is becoming of women but unbecoming of men. The implication is that 'feminine' men are weak (because women are the weaker sex), and therefore they pander to weak geopolitics of pro-migration and border porosity. Similarly, endorsement of progressive sexual politics or environmental politics is also seen as left's emasculation bordering on perversion. The pointed implication is that progressive women are 'loose', devoid of beauty and femininity (ugly and fat), and hence, devoid of family values, and therefore compelled by the need to prove their left-oriented sexual politics, push their men to have sex with other men. There is an attempt to not only 'fix' gender where womanhood is equated with traits of beauty, thinness and traditionally familial, but also a sexual narcissism that simultaneously disparages women when they don't meet the warped standards of femininity, but powerfully 'castrate' masculinity if they happen to be against homophobia. The desire, nay the devotion, of Alt-right women to pedestalize phallocentric versions of sexuality in a socially programmed way is the Stockholm syndrome, where women wilfully align with their exploiter; the left is seen not as a liberator from oppressive fixed categories like impossible standards of beauty and nurture but a destabilizing force that distorts womanhood and distorts manhood—ugliness begets ugliness ('ugly' feminists attract 'ugly' sexual politics) and femininity begets effeminate politics (effeminate men support homophobia).

The ugly feminist and the effeminate man support other monstrosities such as 'carbon neutral apartments' and Third World immigrants. For the Alt-right, there is something castrative about the desire to protect the environment and not exploit it; after all, modernity, voracious consumption and commodification of the environment, industrial capitalism and patriarchy have been seen by critical philosophers as conjoined. Similarly, Third World immigrant is a metaphorical code word for non-White, uncivilized heathens, and if the 'West' is to be seen as the traditional colonizer (male/exploiter), then the Global South is the colonized subject (women/exploited). Therefore, the 'invasion' of the Global South/the colonized subject/women is a powerful destabilization of White masculine West, a castration that renders Europe and America devoid of narcissistic control of their White identity and White future that will surely be lost to the mixed racial interactions brought forth by the virile and fertile Muslims and Mexicans. The nations of the West are the familial home for beauty and Whiteness of Western civilizations, a safe haven for White women provided to them by men. Lokteff celebrates White masculinity by discursively stitching gender, race, migration and nation building into a celebration of White masculinity of the correct kind. The perfect White man does not wear skinny jeans, is emphatically heterosexual, is a provider that contains women because she wants to be contained within the home and the nation, both of which are beautiful gifts that men can give women. In that context, it is to be understood that 'the man' must protect his wife, his home, his nation, his civilization; therefore, the act of racism against migrants, the act of walling, border control, anti-immigration and anti-refugee resettlement politics are masculine acts undertaken by strong men to save the beauty, purity and femininity of the West as the home of civilized White men and women.

The political sphere of the conference where ideologies are built, strategies discussed and successes honoured is also the site for race-appropriate mating game. Lokteff gushes over the 'watering hole' properties of the Alt-right conference, where virile men can meet beautiful women in a primitive enactment of the 'eugenics' of heteronormative sexuality— 'women in need' of racially/sexually 'appropriate' mating partners and men gloriously meeting that need. The 'watering hole' not only brings together a specie bonded by the desire to dominate and predate other species (migrants, Muslims, independent women), but serves as a cite for careful racial/sexual selection so that the greatness and purity of the White pedigree is carefully nurtured. The key to the preservation of White heterosexuality is the careful cultivation of a femininity that is soft and physically un-intimidating; so that, when such women do make a point, men rush in to implement them as a chivalrous gesture and an ode to femininity. Lokteff herself embodies a carefully cultivated demure grace throughout her hard-hitting speech as she belittles, with a gentle smile, the left, the men on the left, and belittles women on the left as fat and ugly. It is meticulously honed that aggressiveness is not a desired attribute in right-wing women; it is unbecoming and off-putting to men and does not bring constructive change. Men must display aggression in saving, protecting and providing. Alt-right women, on the other hand, must show their strength in restrain, poise and sensuality. In other words, an ideal Alt-right woman is a lioness only in her sensuality and poise, not in aggression—it is lost to Lokteff that in the animal kingdom, the lioness, although smaller than the lion, is actually faster than it and does the bulk of the aggressive job of organizing a hunt and bringing a kill to feed the pack, while the 'lions 'lion' around in the shade' (Pociask 2018).

Ayla Stewart, Alt-right's sweetheart mom that Lokteff endorses emphatically, is a YouTuber and a blogger. Stewart has over 11,000 subscribers on YouTube and over 200 videos. Stewart, however, is quick to clarify that she does not align with all aspects of the Alt-right ideology as she is open to having friends from all races and she is not fighting for a pure White ethno-state (JLP Show 2018). Stewart has made it her mission to disseminate the importance of large White families, home-schooling, restoration of pride in White culture and critique of public schools in the USA. Her website: 'Wife with a Purpose: Trad Life: The Restoration and Preservation of Traditional Family Values' lists its contact address as '140 Haunting the Nightmares of Feminists Plaza Vinland, North America' and claims that Stewart is 'the most censored Christian mother in America' and a 'fake news target and stalking survivor'. The website proudly claims that Stewart was one of the first to be de-platformed from Twitter and hounded for supporting president Trump's agenda, which she lists as:

> Faith, family, freedom
> God, guns, guts.
> Borders, Bibles, Babies. (Wife with a Purpose 2019)

In a YouTube interview for the JLP Show hosted by Jesse Lee Peterson, who himself is Black, Stewart and Peterson chat amicably about the need for multiple White babies and the restoration of traditional family values. The JLP Show webcasts interviews with White guests on issues like White history month to curing LGBTQ communities and has a large White fan following. In the interview, Peterson quizzes Stewart on White history month, family values and Christopher Columbus as a White hero. Peterson starts by wishing Stewart a happy White history month and asks her to comment. In response, Stewart says:

> I am feeling wonderful about it! We have been really shamed as a race and a people in our public schools to not be proud or happy or content with our culture and what we have done as a people. We have been culturally conditioned to hating ourselves, most white people who hear anything positive about white culture have an immediate reflexive reaction of negativity. (JLP Show 2018)

Peterson then asks Stewart about her large family and comments, 'Thank you for having White babies!' Both Peterson and Stewart laugh, and Peterson expresses concern that if White people become a minority and people of colour takeover, this country will become 'a 'S' hole country!' Stewart then goes on to explain her stance regarding babies, family values and public-school education.

> Yes, I have a similar concern and it is happening everywhere not only in America, but Sweden, Germany, Canada, and Australia— people are not having babies, this is such a great way to maintain our lineage, heritage and honor our ancestors, and keep our country strong. You grow so much when you have children, these liberals are just choosing to keep dogs and going to Starbucks and that is their whole life, they never learn any of the values that God intended us to learn through having children, multiple children, and raising them in traditional ways...we homeschool our children because, we did not want them to be indoctrinated with liberal propaganda, which is not only anti-white, it is also, anti-God, if someone is a person of God, they will be smeared in the public schools. (JLP Show 2018)

Peterson went on to ask Stewart about her views on today's men and Stewart replied, 'Unfortunately, men have been feminized, weakened (not all), rendered subservient to the feminist tyranny that we live under in our current society.' When Peterson asked, 'Can this be overcome?' Stewart explained that it could be done if men would 'be a rock', 'be a harbor in the tempest', 'be a man again', 'cultivate your manhood', 'don't eat soy', 'do right by your wife and children' and 'don't let your mother, wife, or sister, the women in your life push you around' (JLP Show 2018). Clearly, Stewart's agenda and fan following feeds on the marketing of traditional gender roles pitched against feminism, her mock address proclaims are home as a site of 'nightmare for feminists'. All the usual conservative hot-button issues ranging from God to gun, to family, anti-abortion and border control are listed as agenda. The interview between JLP and Stewart is a combination of self-inflicted racism and self-inflicted misogyny that is almost bizarrely psychotic. The Black man's enthusiasm for White babies and a woman's penchant to be compliant towards the 'manly man' is a bizarre mirror image of each other; it is a commentary on the insidious infiltration of patriarchy and Whiteness as paradigmatic discourses that create a self-disparaging identity politics of racial and gender submission, a willing consent to exploitation that uplifts the hegemony of racist and patriarchal discourses. The urgent need to procreate in large numbers so as to populate the world with White children is expressed by both parties, what is interesting is that JLP echoes President Trump's comments about African immigrants coming from 'S' hole countries (Yee 2018), claiming emphatically that biological reproduction of the White race is the only possible way for saving America from 'degenerating'— it is interesting that JLP has no comments about the contribution of Black people in the growth and advancement of the country. JLP's enthusiastic endorsement of White supremacy is an optical illusion that strategically creates blindness to the oppression, marginalization and the historicity of racism against Black population in America. JLP therefore, becomes the alter-ego of Whiteness; he self-positions his Blackness within the larger narrative of White supremacy to provide strategic legitimacy for his historical racial oppressor thus, willingly consenting to Alt-right's racism. Stewart takes great pleasure in casting her opponents as frivolous beings who spend their lives in Starbucks, taking care of dogs rather than learning life's experiences through the 'holy' duty of procreation.

In a separate YouTube video on immigration, Stewart blames feminism for the volumes of immigrants pouring into Europe. Her argument is that refugees and migrants make no logical sense for an international order that is based on nation states with boundaries; yet, German people wait at the stations carrying signs welcoming immigrants, immigrants who will 'come and throw garbage everywhere'. The reason is emotional and not logical; the emotion being White guilt—predominantly, White nations should feel guilty for colonialism, for having resources. 'No one asks India to share!' 'Nobody says that China needs to share for the prosperity they have been having because we are buying all their crap.' The reason why Western society, according to Stewart, is based on White guilt is because

Western societies for many years have been constructed on a false foundation of feminism, which is an ideology based on emotion rather than logic. These are societies, argues Stewart, where women are considered better than men, here single mothers are worshipped as heroes, here environmentalism and global warming are important issues and social justice warriors are praised. These are, according to Stewart, feminized, illogical and emotional issues practised by people who are indoctrinated with the emotion of feminism. Feminism strips men off their masculinity, emasculates them and renders them emotional. An emphasis on emotion/feminism renders the world out of balance, creates a chaotic and illogical world. According to Stewart, a world cannot be based on nurturing. Border porosity, openness to migrants and refugees are an example of that illogical, emotional feminist nurturing. Women's emotion and nurturing are useful within the family and for occupations in which women 'naturally' excel, such as teaching, nursing, relief and aid work, but the whole world cannot be treated that way. Men, on the other hand, are 'naturally' good at building structures, industries, acquiring resources, leading, protecting and providing, and 'the White Christian man has done it the best.' A feminist society robs men of their natural strengths such as leadership and logic; this creates feminized men, 'hipsters with man buns walking around talking of their feelings', 'we need manly men in society' (Stewart 2015), otherwise, our political priorities will be illogical, such as politically prioritizing migration, environmentalism and global warming. Lokteff and Stewart are what is known in Alt-right circles as 'trad wives', short for 'traditional wife', who embody feminine and wifely qualities such as submissiveness, chastity, willingness to do household chores and want many children. The trad wives carefully manage their blogs and websites with photos that display themselves in comfortable homes engaged in wifely duties like baking while looking picture-perfect in dresses or skirts. The very essence of feminism, which is about critiquing socially normalized gender roles and expectations such as men as rational, women as emotional, men as protectors, bread winners and providers, and women as receivers of provisions and protection, is used and misused in confused yet strategic ways (Butler 2011; Butler and Weeds 2011; Hughes and Witz 1997). Therefore, emotion is considered inherent in women and a positive attribute when directed at husbands and family, or in schools as teachers and in hospitals as nurses, and this emotional economy is attributed to feminism. When this 'feminism' as a praxis of emotions is extended into geopolitics, Stewart claims, it produces weak policies of border porosity, environmental protection and preventing climate change, rather than virile forms such as strict immigration policy, conquest of resources and war. It is interesting how feminism and normalized notions of femininity are confused, the former being a critique of the normalization of socially assigned nurturing roles to women, and the latter being the conformity to such assigned roles. Feminism critiques the socially normalized attribution of emotion to women and logic to men claiming that these are structured, superimposed and normalized. Stewart incorrectly assumes that feminism fosters emotion, and hence, men raised by feminists are emotional, and geopolitics administered by such men is weak and emotional. On the contrary, feminists argue (Butler 2011; Butler and Weeds 2011) that conflation of emotion with women is a patriarchal construct. In other words, emotion, nurture and caregiving are important attributes' but they are not necessarily tied to the biological female—gender (femininity, masculinity) is a social construct, a social pigment injected into the biological cell. Ultimately, the moot point for Stewart is the acceptance of societally dichotomized bio-gender roles, otherwise, men are not 'manly' and are rendered illogical, emotional, feminine, emasculated, skinny and unmanly. Men should be macho, and women should be feminine, that is how nature, biology and God created the world, and feminism disrupts that order into a chaos of feminine men. Trad wives do not aspire for a world where woman (and men) can aspire to be logical *and* emotional, strong *and* nurturing, homemakers *and* geopolitical thinkers, builders *and* caregivers. In Alt-right women's self-directed misogyny, the 'lioness' is strongest when it is sensuously compliant, gracefully non-aggressive and homely, not worldly.

In a promotional video on YouTube, the Proud Boys—a White supremacist, male chauvinist group founded by Gavin McInnes (often with troubled ties to the Alt-right)—claim that 'there is only one criteria for membership, you will have to accept that the West is the Best,' and of course, you have to be a biological male.' In the Dallas chapter of the video, a new member is recruited and asked to repeat an oath: 'I am a proud Western chauvinist and I refuse to apologize for creating the modern world.' One member clarifies that 'we are not anti-women in the workplace, we are just pro-house wives, why won't women come up the pedestal that we have created for them, I don't understand.' Regarding feminists and liberals, McInnes facetiously says that it is like your four-year old punching your knee and you saying, 'please stop saying 'smash patriarchy', 'smash capitalism', it is not good for you, I want you to be happy, I want you to get married and have children, I want you to enjoy yourselves, but this feminism, this punching my knees is not good for you, I can take it, but this is not good for you, please stop being liberal, you are hurting yourself' (Zadrozny and Siemaszko 2018). If the trad wives are the procreators, mothers, caregivers and cooks, the Proud Boys serve as the 'rational' and masculine counterparts who are the 'manly men', not the dog-walking, Starbucks-going type but the one's that bring modernity. Like the trad wives, the Proud Boys cast feminism and liberalism as weak, emotional, infantile and knee-jerk value systems born out of unhappiness, inability to attain marriage and become parents.

Lauren Southern, a Canadian born far-right activist, having close ties to the Alt-right, talks, 'Boobs, feminists, and migration,' on YouTube (Rebel News 2015). A White male host opens by claiming that they will be photoshopping some cleavage on Southern, an idea that Southern approves claiming that she has never done it on YouTube video because the internet will go crazy as her viewers are 'good conservatives'. Southern shot into internet fame working for Rebel media that trolled and sabotaged feminist rallies (SlutWalk movement) in Canadian cities organized to protest rape culture. While most protestors refused to talk to her, Southern followed them around seeking individual interviewees and expressing disagreement with the main argument of the rally that rape culture is normative in most Western societies. Southern was followed by 'Men Going Their Own Way' (MGTOW) followers carrying signs claiming 'Feminism is a refuge for women's sexual failure' and 'Feminists say any sex between a man and a woman is rape.' Throughout Southern's interview, the MGTOW men were strategically placed to capture camera footage and to launch a visual offensive against the protestors. At one point, Southern stops to interview the MGTOW members who claim that their organization is a reactionary one that takes bachelorhood into a version of activism, and as part of their activist stance, the MGTOW men have decided to not engage in relationships with women because of the baggage that feminism brings due to the drama of the family courts, and because of constant allegations of rape (Rebel News 2015). Lauren Southern is for Rebel media what JLP is for the JLP Show—consenting to self-exploitation by positioning one's identity within the narrative of the oppressor. In JLP's case, it was Black positionality that champions White supremacy; Southern, on the other hand, attempts to undermine a feminist movement through her troll journalism that heckles feminists for wearing scanty protest attires. Southern provides a lot of footage for MGTOW men who complain that promiscuous women often change their minds about sexual content. Important issues such as gender relations, sexual consent, rape and custody battles deserve discussion and robust participation of both men and women from all sides of the political spectrum. However, what Alt-right's YouTube activism achieves is a selective propagation of the master narratives of White supremacy and patriarchy using Black men and White women as anchors, who, by virtue of their racial and gender marginality, turn upside down the very notions of racism and patriarchy. Their endorsement of the structures of oppression creates an oppressor–oppressed toxic bond, where the latter legitimizes the former even when the former disparages and oppresses the latter.

Milo Yiannopoulos, a vocal spokesperson for the Alt-right on internet, Twitter and university campuses, when interviewed by Studio number 10 claimed that feminism is a form of cancer and has run its course. When one interviewer claimed that she was a proud feminist, Yiannopoulos retorted, 'I am sure they will cure you soon, there is chemotherapy for that' and then went on to clarify that what feminists characterized 'as hate, and abuse, and harassment is a hysterical drumming, it is sort of a moral panic' (Yiannopoulos 2017). When the same journalists asked Yiannopoulos why he called Donald Trump 'daddy', Yiannopoulos replied:

> I called him that because it sort of annoys everybody, but also because he reflected the role Donald Trump was playing in culture and society at that time, he is one of those people who slightly made you cringe at times, made you little embarrassed at times, but was basically right, basically had your interest at heart, and would look after you anyway. I found a lot of female voters who you might not have imagined would vote for Trump because, of perhaps his locker room talk or whatever, voted for him anyway, and they loved him, Why? Because he is this strong masculine figure who projected strength and maybe, a little machismo versus the previous president who was useless and never inspired a…. there were no women fainting on the aisles or getting light headed on the chaise lounge for Obama in the end, but they were for Trump, and I found that fascinating, and that is why I called him Daddy. (Yiannopoulos 2017)

An intricate web of chauvinism is afloat here. On the one hand, Whiteness uses Blackness and patriarchy uses women as foot soldiers for legitimization of the supreme identifiers of Western modernity (being White and male). On the other hand, Yiannopoulos, who is openly gay, aligns with 'daddy' (Trump) whose administration has attacked LGBTQ rights on healthcare, education and employment (Malaea 2019). Yiannopoulos excavates Trump's charisma as 'machismo' and 'strongly masculine' even when his position as a gay person should in itself be a disruption of patriarchal gender normativity such as machismo in men and fainting fits in women. Despite his positioning in a marginalized sexual identity, Yiannopoulos is very much a White, Western, 'straight', patriarchal figure that worships toxic masculinity as strongman 'daddy' figures, who albeit embarrassing, are powerful providers ('would look after you'). President Obama is cast as the alternate-to-daddy version, the effeminate one that does not attract admiring women. The trad wife's vision of the world is accentuated here, nurturing qualities are feminine and meant for homemaking and child rearing, but geopolitics is best left for the big daddies that can display sabre-rattling machismo. Feminism is a disease in that context, a hysterical misfit of a movement that destroys stable power relations (like patriarchy, heterosexuality) by characterizing 'normal' behaviour as 'hate' and 'abuse'. Geopolitics based on diplomacy, moderation and negotiation is characterized as feminine caregiving rather than ruling—ruling requires manning up by not eating soy and 'projecting strength'. Feminists are neither feminine, nor capable of dispensing geopolitical machismo, and they are a blight, a sort of existential angst of hysterical women caught in a moral panic. There is cognitive dissonance in the way identity is cast to create acceptable and unacceptable differences. Trad wives identify with patriarchy endorsing the need for women to be demure and soft but speaking tough when it comes to endorsement of normative gender roles; they argue that traditional gender roles do not make women submissive to the patriarchal order, just produce appropriate and God-given division of labour between men and women. A Black anchor endorses White supremacy by urgently proclaiming the need for increasing birth rates within the White race; he thinks that it is a necessity if the civilized order is to be prevented from going to 'shit'. A gay person endorses heteronormative notions of masculinity as attractive and desirable quality for leadership and geopolitics and disparages any deviation from that norm as uninspiring. In other words, a manly man inspires women, such a manly man is White, he provides and rules, and any social movement (like feminism) that disrupts this template is madness, not civilization.

The proliferation of Alt-right's stance on feminism, masculinity and sexuality has led to the proliferation of misogynistic websites and blogs like the Return of the Kings that is replete with articles titled: 'Seven Ways that Modern Women Treat Men like Dogs: Do You Take Abuse from a Woman?', 'If You Hate the Patriarchy, Give Us Back Our Electricity: Feminists May Hate the Patriarchy, but they Don't Hate Male Inventions', 'How to Fight Feminist Organizations like, "Muslims for Progressive Values: They Are Ushering a Matriarchal Society"', 'Seven Ways Women Are Just like Abandoned Dogs' and 'Women Lie about Everything.' It is interesting that the misogyny drifts from targeting feminists to targeting women; somewhere the line dissolves. An article on patriarchy and electricity that is posted on the same website is replete with pictures of 'angry women' demonstrating or protesting, most pictures show women with bright hair colours (blue, green) with contorted facial expressions. The article claims:

'Down with the Patriarchy!' shouts a blue-haired, non-binary, non-gender conforming thing at the top of its shrill lungs. Has the world gone mad? Has the apocalypse finally come? What is going on here? Is there a virus in the water? No, it's just Tuesday at a University in America. And the blue-haired, shrieking thing happens to be your professor. Have fun at school fellas!

With the advent of technology (all of it invented, improved and maintained by the dreaded patriarchy), work has largely evolved into pushing paper, dialing the phone, reading, writing and communicating. Women recognized that with the physical barriers to 'bread-winning' having been largely cast aside, they could potentially do these sorts of jobs just as well as the men.

They lobbied their husbands and other powerful men to let them enter the workplace and compete for jobs alongside the men. And men, being reasonable, gracious and accommodating towards the ladies supported their ambitions.

Backstabbing, gossip, rumor mongering, slander… that's how ladies compete with one another. Complimentary to the face and cunning behind the back. And now the men, rubbing their heads in agony, slowly coming to their senses, are realizing the drastic mistake they made in accommodating the demands of the perpetually unsatisfied feminist agenda.

College, once a haven for free thought, challenging ideas, and ritualistic debauchery, has devolved into a paranoid, politically correct surveillance zone where anyone who dares not conform to the feminist lunacy risks total ruin. (Blackmire 2018)

The Alt-right targets university campuses because they view these as sites for left-liberal discourse production, and the question: 'Is there a virus in the water?' The implication is that 'madness' is rife as feminist professors proliferate like blue-haired viruses teaching about feminism, which is swiftly deconstructed as a movement of women clamouring for office jobs because with the economy going White collar, women who are physically weak (unsuitable for agriculture, mining, industry) were able to clamour for office jobs to which powerful men 'kindly consented'. But the face of feminism at the workplace is seen as 'backstabbing and gossip', which is attributed to women's inherent nature. Now that feminists have colonized workplaces and college spaces, the 'madness' virus of surveillance, paranoia and political correctness has spread. Feminism, viewed through the Alt-right's lens, is an absurd, false ideology, unnatural, entitled and born out of patriarchal graciousness; it is a celebration of ugliness, fatness, political correctness and disruption of the natural biological division of labour that does not respect the power and innovative genius of man.

Blue-haired Virus Called Feminism

In Chapter 2, I argued that liberal philosophy fails to unequivocally explicate the distinction between acceptable and unacceptable difference. Unacceptable differences based on privilege were created through horrible systemic injustices such as class oppression, racial oppression and patriarchal oppression. Liberal multiculturalism believes that freedom or happiness is contingent on the accumulation and preservation of objects/ private property, and hence, it is unwilling to disrupt the status quo (class, gender, racial) because, while it does not articulate it as thus, it assumes that accumulation on class, racial and patriarchal lines is something that is inevitable—inequality is inevitable. Liberalism, therefore, agrees that concentration of happiness (possessions, wealth, private property) is something the state should not police or disrupt; instead the liberal state can affirm (multiculturalism) some unequal groups that have entered realms of acceptability. Individual freedom, therefore, provides solid ethical underpinnings to movements like Alt-right based on patriarchal hegemony because it never threatens to dismantle the history–geography of inequality produced by these hegemonic positions. The Alt-right, however, attacks feminism as it views it to be an ideology nested within liberalism, multiculturalism and identification of man as the exploiter. Feminism's popularity in progressive groups, political parties, university campuses, movies and pop culture makes it an important competitor in the marketplace for production of Identitarian acceptability. Scholars (Eisenstein 2005; Fraser 1995; Shaw 2018) have argued how liberal feminism's singular focus on conquering spaces of production/work/economy makes it vulnerable for co-optation by capital, particularly, neoliberal capital (free market globalization), often limiting the scope of feminism to diversity quotas in jobs and schools without fundamentally attacking patriarchal normalization of 'work' as masculine/emancipatory and caregiving as feminine/oppressive. This uncritical pursuit of 'acceptability' through economic rights at the work place makes liberal feminism susceptible to competition and onslaught by movements like the Alt-right that view women not as humans, but as individuals competing with individuals (men). Globalization and outsourcing, neoliberalization and free trade, and financial liberalization have ushered a post-Fordist society that has seen the dismantling of traditional manufacturing, shrinking middle class and increase in inequality in the Global North (Harvey 2007a and 2007b), often challenging traditional patriarchy at the mill, factory and the mine through the process of structural adjustment leading to overhaul and near disappearance of these sectors. The simultaneous outsourcing of manufacturing jobs to the Global South and proliferation of sweatshops and economic processing zones have created an army of feminized precarious workers that are exploited through the new flexible regime of casual hire and fire and temporary and informal status (McDowell 2003). The visual presence of women in many globalization related jobs in the Global South (like call centres and export processing zones) has led many liberal feminists to claim that the feminist revolution launched to overcome patriarchy at work has been very successful. The Alt-right too has internalized this liberal feminist discourse attacking the 'perceived domination of society by feminist ideology' (Shaw 2018, 187), seeing it as a challenge to the patriarchal order and the rightful position of the White man in the sexual economy. The manosphere (Ging 2019), that is, the spaces of blogs, YouTube, Twitter and Instagram has become the site for neo-masculinist/White supremacist assertion. The manosphere serves as an apt site as it requires very little organizing, leg work and intellectual analysis, and instead involves a seamless transition from computer games in mancaves and White boy's clubs to the world of perceived emasculation, thus, fuelling misogynistic vitriol against feminist takeover. Academics have indicated correlations between absence of college degree and economic vulnerability, and strong correlations between economic vulnerability and exclusionary politics based on misogyny and anti-immigrant xenophobia (Cohen, Luttig, and Rogowski 2016). Donald Trump is seen as an antithesis to this namby-pamby pro-feminist man, one who is unashamed in his misogyny, and therefore manifests a theatre of testosterone by making his mancave and locker room the centrepiece of his governance and geopolitics and, sooths the class and identity vulnerabilities of the post-Fordist, neoliberal White man. Trump is embarrassing as a 'daddy-man' in public, embarrassing because he is rough around the edges in his political incorrectness (anti-feminist, anti-Mexican, anti-Muslim), incorrectness that the Alt-right wants to embrace.

The trad wives and the 'cad girls' (like Lauren Southern) are the feminine face of the Alt-right's neo-masculinist co-optation of spaces such as home, college campuses and streets that have traditionally been sites of feminist protest. Feminist scholars have argued strongly against the separation of spaces of work (production) and spaces of care (reproduction), arguing that this is a capitalist–patriarchal sleight of hand that renders caregiving as emotional, feminine and unpaid, and hence, not within the realm of what society recognizes as 'work'. The trad wives have been deployed to restore the 'natural' order of things by proclaiming the demure, graceful, apron-clad lives of the good cook, and the mother telecasts and podcasts through blogs, web pages and YouTube videos. The infiltration of trad wives into the manosphere of the Twitters, podcasts, YouTube interviews and Alt-right conferences are not seen as subversion of the sexual economy, but rather, a dutiful feminine role of using the master's tool to restore the master's position in the sexual economy. Women (trad wives and cad girls) swooning over Donald Trump and arguing for violent geopolitics of anti-immigration and Black men extolling the importance of high reproductive rates among Whites become foot soldiers in restoring the natural biological sexual order of society that has gone awry. Alt-right women criticize feminism for disrupting natural differences that should be carefully cultivated for a society based on eugenics—geopolitics should be patriarchal and not nurturing; that is why White men were able to build European civilization as a romantic gesture for White women. Alt-right women dehumanize feminists as women who could not find a husband or who could not get laid on account of being 'fat', 'ugly', 'blue haired' or a 'professor'. Shaw indicates how the neo-masculinist trends within the Alt-right conflate economic vulnerability with sexual resentment; while they take anti-state, anti-welfare position, they simultaneously, want the government to provide for individual sexual needs. The ability of women to protest against rape culture is seen as an affront to the ' man's right to sex', the ability to control the body, decide on sexual choices, decide on sexual identity and reproductive decisions are seen as a claim to power that is emasculating for the patriarchal sexual economy. The feminist's claim to power is seen as creating an 'unacceptable' difference: the feminist and the man who supports her (the skinny jeans, man buns, Obama type). The feminist identity is, therefore, an aberration to the norm, a blot, a contortion, an ugliness that must be deranged in its blue-haired intellectual manifestation that stands outside of anything that is normal. College and the street must be reclaimed by the manosphere to restore the 'ritualistic debauchery' (Return of the Kings 2019) of drunken frat parties, voyeurism and commodification of bodies that realign women to be blonde, thin and pleasing.

In feminist theory, the subject or subjectivity is situated and located in the body, and therefore, all political, sociological, economic and cultural struggles are situated and begin at the body; the gendered frame is, therefore, the primary site of embodiment, and simultaneously, a problematic signifier in patriarchal history (Braidotti 1993; De Lauretis 1990). Embodying women or locating women is an ideological political act that feminism must deconstruct. Abu-Lughod in the context of Afghanistan asks, 'Why was knowing about the culture of the region—and particularly, its religious beliefs and treatment of women—more urgent than exploring the history of the development of repressive regimes in the region and the United States' role in this history?' Embodying for Abu-Lughod (2013, 31) is 'cultural framing', where the Afghan women become the 'cultural mode of explanation' for war on terror, rather than the imperialist geopolitics of American hegemony. Butler (1988) clarifies that embodiment or the act of doing gender (Beauvoir 1974) involves a performance of repetitious stylized gestures, movements, manner of talking and dressing and an act, which is imbibed by women and expected in society. Similarly, aesthetic representation of women's bodies as a site of co-optation and resistance has been discussed comprehensively in feminist literature (Fluri 2009; Gökariksel and Secor 2010; Oza 2006; Secor and Gökariksel 2009; Sharp 1996). Therefore, struggles for control over the body in feminism represents struggles to create alternative embodiments where women have sovereignty over their bodies. Disembodiment is disempowering, it represents alienation and annihilation, a cruel disjuncture of body from mind (Bray and Colebrook 1998). The 'cultural framing' and 'the act of doing gender' is deeply contradictory; on one hand, the trad wives and cad girls are demure, graceful, 'good cooks', 'accomplished mothers' and thin and blonde, on the other hand, they are articulate YouTubers, loquacious bloggers, eloquent conference speakers and probing interviewers. The contradiction to the 'acceptable' framing or 'expected' stylized gestures of gracefulness, demureness and thinness is absorbed in the manosphere only when the alternative cultural framing of activist, anchor, interviewer and blogger is used in the service of extolling the toxic neo-masculinist White supremacist paradigm. This alternative framing or beyond the 'expected norm' of doing gender (where Alt-right women further neo-masculinist propaganda) is not dismissed as ugly, fat, aggressive, blue haired and crazy because the alternate or exceptional roles that the trad wives and cad girls play is an embodiment of disembodiment. The Alt-right women use their bodies to do gender and culturally enframe and embody a neo-masculinist cultural body of White masculine supremacy; in this process of embodiment (of the White man), their personhood is systemically disembodied. The act of doing/fixing White patriarchy disembodies the trad wives and cad girls as women—they become extensions of the White male heterosexual cultural economy (just like JLP, the Black anchor and Milo Yiannopoulos, the gay Alt-right spokesperson). The Alt-right women naturalize patriarchy when they claim that women are not inferior, just different—the difference being that women are good at caregiving, while men are good at civilization building. The disembodiment is apparent when they delegitimize the labour of caregiving as emotional and, hence, an impractical and useless epistemology when it comes to governance and geopolitics (like pro-immigrant policy and openness to other cultures). The Alt-right women devalue/disembody nurturing as 'feminine' and unsuitable strategy for powerful men. Women embody patriarchy and simultaneously disembody their personhood through devalued cultural framing and stylized gestures of doing 'Alt-right style gender'. This embodiment of disembodiment is a cultural/political/ideological act, it is an act of 'locating' that the Alt-right accomplishes with finesse. In that context, embodying women and feminists as 'abandoned dogs', 'backstabbing', 'gossip', as 'those who hate men, but love inventions made by men' and as those who abuse men' are misogynist acts where women (along with immigrants and Muslims) become the 'cultural mode of explanation' for unemployment, alienation, shrinking middle class, outsourcing, sexual frustration and a general sense of emasculation. Liberal individualism and its endorsement of rational pursuit of profit, property, accumulation for accumulation's sake that allows for a neoliberal geo-economy and a military industrial complex invested in imperialist geopolitics of war that contribute to growing inequality, concentration of wealth, outsourcing and unemployment, rather than health, education and infrastructure is overlooked. Alt-right's lack of interest in the spread of global capitalism, politics of war on terror, American exceptionalism, and instead, a tunnel-vision for attacking feminism, immigrants and Muslims displays an inability for analysing the historicity of systemic oppression. Like liberal feminists, they too make the mistake of buying into an objectivist ethics, a liberal individualism that believes in emancipation through work, owning a home and accumulation of stuff, all of which require the preservation of a skewed sexual economy where caregiving (reproduction) and work (production, governance, geopolitics) are gendered. Just as Afghan women become the 'cultural mode of explanation' for war on terror, rather than the imperialist geopolitics of American hegemony (Abu-Lughod 2013), feminists become the cultural mode of explanation for the breakdown of the biological order of procreation, maintenance of the supremacy of the White man and White civilization, and erosion of Anglo-European culture through immigration and refugee resettlement. 'Return of the Kings' blog claims,

> They lobbied their husbands and other powerful men to let
> them enter the workplace and compete for jobs alongside

the men. And men, being reasonable, gracious and accommodating towards the ladies supported their ambitions…And
now the men, rubbing their heads in agony, slowly coming
to their senses, are realizing the drastic mistake they made in
accommodating the demands of the perpetually unsatisfied
feminist agenda. (Blackmire 2018)

The 'mistake' occurred in allowing women to enter the sphere
of production because apparently this was the feminist agenda,
that is, taking over the 'office', or in other words, taking over
the public sphere of the market, the government, society, politics, geopolitics and the rest. The same Alt-right men that claim
to put women on a pedestal deem them as epitome of caregiving, child rearing and motherhood, and find it an 'agenda' and
a 'mistake' when the hallowed heroine steps 'out' of her home.
The nurturer is quickly demystified as backstabbing, rumour
mongering, cunning and slandering as she steps out of her
biologically and culturally ordained gender role. The patriarch
(both Alt-right men and Alt-right women) never takes a look
at his own gaze; why did the nurturer stop nurturing once
she stepped out of 'her domain'? Was caregiving ever valued
anywhere? If caregiving is indeed affirmed and pedestalized,
why can't the office/the society/the market/the government/
governance/geopolitics not be nurturing environments? What
is it about liberal individualism that celebrates graciousness and
accommodating nature of men towards the ladies as chivalry
but delegitimizes office-going women's drive for efficiency and
competition as cattiness, backstabbing and gossip?

Soft Women Saying Hard Things

In this chapter, I take a look at how misogyny and Whiteness
intertwine to create a template of perceived trauma and demand
for valourization on the part of Alt-right men. Some scholars
argue that the Alt-right's neo-masculinist angst arises out of
contemporary contexts of neoliberal free trade, outsourcing,
growing unemployment, declining middle class, increasing
racial diversity through immigration and an increased fear

of disappearance of economic opportunities arising out of competition from women and immigrants. I argue that liberal individualism and multiculturalism provide comfortable breeding ground for neo-masculinist identity angst. Since individual liberalism is the political soul of the body politic of capitalism (the USA and European style), the pursuit of happiness through consumption, accumulation, and acquiring private property must remain sacrosanct. In other words, since capitalism is about the persistence of class inequality mediated through classical economic liberal ideas of self-interest and competition, a political soul (individual liberalism) that enlivens capitalism must, therefore, not disrupt systems of social inequality. Instead, a liberal individual must become competitive through self-interest and hard work to rise to the top of the heap and take advantage of unequal class relations by becoming best in the competition among unequals. Becoming best requires the continued existence of tiered social life where other individuals, groups and classes feature lower/last in the pursuit of affirmation through commodity consumption, private property and identity affirmation. A system based on inequality does not problematize inequality as a product of systemic oppression; inequality is rather a given condition within which an individual provided with 'equal' opportunities and demonstrating aggressive competitiveness can pursue happiness. A political philosophy of individual liberalism that dovetails with the body politic of capitalism must keep this inequality alive and give it a positive spin as well; otherwise discrimination, marginalization and inequality will be self-conceptualized by the oppressed as exploitation. Multiculturalism is the positive spin that 'affirms' capitalism's oppression—if African Americans have been systemically oppressed by plantation capitalism, then contemporary capitalism may affirm Blackness as acceptable diversity, 'valued' through small diversity quotas in jobs and colleges, but not valourized through massive systemic economic overhaul such as land reforms and property or wealth redistribution.

In the absence of systemic analysis of historical and geographical contexts of oppression, any identity can claim marginal status (based on dwindling numbers, perceived trauma from aggressive immigrants and people of other identities) and affirmation under multiculturalism. Identity decontextualized from the historical–geographical contexts of their actualization is identity individualized and is meaningless and vacuous. But since multiculturalism backed by individual liberalism is also meaningless and vacuous in its superficial affirmation of diversity, it lacks the power or moral consciousness for discriminating between acceptable marginal identities that need affirmation and unacceptable marginal identities that need to be marginalized. In that context, when neoliberal capitalism induced neo-masculinist trauma manifests as Alt-right patriarchy, neoliberal capitalism cannot be cited as the systemic cause for identity annihilation because capitalism is a given good. Then, it becomes easier for the Alt-right to locate feminists, Muslims and migrants as the site of marginalization. Instead of citing capitalism induced inequality as the historical–geographical process that marginalizes women, feminism and changing gender roles, women's entry into the work force in offices, colleges and universities become the systemic sites of attack. In the face of this trauma of neglect of the White man, it will not be far-fetched or impossible for neo-masculinist groups to claim acceptability and cultural affirmation; Trump's election victory riding on a neo-masculinist identity wave is ample proof of this fact. It will also not be an aberration to assume that such movements (neo-masculinist) may gain mainstream popularity, transcend their presence in the fringe and clamour for protection under the multicultural agenda. It is true that these neo-masculinist trends within the Alt-right critique establishment–conservatism and liberal multiculturalism, but what we as a society, and they as a 'fringe' group fail to realize is that these identity affirmations are dangerously close to the multicultural project because of the common shared traits of superficiality, individuality and disinclination to 'out' systemic causes of oppression. As I argue in the introduction to this chapter, two things make an identity oppressive and 'unacceptable', that is, its inability to recognize its own complicity in producing historical–geographical devalourization of 'others' (women, people of colour, indigenous groups, colonial subjects) and the arrogant self-valourization based on devalourization of 'other'. Liberal multiculturalism is complicit with the first, thus creating fertile conditions for liberal misogyny to flourish under 'cultural' movements like the Alt-right.

While multiculturalism as a progressive praxis may openly critique far-right neo-masculinist movements like the Alt-right as unacceptable, and while the Alt-right itself may denounce 'minority-appeasing' pretentions of multiculturalism, yet it is in the liminality of these contradictions that unacceptable Identitarian movements like Alt-right find comfortable breeding grounds. The Alt-right's anti-women/anti-feminist stance find comfortable breeding conditions rooted in classical liberal ideas such as man as the rational, competitive individual, man as the individual and women as the familial. In these spaces of contradictions, Alt-right views feminism as an antithesis to liberal capitalism, where feminists revert the acceptable identity of capitalist geography by leaving home (sphere of the familial) and treading into work/politics/governance (sphere of the individual). It is ironic that liberal feminist agenda is exactly just so—dissolving women from their communitarian ethic and producing the workfare woman-individual that populates the masculine sphere of work—this may seem contradictory to what the Alt-right wants; yet, both Alt-right and liberal feminism (as well as liberal multiculturalism) believe in the production of the efficient individual that realizes its life potential through workforce competition within capitalism. The difference being liberal feminists want more women to become individuals and Alt-right wants to keep workspaces intact for men. And therefore, while they push against each other, there remains a narrow, liminal space where the core of realization of one's personhood is similar for neo-masculinist movements, liberal feminists and multiculturalism, and this core is self-valourization as individuals. Wherever this individuality is threatened, an 'other' must be quickly constructed so as to fortify one's self-valourization—multiculturalism's 'other' becomes terrorism and fascism without proper systemic analysis of self and the other (that is, is there no terrorism and fascism within multiculturalism?), liberal feminism's 'other' becomes the patriarch at the workspace (often neglecting that women's participation through work is not always patriarchy-challenged, but rather a fitting within the rubric of productivity, efficiency and profit, which are the inherent building blocks of patriarchal capitalism), Feminists and women become Alt-right's 'other', and often, the boundary between the two is not very clear to the Alt-right's membership itself.

The 'trad wives" and what I call in this chapter the 'cad-girls' are ingeniously crafted. The trad wife is the antithesis of the workfare liberal feminist, apron-clad home-maker and child-bearer—the familial that must support masculine capitalist individualism by grasping the levers of family and community well so as to not disrupt the social order of things. While the trad wife balances the patriarchal economy by valourizing patriarchy as the normal order of work and geopolitics, she must 'gracefully' tread gendered spaces like YouTube's blogosphere and conferences and commit gender blasphemy by stepping outside the familial, but doing so in a way that valourizes the individual man by singing praises of his creative and protective genius. Trad wives claim that women's identity in society is not reduced by patriarchy but given respectful distinction by pedestalizing motherhood and nurture. At the conference and cyber space, the trad wife is the Madonna of individualism even while she proclaims the feminine virtues of the familial. In turn, the Alt-right man claims that he does not mind women at the work space (they prove it by promoting work-oriented 'cad girls' as internet show hosts that heckle other women and feminists), but why would women not want to take a rest and be a queen at home if her man wants to give her that? The trad wives and Alt-right men together cast a gender template where both extoll the importance of women in charge of reproduction and men in charge of production. The 'other', therefore, are women who want to do the opposite; men who support women wanting to do the opposite and feminists who are viewed as symbolic of that opposite. Feminists are the deeper outcasts because not only is their intellectual praxis viewed as destabilizing the place of work, but their philosophical praxis is seen as destabilizing heteronormativity, challenging sexual control and rape culture, and challenging conventional standards of beauty and body. Feminists are, therefore, seen as distorting all aspects of the individual (his self-realization as provider through work, his self-realization as man through his right to demand sex, the self-realization of his masculine gaze through standardization of female beauty as thin, White and blonde). As neoliberal order proceeds and capitalism reorients as an economic system encumbered by outsourcing and job loss, the college going capitalist man's existential angst wrapped up in the possibility of economic rejection from the market also sends a jolt to the other dimensions of his self-realization (i.e., as a heterosexual man); this combined with increase of women at the workforce and rise in LGBTQ movements create new anxieties. However, as the Alt-right's neo-masculine stance in the manosphere demonstrates, this anxiety is not manifested as social movement of the poor and middle class for greater redistribution, free college tuition and free healthcare. Instead of launching a powerful onslaught at neoliberal capitalist individualism that reduces men (and women) to workers/producers/fathers/ husbands, the Alt-right prefer lazy and reactionary analysis of manhood's trauma and its desperate need for identity valourization by eliminating feminists. The analysis is lazy because containing women at home will not take care of the fact that capitalism is systemically crisis prone and will always devalue labour through wage suppression, outsourcing, unemployment and wage stagnation. No matter how many women become homemakers, how many migrants are turned away, how many feminists are vilified and how many women's studies department are closed, the pursuit of happiness within liberal capitalist individualism is a short-term illusion until the next systemic crisis hits (Harvey 1978, 2014). Just as liberal feminism must rethink 'the women as the workfare individual model' and just as multiculturalism must rethink what cultural valourization means without economic redistribution and analysis of historic exploitation, the Alt-right needs to rethink what it means to be a man. As I write this, coronavirus reigns all over the world and social distancing has been enforced in the USA, we are faced with an existential question: What does it mean to be human? And therefore, by extension, what kind of society do we want? Do we want a society where social distance becomes a norm rather than a calamity? Do we want a society where we compartmentalize happiness as an individual prize not to be shared by any other? Do we want a society where our manhood and womanhood are realized through the devalourization/reduction/diminution/commodification of other humans? Inability to realize one's complicity in the violence of devaluing others and the arrogant valourization of one's identity at the cost of others are forms of social distancing that may create temporary clubs of us (Alt-right men) versus them. But this is not society created, it is society quarantined, which itself is an oxymoron. If individualism means sacrificing society, if being man means devaluing women, what happiness are we pursuing and for whom?

5

Alt-right and Islamophobia as Disembodiment

Islamophobia as 'Culture Talk'

If Alt-right fora and the different threads of discussion are followed closely on YouTube and other media platforms, it becomes clear that Islamophobia is a major red-pill (radicalizing) moment for the Alt-right and other associated Islamophobic groups. Islamophobia presents as a multifaceted opportunity where the fear of Sharia Law, the veil and the immigrant status of Muslims combine to produce a cultural construction of the exotic other, much like the 'blue haired virus' called feminists as argued in the previous chapter. The Muslim is embodied as outside the pale of Western civilization, antithetical to Western values, violent, sexist and homophobic. This construction of the Muslim other runs parallel to the feminist other constructed as fat, ugly, aggressive, abusive and incapable of raising children or having families. In producing (embodying) the

Muslim, the Alt-right simultaneously unproduces (disembodies) her as an entire culture that must be 'located', 'opposed' and 'cast outside' of Western liberal democracy (Gregory 2003). Consider this excerpt delivered after the Orlando shooting in which an American born Muslim man shot people at a bar in 2016. The excerpt is from a speech by a charismatic speaker, Stefan Molyneux, who runs a philosophy channel on YouTube (Molyneux 2019b).

A sheik [invited as a speaker in Orlando] claimed that the killing of homosexuals is the compassionate thing to do...One Donald Trump supporter punches someone, it's the whole campaign, it's all the way to the top, if Donald Trump had called the murder of blacks, if a Donald Trump supporter went out and murdered blacks, it would go all the way to the top, if a Muslim goes out and kills homosexuals [as in the Orlando case], huuuh, nothing to do with anything... the Westborough Baptist church hates gays, they hold signs, and everyone hates on them, who is criticized more?...Turkey is holding back three million largely, Muslim migrants that they threaten to unleash upon Europe if they are not allowed free entry and free movement into Europe over time...half of British Muslims think that gay sex should be illegal, half of British Muslims think that gay sex should be illegal! In England polygamy is illegal, but Muslims can have tones of wives...this is called integration! Where is the media? Where are the liberals? Are they scared? Are they complicit? Oh wait! Muslims vote democrats, media loves the democrats... we don't have the same standards for everyone, universalization is foundational to Greco-Roman Judea Christian ethics, universalization, that was the goal of Socrates and Aristotle, we are all subjects to the same rule, the golden rule....

Molyneux's philosophy channel on YouTube—Freedomain— spends a lot of media time and space endorsing and establishing a correlation between race, income and IQ (Molyneux 2019a), claiming that racial IQ data is about ten trillion times more validated and reliable than climate change data on future temperature increase. Molyneux, while clearly anti-liberal (anti-democrat) and pro-Trump as the excerpt above denotes, is an entrenched supporter of what he considers universalizing principle of Western civilization, that is, science, enlightenment, empiricism, free market democracy, rule of law and freedom of speech. While not fitting into the traditional social–cultural–economic establishment-conservative mould, his philosophy is slightly more of a sophisticated variant of the cruder version of the Western supremacy paradigm that the Proud Boys club denotes. Molyneux uses a more pedantic variant of Spencer's White-partition ethno-space logic to convince his audience the scientific and biological basis of ethno-racial correlation with intelligence. This biological determinism then projects and diffuses into a more cultural/ethno-religious determinism, for example, Molyneux (2019) claims that there is no Shakespeare coming out of Sub-Saharan Africa, not because they 'are lazy, or bad, or lack moral qualities', it is their ethno-racial IQ on average (implication being that it is just an empirical fact that this average is lower than the Anglo-Saxon race), therefore, he argues that the smartest Blacks have tried to leave Black countries in order to go to White countries so that their 'intelligence will gain traction through the meritocracy of the free market'.

Blaut (1992), in his critique of Eurocentricity, has argued how biological racism of the past (measuring skulls to correlate with intelligence and later on genetics with IQ testing) transitions to religious racism, that is, biology being equal, some religions are more civilized (better) than others, and then, more contemporarily (in a more secular world), into cultural racism, which is the world view that certain cultures are able to promote a modern, and better way of life than certain others. Blaut argues that Weber's (2013) *Protestant Ethic and the Spirit of Capitalism* is a Eurocentric theory of cultural diffusionism that contends self-interest and hard work as inherent to Protestantism. Therefore, Protestantism is the moral underpinning for the emergence of industrial capitalism, and by extension, economic rationalities of self-interest and cultural–political rationalities of individual freedom. Blaut critiques Weber to indicate that emplaced within his Eurocentric bias, Weber implicitly argues that forms of religious morality other than Protestantism are unable to birth industrial capitalism. If industrial capitalism is the essence of modernity, then, according to Weber, Western Europe and America become modern cores surrounded by stagnation. Therefore, modernity must be 'brought to' or diffused from the 'West' to the rest, the rest needs the West for their upliftment (much in the same way as the Alt-right argues that Western civilization is supreme). Said (1979), Gregory (2003), Mamdani (2004), Abu-Lugodh (2002, 2013) and Bilge (2010), in their deconstruction of orientalism, indicate that the cultural construction of the racial other is more than just an aversion to a certain race, it is a mixture of aversion, confusion, ignorance and exotification of the entire life-world of the racial other to create 'imagined geographies' (Said, Gregory), 'culture talk' (Mamdani), 'cultural framing' (Abu-Lugodh) and 'feminist orientalism' (Bilge) through an assemblage of racist tropes and missionary zeal where the other's body, mind, private and public worlds are produced and unproduced as an unmodern, unequal, profane, veiled outside to the 'West'. The cultural-other either needs subjugation to the 'West' or needs the 'West' to be its saviour. This placing of the Muslim other as an unequal race is more than just colour coding, it is the simultaneous production and unproduction (embodying them as possessing certain attributes and, simultaneously, disembodying them as inhuman because of those very attributes) of Muslims as a people as unmodern, sexist, homophobic, barbaric and antithetical to Western values. Because this was a talk given to an Australian audience, Molyneux (2019b) goes on to argue that indigenous people (in this case Australian aborigines) live in their constructed, mystical certainties that contradict the empirical based realities of the White population with whom they share the continent. This contradiction, Molyneux argues, is deep because it cannot be denied that the White civilization allowed curiosity to flourish, and hence, paved the way for Platos, Aristotles, Spinoza, Socrates and Francis Bacons. Europe and North America (Molyneux clearly articulates that Mexico needs to be crossed out) are responsible for the enlightenment epoch and 98 per cent (no source is provided for this data) of the scientific discoveries that led to the creation of the modern world. Much like Weber, Molyneux's final thesis is that race equals culture, equals science, equals modern values of free market and free speech. Individual freedom, self-interest, meritocracy, free market capitalism, as I have argued in the previous chapter, becomes the universal solvent through which Alt-right's phobias, attacks and ideological template is distilled.

Molyneux speaks in the backdrop of the Orlando shootings and Trump's rise to power, he, therefore, lashes out at multiculturalism, which he understands as Muslim appeasement by liberals (as in political party) and the liberal media. Mocking integration as a form of favouritism towards the Muslim minority in Europe and England using anecdotal, stereotypical and highly selective information (not backed by credible sources) on polygamy and migration, Molyneux argues that Muslims are allowed, encouraged and given the right to be outside the paradigm of 'universalization'. 'Universalization', according to Molyneux refers to Western individual liberalism based on cultural (separation of church and state, rules of marriages and divorce), political (freedom of speech, to vote) and economic values (self-interest, competition, pursuit of profit) that he believes is the basic template of Anglo-American civilization. Molyneux thunders that the Muslim population living in the 'West' are incapable of adherence to the universal principles of liberal individualism and liberals in Western host societies are disinterested in disciplining Muslims into accepting those principles, thus leading to the chaos and violence of situations like the Orlando shooting. It is lost to Molyneux that modernity need not be Western, indeed, the cradle of human civilization in the banks of Tigris and Euphrates (modern Iraq) was not Western, some of the most ancient forms of modernity and development in science such as numbers, algebra (Arabic), zero (India), irrigation technology and urban planning (Indus valley), industry (silk, gunpowder—China) originated outside the 'West'. It is also lost to Molyneux that IQ is a function of ethnicity and race because certain ethno-racial categories are often socially produced and entrapped in spaces with low accessibility to tools, technology and sources of knowledge because of the historicity of colonization, plunder, and enslavement that take many generations to overcome. It is also lost to Molyneux that IQ testing is itself culturally biased, and indeed plenty of postcolonial work have deconstructed what it means to be scientific, what counts as science (Harding 2006; Spivak 1999), how 'science' and 'modernity' have negatively impacted societies, environments and communities (Harding 2009), and conversely, how there is a need to understand traditional knowledge not as mumbo jumbo or mystical hogwash but as local knowledge that is contextual and nuanced (Shiva and Mies 2014). It is also lost to Molyneux that just as the entire older White population cannot be blamed as sexist and racist because, of President Trump's proclivity towards racist and sexist statements, similarly, the entire Muslim population cannot be blamed for homophobia. In this chapter, I argue that these gaps are not really loopholes in the arguments of charismatic and intelligent YouTube superstars such as Molyneux or the Alt-right; these are carefully crafted orientalist discourses underscored with passion, poise and anecdotes to 'scientifically' and 'culturally' disembody the Muslim as the antithesis of the West so that Islamophobia can be legitimized as a 'scientific' critique of all things terrifying.

Islamophobia as Orientalism

Edward Said (1979) contextualizes the 'Orient' as a historical–geographical creation, a production through discourse, knowledge making, sedimentation of thought process, imageries and vocabularies creating the West's 'other'. The orient is, therefore, not only geographically adjacent to Europe, it is the site of its colonial control and its cultural competitor. The orient helps define Europe's personality. Orientalism is the formalized business of dealing with the orient 'by making statements about it, authorizing views of it, describing it, by teaching it, settling it, ruling over it'. In other words, Orientalism is a Western style for dominating, restricting and having authority over the Orient (Said 1979, 3). Using Foucault's ideas of discourse and Gramsci's concept of hegemony, Said demonstrates that considerable material investment goes into discursively, materially, theoretically, practically (libraries, archives, universities, bureaucracies), producing Orientalism through which Western consciousness is filtered. Said details the breadth and range of Orientalism:

> A specialist in Islamic law, no less than an expert in Chinese dialects or in Indian religions...we must learn to accept enormous, indiscriminate size plus an almost infinite capacity for subdivision as one of the chief characteristics of Orientalism—one that is evidenced in its confusing amalgam of imperial vagueness and precise detail. (Said 1979, 50)

This 'imperial vagueness' and 'precise detail' simultaneously produces the Muslim, the Arab, the Middle East, and simultaneously obliterates her through an assemblage of racism, stereotypes, imperialism and ideology casting her as the totalitarian, the violent, the terrorist counter positioned against the democratic, modern and freedom-loving Israelite. Mamdani (2004) indicates how September 11 becomes a new facet through which simultaneous production and obliteration of the Muslim is achieved. This contemporary orientalism, according to Mamdani (2004, 17), is 'culture talk' that assumes every culture to have a fundamental, crystalized, solid core, an essence. Culture talk then rationalizes the political consequences that emerge from that essence. In the context of post-September 11 orientalism, Islamic terrorism is the political consequence of a 'violent' 'premodern' culture. According to Mamdani, there are two narratives of this orientalist culture talk, one in which all Muslims are just bad because their culture is degenerate, and according to another, there are good and bad Muslims and politics should be about vanquishing the latter. However, in both narratives, 'history seems to have petrified into lifeless custom of an antique people who inhabit an antique land' (Mamdani 2004, 14). This ahistoric, apolitical, nebulous-yet-concrete, antiquarian-yet-post-September 11 gaze is a systematic production and simultaneous obliteration and, hence, disembodiment of the Muslim. Abu-Lugodh (2002, 5), in a similar vein, cautions liberal feminism's penchant for saving the Muslim women. She argues that well-meaning liberal feminists speak on behalf of Muslim women in the language of human rights. The question for Abu-Lugodh is what should the Muslim women be saved for? She warns us of the dangers of pity and the 'patronizing arrogance' that social change should look one and same for all. She argues that just as the orientalist gaze focuses on sexism in Islam, if the gaze were to be self-directed, it would not be hard to find commodification of women in 'Western societies' for selling consumer products, it would not be hard to point out the glass ceiling and the percentage of women-headed households that are poor in Western societies, it would not be hard to demonstrate large volume of cases of sexual harassment at the workplace in Western societies, and to point out how late most Western nations were in giving women the right to vote, and how many Muslim nations have women as national leaders. But the point, according to Abu-Lugodh, is that while we revert our gaze and look at our own sexism, it will be a fallacy to attribute all of this to Christianity because commodification, harassment, and glass ceiling are complex processes having complex causes.

The orientalist gaze simultaneously produces and destroys the Muslim. Racist interpretation of the Koran and the Sharia Law is one way for achieving this. Center for Security Policy published a report in 2010 titled *Sharia: The Threat to America,* where the report talks at length about 'stealth jihad' (p. 8). 'Stealth-Jihad' is a concept increasingly popular among right-wing groups, it involves a belief that there is a slow penetration of the 'Islamic way of life' through prayer rooms in public schools and airports, construction of mosques in 'Western cities,' slow conversion of Christians, Jews and members of other communities to Islam and, finally, towards the imposition of Sharia law in Western societies. Also described by the term 'civilizational jihad', (p. 8) it refers to a multi-layered approach at cultural subversion from within by co-opting important political leaders and key members in state departments that influence policy (p. 17). The insidious grasp of 'stealth jihad' is described as thus:

> The U.S. government has comprehensively failed to grasp the true nature of this enemy—an adversary that fights to reinstate the totalitarian Islamic caliphate and impose sharia globally (p. 9).

> (p. 10) Steeped in Islamic doctrine, and already embedded deep inside both the United States and our allies, the Brotherhood has become highly skilled in exploiting the civil liberties and multicultural proclivities of Western societies for the purpose of destroying the latter from within (p. 10).

Similarly, Counterjihad is a transatlantic alliance of far-right groups that seek to oppose Islamization and the Sharia. They hold regular conferences across Europe and the UK, and their blog titled 'Gates of Vienna' is so named because the tide of 'Ottoman expansion' was turned at the gates of Vienna in 1683. They blame the 'Islamic control' of Middle Eastern oil as the primary reason for the rise of 'Islamic colonization' of London, Paris, Marseille, Brussels and Rotterdam. They thunder against Islamic urban enclaves and no-go zones of radicalization and Sharia in Europe. The resistance to the spread of Sharia is seen as the resistance to the spread of Islam (Bodissey 2005). The local and the global geopolitics of Sharia is outlined as:

> Thus the goal of Counterjihad groups is to stop the spread of sharia within their own societies. Activists realize that initiatives against sharia must be mounted on two distinct fronts: at the national level (in the legislatures and judicial systems of individual democratic countries) and in international bodies (the European Union, the United Nations, etc.).

> The latter front is particularly important, since the EU and the UN are undemocratic and unaccountable to the people they purport to represent. The Organization for Islamic Cooperation (OIC), which functions as the collective expression of the world's Muslim-majority countries, wields a disproportionate amount of influence at the United

Nations, and vigorously pursues its sharia-based agenda there. (Bodissey 2005)

Islam and its Sharia jurisprudence are imagined as a violent, aggressive, political and legal takeover of 'Western democracy and culture' at the local level through city-based infiltration from within described as 'Islamic colonization'. A larger global takeover is imagined through a transnational takeover of the European Union and the United Nations. The 'culture talk' clearly distinguishes the essence of Western societies as liberal and multicultural and indicates that these are weaknesses that West's 'other' Islam is likely to use in its spread of cultural dominance through the Sharia. Democracy, multiculturalism, civil liberties, regime change and individual liberties are counter posed against Islamic jurisprudence, the Sharia. The orientalist gaze confers a desirable essence for Western culture where its values embody emancipation and freedom as against Islam's savage essence and its expression, the Sharia.

Pamela Geller, founder of SIOA and co-founder of AFDI, in her speech reinforces this civilized versus savage narrative: 'In any war between the civilized man and the savage, support the civilized man. Support Israel, defeat Jihad!' (Geller 2012). The AFDI (http://afdi.us) website is replete with mugs, postcards, and T-shirts depicting the cartoonized figure of Mohammad as an angry, turbaned and bearded man saying, 'You can't Draw me' to be sold for $50 apiece. A poster depicting Mohammed drawing a self-portrait calls for 'Mohammad art exhibit and cartoon contest.' The same website uses out of context and selective verses from the Koran to cast Mohammad as a sexually promiscuous misogynist, a paedophile and a violent man deploying draconian punishments.

Gatestone Institute that calls itself a non-partisan think tank and declares its objective to educate the public on what the mainstream media does not report, they document articles on topics like 'Islamization of France' or 'Muslim persecution of Christians'. Articles quote statistics on how churches are being closed down in Muslim majority countries, or how the Christian population

is shrinking in 'Western' nations, and how Muslim fundamentalist clerics are rabble rousing and lynching poor Christian boys
(Ibrahim 2017). These news items are listed with dates and places
but with no reference to any source or news organization, which
makes it impossible to confirm their credibility.

The villainy of the antiquated degenerate religion, and the
violent, misogynistic, premodern, oppressive and terroristic proclivities that emerge from its essential core is a natural 'other'
to the emancipated modern West. Culture talk obfuscates
political economic analysis of Western imperialism, history of
slavery, occupation of Palestine, killing of Native Americans
and meddling in the Middle East. It also obfuscates domestic
violence against women, commodification of women's bodies,
serial killings, mass shooting in schools, paedophiliac priests,
and shooting of Black people in 'Western societies' as stray
incidents of mentally unsound people. 'Western villainy' is
not systemic, not racist, not an expression of his/her cultural
essence because his/her culture is emancipated, advanced and
peaceful. The Muslim, however, cannot be saved because her/
his religion and culture is villainous at the core. As Gregory
so poetically said, 'Violence must be lodged in their genes not
the geographies to which they have been brutally subjected
(Gregory 2003, 15). Therefore, her/his annihilation can only
be achieved through her complete disembodiment, a complete
stripping from whatever we hold good in humanity.

Islamophobia as Racism

The aggressive, virile, violent and war-like predisposition of
the 'Muslim race' has long been the topic of introspection
of many academic works validating the socio-biological pro-
pensities behind skin colour. The awe-inspiring spread of the
Persian empire, the colonizing propensity of the Ottoman Turks
threatening the very existence of Christendom, the temple-
destroying, man-killing and blood-boiling disposition of the
invading Mughals reducing the peace-loving Hindu culture
of India are well documented (Morison 1908; Palgrave 1872;

Temple 1910). Stoddard (1923) in his then famous and now infamous book, *The Rising Tide of Color Against the White-world Supremacy*, calls Islam the seat of Brown renaissance equating at once, phenotype with religion. The Muslim is immediately disembodied as a homogenous 'Brown' figure rising against the White world. Using commentaries of White 'orientalist scholars', Stoddard lists the characteristics of the Muslim or the Moslem. The Muslim is fixed and 'secure as a rock' (Stoddard 1923, 59), and from the fixity of her position she revels in the restlessness of others (meaning Christians). The Muslim is fixed but not rigid: '...the Mohammedan world has availed itself of White institutions such as the newspaper in forging its new solidarity....' The newspaper has a race, it is White and modern, the Muslim and his race are seen as benefitting from White inventions because he is culturally vacuous, incapable of innovation and enlightenment. The Arabic numeral, algebra, trigonometry, cryptology, fountain pen, pin-hole camera, astronomy, cartography by the same racial logic, however, do not become Brown institutions stolen and usurped from the Muslim by the White man, they are just disembodied into oblivion. So, the Muslim is fixed but open to White institutions that allow him to consolidate his army and hence, spread to Africa (Stoddard's paranoia becomes palpable here). The Muslim is proselytizing, his ardour and passion for converting a non-Muslim is so deep that he will without hesitation give his child in marriage to admit the neophyte, and once converted, Islam and the Muslim have such a hold, such a tenacity, there is no giving up. The Muslim demonstrates a pan-Islamic missionary zeal for the spread of the 'Caliphate' and spell doom for the White man (Stoddard 1923, 83).

> Elsewhere, from Morocco to the Dutch Indies, there is in the racial sense, as Townsend says, 'no white anything,'...These are indeed fragile foundations. Let the brown world once make up his mind that the white man *must* go, and he *will* go.

Tracing the development of this European concept of 'race', Rana (2007) notes that its development is often placed at the

15th and 16th century with the discovery of Native Americans in the new world, which placed them in religious opposition to Christianity, and hence, as the heathen race. In the European continent, the expulsion of the Moors and their later conversion created another template of 'race'—the Moors were a heterogeneous category of Arabs, Berbers and West Africans with the underlying religious characteristic of being Muslim. Religion, therefore, was an important attribute in racializing groups that were diverse in phenotype and appearance. Conversion of Muslims or Jews to Christianity produced a class of crypto-Muslims and crypto-Jews (new converts) facing tremendous hostility. So, in the racial triangle between Indians, Muslims and Christians, Rana (2007) argues that while Native Americans were reconfigured as 'Muslims' because in the colonial eye they were barbaric, sodomites, sexually-deviant and depraved with strange rituals and marriage traditions like the Moors. Moors (the Muslim) are a religious category who serve as the basis for racializing Native Americans, and also, simultaneously producing 'the other' of Christendom.

YWC is registered as a non-profit student organization that opposes multiculturalism. Its Founder-President Kevin DeAnna claims that the organization now has chapters across dozens of university campuses in the USA and abroad. In an interview video posted on YouTube, DeAnna claims that

> Western civilization is a compound of Christian, classical, and then the folk traditions of Europe…we don't just define it as just democracy, rule of law, and these universal institutions, we say that it is a specific culture that comes from a specific historical experience. (DeAnna 2012)

The antithesis of 'the other', the Muslim, is the 'Western civilization' constituting Christians of Europe who settled elsewhere. It is a specific ethno-racial compound, not abstractions like universal principles of civil liberty. Abstractions like universal principles of democracy and rule of law tend to create the embodiment of a 'citizen'. A citizen can be an American, a Swede, a German or British, and also, be a Muslim. But if the 'we' are embodied as Christians and part of the Western civilization, then the Muslim is instantaneously disembodied as outside of it and stripped off abstractions such as 'citizen' or 'human'. 'Western' becomes a code for 'White' and 'civiliza-tion' becomes a code for 'race'. Race is conveniently conflated with religion and can then stoke primordial racial fantasies by disembodying diverse groups of people of heterogeneous citizenships, nationalities, ethnicities and appearances into a racialized abstraction residing outside the 'West'.

In another video, former congressmen and advisor to YWC Tom Tancredo explains that 'we are the product of a Judea Christian-Anglo culture...all cultures are not the same, all political systems are not the same, some are better than others' (Tribute to Youth for Western Civilization 2009). In a separate video but from the same montage, Black leaders and preachers are depicted as rabble rousing and calling for the demise of the 'White man'. Muslims in turbans and beard are shown as burning the American and British flags. These video clips are punctuated with clips from Pat Buchanan's speech on blood and soil that binds a culture to a common heritage drawn from the same history, literature and language. The video montage ends with flags from countries in Western Europe, America, Britain and Australia in case the viewer had any doubts about which blood was tied to which soil (Tribute to Youth for Western Civilization 2009). Extolling the pride of the White West, Madison Grant (1918, 16), over 50 years ago, similarly racialized diverse phenotypes.

> Thus the view that the Negro slave was an unfortunate cousin of the white man, deeply tanned by the tropic sun and denied the blessings of Christianity and civilization, played no small part with the sentimentalists of the Civil War period and it has taken us fifty years to learn that speak-ing English, wearing good clothes and going to good school and to church does not transform a Negro into a white man. Nor was a Syrian or Egyptian freedman transformed into a

Roman by wearing a toga and applauding his favorite gladiator in the amphitheater.

Whiteness is carried in the blood and manifests as Christianness and Westernness symbolized by 'civilizational' artefacts like 'good clothes', 'toga' and the church. Therefore, colour (or lack of it) supersedes religious conversion and cultural learning of 'Western ways'. The narrative of the 'Western civilization', it's common heritage, it's history and language that is over-present in the YWC videos, therefore, hinges on the essential core of blood purity that Grant talks about. That is why the Black priest and the flag-burning Muslim are one and the same—race disembodies the Muslim in the same way as it does the Black person, and both are placed outside the 'blessing' of 'Western civilization'. Henry Osborn in a *forward* to Grant's book referred to these racial traits as 'hereditary traits',

> If I were asked: what is the greatest danger, which threatens the American republic to-day? I would certainly reply: The gradual dying out among our people of these hereditary traits through which the principles of our religious, political and social foundations were laid down and their insidious replacement by traits of less noble character. (Grant 1918)

'Noble character' cannot be acquired or learnt by the Muslim because her hereditary traits (race) births a religion, and hence, a socio-political foundation that is inherently ignoble, she can never be an embodiment of the 'West' or Whiteness.

Islamophobia as Anti-immigration

President Trump remarked, 'Why should the United States take in immigrants from "shithole countries" in Africa over people from places like Norway?' (Yee 2018). The disembodiment of the entire White colonial project that ravaged and plundered Africa, killed thousands and produced a systemic postcolonial modernity of poverty, hunger and political instability has never been more profound than through this choice of profanity.

The immigrant is a race in itself (Prashad 2001), and the over-present Muslim immigrant who is not White, or Christian and hence is not part of the 'Western civilization', is always disembodied through the politics of shit, literally.

Patriotic Europeans Against the Islamisation of the West (PEGIDA) rose to prominence in 2014–2015, they are registered as a voluntary organization protesting Islamization of Europe and critiquing the perceived inability of immigrant Muslims from integrating into mainstream society. It held regular rallies in places like Dresden, asking for a ban against mosque construction in Germany and stricter laws on immigration and asylum (Kallis 2016). In that context, Kunzig (2016) reports how PEGIDA and the far-right proclaim 'over-foreignization' of Germany by scrutinizing every aspect of the migrant's daily life. The Muslim's hygiene, her movements and her gestures are subject to racist devaluation. The Muslim litters the parks, they ride bicycles on sidewalk and want to shit into holes in the ground rather than sitting on the Western toilet. In a refugee shelter in Hamburg, Kunzig meets maintenance workers who complain about broken toilet seats because the migrants assault Western modernity with their squatting habits, thus breaking the toilet seats at refugee camps. The immigrant's body is the source of her disembodiment, her Muslimness, her Browness, her movement, hygiene, eating habits, prayer rituals blends into a texture of 'foreignness' that destroys 'our home' (Kallis 2015). In France, the state has started regulating the immigrant's religious practices through the production of a policy practice that has been called 'French Islam' (Davidson 2012; Fernando 2014). Through surveillance, the state decides which aspect of the Muslim's religious practice is compatible with French Republicanism, thus creating a whole trope of 'official mosques' and 'obedient migrants'.

Norway's Progress Party's rise to power and Sweden Democrat's rise to popularity are grounded on similar emotional 'displacement' from what used to feel like 'home' (Crouch 2014). Immigration is dubbed as Arab invasion and both parties run on anti-immigrant plank that couch Islamophobic policies under catchy phrases like the conversion of Europe into 'Eurabia' (Horsti 2017). Norway's Progress Party followed the mandate of many French towns calling for a ban on 'burkini' as the body length swimsuit worn by some Muslim women because the burkini is perceived as a symbol of radical Islam (Furedi 2016). Mosques were torched in Sweden in 2015 and a politician resigned in 2017 for calling Muslims 'the opposite of humans' (Maza 2017). Pan-European Islamophobic coalitions like Young European Alliance for Hope including alliances between the Austrian Freedom Party, the French Front National, Flemish Vlaams Belang and that of the Sweden Democrats are upscaling their national Islamophobia to a regional level through joint meetings across borders.

According to the Southern Poverty Law Center, anti-Muslim hate groups in the USA include ACT! for America, Soldiers of Odin and The Crusaders. These organizations combine anti-refugee, anti-immigration and anti-Muslim ideologies into a heady assemblage of intolerance expressed through social media, marches, demonstrations, hate speech and violence. Some of them have chapters outside the USA in Canada and many draw their origins from Europe. For example, Soldiers of Odin's (the USA chapter) welcome message states,

> Waves of immigrants are pouring into Europe committing mass rape. Sweden and Germany, in particular have faced the brunt of this policy of welcoming hordes of 'refugees.'… when—not 'if'-- this terror reaches our shores, it will be a true INVASION…We are not a nice polite group that will report outrages to the police …WE ARE NOT. We will BEAT THE LIVING SHIT out of any we catch raping American women and terrorizing American citizens. (Anti-Defamation League 2016, 5)

A short BBC film posted on the webpage of 'BombIslam', an extremist group based in the USA traces the Friday activities of Robert, the founder of the organization. Robert and a group of ex-army veterans carrying American flag and the Koran walk towards a mosque in Phoenix, Arizona and stop a Muslim man on the way to the mosque. Flaunting the Koran, Robert calls it the most sexist, homophobic document that condones paedophilia. He then asks the Muslim passer-by to leave this country and go to a Muslim country and take Obama with him. The purpose of their Friday activity, Robert claims, is to harass Muslims and antagonize them because Islam is a ridiculous religion trying to normalize its existence in America; it is also anti-women because Muslim women have to wear a burqa. The latter part of the film shows a Muslim woman, her head covered in a head scarf and a sneering Robert claiming in rage that she thinks 'she is better than us, so we are not allowed to see her hair' (BombIslam.com 2018) (This film has been taken down since 2018, but other similar exploits of Robert Sterkeson are still available on the web page). On clicking BombIslam's webpage, one is greeted with an animated picture of a Mosque being blown up into an orange ball of flames, underneath the title says: 'Sick and tired of Muslims? Then share this page.' Below, the founder posts his mission statement:

'My name is Robert and someday I am going to seize control of this country and end this sick joke we call democracy. I'm running for President in 2024 and when I win, I'm going to kill every last fucking Muslim & Jew on the entire planet. I am completely serious. Every. Last. Fucking'. (BombIslam.com)

Other video clips posted by Robert and his group depicts cartoon superheroes bombing Muslims, doctored videos of President Obama and how he would destroy Muslims if he was not one himself and paranoid videos of White women embracing Islam and reciting the Koran. Robert claims that 'diversity' is code word for 'anti-White' and multiculturalism for 'White genocide' and those not speaking out against them are complicit (Minds.com 2016).

Disembodiment of the Muslim as immigrant is an assemblage of cultural, sexual and racial construction, a Frankenstein, an 'opposite of human' that offends the 'Westerner' and defiles the 'home' of the European–American–British host communities. This marking of the 'Westerner' as exceptional from 'the others', in this case, the non-humans, the Muslim is what Puar (2007) calls 'homonationalism'. The image of the 'pure White women' to be saved and protected from the 'immigrant rape wave' and 'the threatening Muslim male' (Horsti 2017) disembodies the Muslim migrant. 'The home' must be rescued from the assault of mosque builders and public prayer goers, headscarf wearers, halal food sellers that take over the wine and sausage festivals, and the 'ridiculous religion' in general, which makes immigrants inherently offensive disturbing the peace and tolerance of Christianity.

Disembodiment through immigration rests on a fundamental belief that cultures have an essential core and that they are homogenously contained within geographical containers of the nation states. However, how does America, which is historically touted as a nation of immigrants grown strong from the innovation of its huddled masses that arrived by boat loads freeze its exceptional cultural core? How can the power of Islamophobia disconnect American identity from its affirmative history of tolerating and absorbing the immigrant? The answer lies in what the USA based anti-immigrant group Youth for Western Civilization refers to as their intellectual inspiration (DeAnna 2012), Huntington's *Who Are We?*

In *Who Are We?* Huntington (2004) engaged in an intellectual soul-searching about what it means to be American, and what exactly are the nuts and bolts of Judea-Christian-Anglo culture. Huntington claims that F. D. Roosevelt and Kennedy were wrong when they proclaimed American as the nation of immigrants. Instead,

> Their [FDR's and Kennedy's] ancestors were not immigrants but settlers, and in its origins America was not a nation of immigrants, it was a society, or societies of settlers who came to the New World in the seventeenth and eighteenth century...settlers came to America because it was a *tabula rasa*. Apart from the Indian tribes, which could be killed off or pushed westward, no society was there; and they came in order to create societies that embodied and would reinforce

the culture and values they brought with them from their origin country. (Huntington 2004, 39–40)

Thus, within the Huntingtonian paradigm of settlers versus immigrants, the term 'settlers' is the contemporary variant of the older term 'colonialists' or 'conquistadors'. For Huntington, in the settler's world view, the place to be settled is a clean slate because the indigenous inhabitants simply blend into the wild like animals. A 'settler', unlike an 'immigrant' is imbued with that 'sense of collective purpose' (p. 39) 'to create a new society' where nothing existed. And therefore, America is a Judea-Christian-Anglo civilization because the Judea-Christian-Anglo settler *found* America. 'Before immigrants could come to America, settlers had to *found* America' (Huntington 2004, 40). 'Founding' as opposed to integrating, assimilating and blending is an act of establishing supremacy by killing, conquering, pushing out—all of these would be compounded under founding–settling. Native Americans did not 'settle', they never existed outside the state of nature and the savage wilderness. The immigrants that came after the White puritans simply blended within the fold of White protestant America. They did not 'found' America and, hence, did not 'settle' because America had already been claimed, founded and settled. Therefore, the 'original' settler's White protestant race–religious identity, by default, determines the essential core of what it means to be American. This settler–immigrant difference, according to Huntington and the Youth for Western Civilization, is the fundamental core through which the immigrant Muslim can be disembodied as the Muslim. The settler carves geography and history with determination and is the one that embodies a particular identity. The immigrant is embodied or disembodied by the arbitrary will of the settler who decides if the immigrant 'fits in' within the cultural core or disturbs it.

For the Islamophobic movement, the Anglo-Protestant culture is the 'critical defining element of what it means to be American...Protestant beliefs, values, and assumptions, however, had been the core element, along with the English language, of America's settler culture, and that culture continued to pervade and shape American life, society, and thought as the proportion of Protestants declined' (Huntington 2004, 62). Similarly, for European and British-based hate groups, being European or being British has essential non-reflexive core elements of Whiteness and Christianness combined with linguistic identifiers such as English, French, German and Swedish that embody the settler and disembody the 'immigrant'. The immigrant disturbs these 'stable' culture–spatial cores of Western individual liberalism with their religious practices, prayer habits, toilet rituals, accents, food habits and recipes. The Muslim is an immigrant not because she arrived late but because she disturbs the essential core of what is assumed to be the 'settler culture' (Huntington 2004, 62). This settler culture is not really a culture, it is simply ethno-racist ascription to a certain religion, Whiteness and the ability to speak a certain language with accents that are arbitrarily approved by the 'settler'. In this politics of disembodiment, desire to dominate separates the 'settler' from the 'immigrant'. In the paradigm of an orientalist, Islamophobia does not displace the immigrant's culture, 'culture talk' disembodies the Muslim but absorbs her/his culture within the paradigm of multicultural affirmation because everybody likes a bit of kebab, calligraphy and ethnic music. Restricting citizenship, denying asylum, cutting welfare to immigrants (E. H. 2017) disembodies the immigrant, puts her/him in place, separates her/him from the 'settler' and creates the Muslim.

Individual Liberalism, Islamophobia and Disembodiment

In the post-September 11 world and, more recently, the Syrian refugee crisis, Trump's election, Muslim ban and wall-building rhetoric have created the Alt-right and given a new lease of life to right-wing political parties and right-populist movements all over the world. While these movements are not homogenous, yet a common thread is the reliance on the production of fear revolving around this exotic, inhuman and foreign figure of the Muslim. Muslims are dispersed in different nations, many in non-Muslim majority countries, they come in all shades of colour and speak various languages. Yet, the Alt-right movement in the USA and Europe, right-wing academics, think tanks and right-wing populist political parties have successfully produced a fixed subjectivity of the Muslim possessing certain common biological–cultural traits. Islamophobia, therefore, is no longer a fear of those ascribing to the religion of Islam, it is the simultaneous production and annihilation of the Muslim subjectivity. Racialization, immigrant status and orientalism are chosen ideological narratives that produce and disembody the contemporary Muslim subject.

In this chapter, I choose 'disembodiment' as the conceptual tool to explicate how contemporary Islamophobia produces the Muslim. Disembodiment is worse than racialization, misogyny, elitism and colonial occupation because while the racialized, sexualized, barbarianized subject is *de*humanized, a disembodied subject *never* existed as a *human*, she/he always lacked a *being*. While a dehumanized (Black people, women, poor, colonized) subject can use her/his subjugated position as a site to resist racism, sexism and imperialism, a disembodied subject has no claim to resistance, because her/his injustice has not yet been fully conceptualized, she/he only exists in various avatars such as villain, terrorist, rapist and women-hater. Unlike Agamben's (1998) *homo sacer*, a subject position in ancient Rome, whose death did not merit any sacrificial value, the Muslim is disembodied in life, and her/his death is valuable because it is often seen as a true Christian and patriotic act, an act in annihilation of terrorism, a crusade against the savage. The 'Islamic world' is constructed through nebulous orientalist tropes as one that exists outside Western values of freedom, democracy, rationality and the hardworking individual's quest for profit. By framing modernity as civilization, Anglo-America centric and equanimous with individual freedom, the 'Islamic world' is 'placed beyond' and 'outside'. Alt-right and associated right-wing populism's culture talk and cultural framing embodies–disembodies the Muslim as barbaric in her/his cultural habits, gestures, everyday lifeworld, habits of hygiene—she/he is seen irrational in her/his violent disposition, hence, unable to comprehend liberal ideas of freedom and democracy. Wearing Western attire, speaking English or profit seeking within Western capitalism does not offer her/him salvation, colour, name, immigrant status, mode of worship and her/his religion continuously casts them outside modernity and the West. While school shootings by 'White Western' men (Taylor 2019) and fanaticism of Christian religious cults are seen as exceptional acts of mad men and over presence of guns, but contrarily, the same cultural framing places the Orlando shooting (as contextualized early on in the chapter) as associated with *all* Muslims and their homophobic sheik demagogues. While Judeo-Christian is associated with Plato, Aristotle and Socrates to make the Tora and the Bible documents in Western modernity, Al Biruni, Idrisi and Ibn Khaldun and their contributions to empiricism, algebra and cartography does not make the Koran a modern document. While electoral democracy and the freedom to pursue profit are seen as the litmus tests for the liberation of the rational individual, yet the Muslim's duty towards *zakat al-fitr*, which is mandatory charity by giving a percentage of her/his income to the poor, is not seen as a rational act of kindness towards the community. Pollard and Samers (2007) argue that alternative forms of economic modernism exist in Islamic banking, like,

> Islamic bankers have developed financial products that avoid charging interest and shun excessive risk or speculation. The strong communal dimensions of Islamic economics means that many Islamic scholars view forms of profit and loss sharing (PLS)—in which parties share a predetermined proportion of the profits/losses before the transaction is concluded—and interest-free loans (*Qard hasan*) as the most 'Islamic' and most promising forms of contract.

Pollard and Samers (2007) contend that it is not very useful to deconstruct which religion provides the 'most moral' underpinning for a most modern society, because religion is a contradictory complex assemblage contextual to the time of its production, open to interpretation and modernity itself is contested. Weber (2013) wrote the *Protestant Ethic and the Spirit of Capitalism* theorizing that the moral consciousness of the Protestant individual provided the foundational logic for self-interest based industrial capitalism (Eurocentric views equate capitalism with modernity). The purpose, says Pollard and Samers, is not to construct a *homo Islamicus* as opposed to a *homo economicus* but to point out that religious morality is hardly ever as universalizing and homogenous to be a complete antithesis to its 'other' (whatever they maybe). Pollard and Samers remind us of Shakespeare's *Merchant of Venice* and point out that the West has literally forgotten that, like Islamic societies, usury or profiteering from a borrower's need is a crime in both religions.

The similarities of these Semitic religions (Judaism, Christianity, Islam) are rendered invisible, and instead, the Huntingtonian *Clash of Civilizations* is overplayed into crude caricatures of disembodiment. 'Soph on YouTube' is a 14-year-old White girl who is dressed in *chador* and produces mock videos on Muslims. Such is the vitriol that YouTube had to take her down. Such is the depravity that while thousands of subscribers take voyeuristic pleasure in the abuse she unleashes, yet no one questions the sanity of a 'Western liberal civilization' and the 'virtues of freedom of speech' that 'empowers' a minor to speak in such offensive ways. This bit is excavated before it was removed by YouTube; Soph says,

How about this: 'I've become a devout follower of the Prophet Muhammad. Suffice to say, I've been having a f*** ton of fun. Of course, I get raped by my 40-year-old husband every so often and I have to worship a black cube to indirectly please an ancient Canaanite god—but at least I get to go to San Fran and stone the shit out of some gays, and the cops can't do anything about it because California is a crypto-caliphate. (Bernstein 2019)

The Muslim inhabits the days before feminist revolt, before subaltern resistance to imperialism, before slave's revolt against the master and the working class' revolt against the capitalist. Her/his marginalization is yet to be conceptualized, her/his exploitation yet to be rendered a site for resistance, her/his oppression yet to be substantiated as injustice. No reverse embodiment is yet enough of a challenge to the sweeping templates of disembodiment that materially and ideologically un-produces the Muslim. The disembodiment operates through the identity politics of right-wing activism, academia and media to swiftly and trenchantly annihilate any semblance of being or humanity that the Muslim embodies. Islamophobia is constructed as a violation of body, mind and an entire way of life.

I trace the ideology and inspiration behind Alt-right and associated populist parties and movements in the USA and Europe to demonstrate how the Muslim is disembodied through White supremacy, anti-immigrant xenophobia and orientalism. In this chapter, by deconstructing right-wing academic research, speeches, blogs, videos and news articles, I excavate the populist construction of American identity as an ideological–material production of White supremacy within a larger paradigm of universal Western liberalism to which the Muslim is disembodied as an antithesis. Disembodiment as anti-immigrant xenophobia explicates how diverse nationalities of Muslim migrants in Europe and America meld into the Muslim seen as the homogenous alien whose bizarre behaviour in public spaces, manner of praying and using public bathrooms is destroying a sense of home. Disembodiment as orientalism indicates how modernity becomes the solvent by which the Muslim is dissolved into an exotic assemblage of primitive, inward-looking and parochial people produced by her/his 'depraved' religion. For the Alt-right and associated groups, the Muslim, very much like the feminists, only exists in reverse templates of villainy that disrupts the stable order of Western liberalism. According to the Alt-right, liberal media pampers multiculturalism to blatantly disregard universalist principles of Western civilization by unduly favouring the Muslim other. What the supreme settler culture avoids deconstructing is that universalism is actually Judea-Christian particularism, multiculturalism is superficial tokenism avoiding systemic overhaul of racism, civilization is a mental construct and the 'West' is an imagination depending on who gets to define what is supreme.

6

White Fetishism, Ethno-space and Anti-immigrant Xenophobia

Nation, Race and Empire

The USA has had a contradictory flirtation with migration and immigration. Contradictory because the migrant body has been a racialized body, if not inscribed in skin colour, then inscribed in religious–cultural habits, ethnicity or language, be it African slaves, Jewish migrants, Polish Catholics or Chinese indentured labour. The business of nation building has depended on the need to inject labour, energy and acumen, and this economic need has clashed with intellectual theories on race dating back to the infamous days of eugenics, which has extolled the superiority of the White Anglo-Saxon race (Grant 1918; Stoddart 1923). This clash subsequently boiled over into the emancipation proclamation, end of slavery, civil rights movements and demands for social justice. The contradictions boiled over with the post-World War migration, creation of inner-city Jewish, Italian ghettoes and, subsequently, White flight into the suburbs, the contradictions continue to boil with Hispanic and Muslim migration and virulent anti-immigration xenophobia directed at them. Although written in 2001, Howard Winant's characterization of America as 'domestic and global racial theatre' (Winant 2001, 148) still applies. The questions he raises is as follows:

> As it [US] assumed its place as leader of what is called the 'free world,' the country was forced to face its lack of freedom within. U.S. society confronted anew the anti-democratic and immoral racial subordination upon which it continued to depend. It faced once again the racial limits of its culture, its politics, its economic life. Was the United States really 'the land of the free, and the home of the brave'? Were its vaunted 'free market' and 'free enterprise system' really 'free' for all?

The 'anti-democratic and immoral racial subordination' that formed the genetic makeup of the land of the free, argues Winant, is the very recipe of modernity, the intrinsic ingredients of a nation-building project. Modernization and nation building, argues Winant (2001, 20), involves a 'global racial formation project' where internal differences (class, race, gender) must be sorted out to create a 'we', a patriotic amalgam, that must be set aside from the 'they', the nation's other (economic rivals, ideological competitors, cultural others) (Chatterjee 1993; Gellner 2008; Hobsbawm 2012). Nation building in post-World War USA is also an empire-building project where individual freedom, liberal democracy and capitalism based on self-interest and consumerism, and neoliberal free market capitalism can become the template for the USA-led global modernization project (Hobsbawm 2008; Smith 2004, 2005). This modernization and empire building project controls access to American citizenship in such a way that the distinction between the 'we' (citizen) and 'they' (migrant) is structurally and discursively mediated based on a commitment to free market capitalism, individual liberalism, consumerism and liberal democracy. This commitment to the ideals of American nation is filtered through a cultural–racial prism of colour and religious identity to produce various gradations of 'others', for example, high up on the list are the Nordic Whites (Trump 2018) and lower down are professional visa allocated South Asian software professionals, and still lower down, and even 'outside' are Mexicans and Muslims, although all these categories may be equally committed to the values of American identity. A post-World War II American nation attempts to connect racial bodies with access to American citizenship in such a way that labour–capital mediation (needs of industrial, modernity capitalism and profit making) can proceed unhindered while, simultaneously, preserving the integrity of a cultural ideology that is still committed to the ideas of settler colonization (White Protestant pioneers as culturally superior). Discourse and policy attitude towards the migrant/racial 'other' is, therefore, what Winant (2001) argues, is the link between structure and signification, that is, what race means within a set of discursive formation like immigration policy (this discursive expression is the signification), and its relation to how social structures are organized, for example, access to jobs, nature of education, textbooks, and access to healthcare. I argue that this link between structure and signification is a problematic and contradictory one. While the structures of free market capitalism, individual liberalism and democracy recognize the profit-seeking modern man that can be a labour, innovator, investor or capitalist, in other words, a self-interested individual, racialized imaginations, on the other hand, that define immigration policy casts this very profit-seeking individual as premodern, barbaric, uncivilized, exotic and alien. Hence, structures of a modern nation-building project clashes with cultural/racial signification (meaning making). The nation promises freedom and democracy to its citizens, but the global project of empire building demands 'anti-democratic and immoral racial subordination' (Winant 2001, 148) of the global 'other', so that access to freedom—American style is carefully calibrated to maintain the settler–immigrant gap. Muslims constitute the 'global-other' for Alt-right imaginations in the USA and Europe, and Mexicans constitute the 'regional other' for the Alt-right in the USA. Huntington (2004), in *Who Are We?* (which is often cited by Alt-right leadership as the one of the top inspirations for its ideology), claims:

Assimilation is particularly problematic for Mexicans and other Hispanics. Their immigration poses problems unprecedented in America (p. 185)

The persistence of Mexican immigration and the large and increasing absolute numbers of Mexicans reduce the incentives for cultural assimilation. Mexican-Americans no longer think of themselves as members of a small minority who must accommodate the dominant group and adopt its culture. As their numbers increase, they become more committed to their own ethnic identity and culture.

...The negative feelings and hostile attitudes of Muslims toward America gathered force in the 1990s and became dramatically evident after September 11...The antagonism of Muslims toward the United States stems in part from American support of Israel. It also has deeper roots in the fear from American power, envy of American wealth, resentment of what is perceived as American domination and exploitation, and hostility to American culture, secular and religious, as the antithesis of Muslim culture (p. 360).

In the post-World War empire and identity building project, the immigrant, according to Huntington, is a racialized body. It is not enough that the immigrant can labour hard and through social mobility absorb into the mythical American middle class; for Huntington, the Hispanic and Muslim identifiers are resilient in a way that the German, Irish and Jewish of the World War era were not. The 'new immigrant', owing to its large numbers and cultural peculiarity will always contest the American nation-building project tearing away from cultural assimilation.

White Picket Fences and the Ethno-state

For the Alt-right, the question of migration is tied to ethnicity/ race, preservation of Whiteness as a civilization, immigration policy and border wall, and hence, wrapped up in what some have described as 'White nationalism' (Johnson 2017), and others have described as the creation of a White 'ethno-state' (Spencer 2017). In *Counter Current*, a major web-based White nationalist journal, the editor Greg Johnson makes the following statement on the future of Whiteness and immigration:

> Replacing non-whites with whites is never lauded as diversity or multiculturalism. When it happens in a non-white neighborhood, it is described as 'gentrification.' When it happens in a non-white country, it is condemned as 'imperialism' and 'colonialism,' or even 'ethnic cleansing' and 'genocide.' Non-whites get to keep their spaces, but whites don't. What is theirs, they keep. What is ours, is negotiable.

> White Nationalism is identity politics for white people, and it will inevitably arise when formerly white societies become multiracial societies. It will only cease when multiculturalism is replaced with racially and ethnically homogenous white societies again.

> ...In fact, when White Nationalism first emerges, it is seldom willing to directly confront the taboo against racial identity, so it embraces civic rather than racial nationalism and pursues white interests under the guise of universal principles like rights and legality. Nevertheless, even the most sheepish and bashful, even the most self-contradictory and self-defeating White Nationalist sentiments were powerful enough to carry the Brexit referendum and Donald Trump to the US presidency. Indeed, such implicit White Nationalism is the animating principle of the growing populist-nationalist movements across the white world.

> For instance, I believe that White Nationalists should seriously promote a new immigration/emigration policy that aims to return to the ethnic *status quo* of 1965, which was in many ways the peak of American civilization. The goal would

simply be to erase the catastrophic error of opening our borders to the Third World. This transformation could take place gradually, with 2065 as the target date for completion. This sort of proposal could even meet with the approval of many non-whites because it gives a place to their kind in America's future. As long as whites had complete freedom to disassociate with other races, the result would be a *de facto* White Nationalist society for the vast majority of whites.

But there is no guarantee that such a racially segregated society would not eventually grow complacent, then delusional and profligate, repeating all the mistakes that are destroying us today. Thus, White Nationalists will have to keep moving the goalposts toward the complete realization of the ethnostate. There's no reason for us to ever stop extolling the idea of a completely homogeneous society because, even the most timid civic nationalists know, in their heart of hearts, that America would be a better place with no blacks or Mexicans or Muslims whatsoever. (Johnson 2017)

For Johnson, therefore, White nationalism is an acceptable identity movement because Whiteness as a race/culture is under the onslaught of migration from Third World communities seen as neo-colonialism, a process that contributes to the shrinking of spaces that White people control ('nice neighborhoods, schools, businesses, communities, and countries' Johnson 2017). White nationalism as an identity movement would aim to establish a 'White Nationalist society' based on racial separation, however, demanding racial separation would be a form of 'timid civic nationalism', which will work temporarily. In the long run, racial apartness within the same nation state carries with it the possibilities of 'repeating all the mistakes' such as mixed schools, mixed public spaces, interracial marriages and affirmative action resulting in complacency and profligacy among the White race. Therefore, the timidness of civic nationalism must be overcome to ultimately launch a virulent form of White identity based national movement that restores White settler's status quo by creating a White nation devoid of 'offending' black people and immigrants such as

Mexicans and Muslims. 'Mexicans' being a metaphor for mostly all Latin American nationals and Muslims referring to a catch-all container box for people of various shades and nationalities ranging from Iran to Indonesia. Clearly, not all immigrants are unwelcome in the White nation, those with Brown or Black skin are, and in this colour scheme, even the Whitest of Muslims (for example certain Turkish, Lebanese, Iranians) are painted Brown. As discussed in the previous chapter, Islamophobia becomes an embodiment of race and Mexicans become a metaphor for undesirable immigrants and black people for undesirable elements. Brexit and President Trump's election to power are cited as evidence for the immense support of a mild variety of White identity movement, which is foreseen as the precursor to larger geographical separations and even the creation of White ethno-states in the image of Zionism and Israel. In articulating what this White nation might be, Richard Spencer (2017) in a podcast interview, discusses the ideology and imagination behind his now immensely popular concept of the ethno-state:

> The ethno-state is an ideal, but that does not mean that it will not come into being. The left has always had big dreams... of communism, the Jewish identity movement, had in the 19th century, this dream of Zionism, which was treated as totally impractical and impossible etc. when it was just an idea...the right has always been reactionary, it has reacted to the left, and it has dismissed utopias...the right also needs big dreams, we need to be just as utopian as the left, we need ultimately, have an idea of what we ultimately want, where is this ultimately leading? Even if it is not going to be achievable in our life time, like true communism in the left's mind has never been achieved, but it [ethno-state] will be a motivating ideal. Yes, I would like a state in the European continent from Portugal to Vladivostok, whether something like that can take part, could arise in north America, that too would also be wonderful, but right now it is to define it as an ideal...But the way I understand the ethno-state is post-America, I don't think it can arise as a policy initiative by the Republican party or the Democratic party...we [Alt-Right]

want to conserve the white race as a being that has a history and future, and that has culture that is inherent to it and cannot be separated from race, there is a conservation element to it, much like we want to conserve living things that have history, much like the Red woods and breeds of animals...I want white people to flourish...because we have a unique history that we do not share with Africans ...of course white privilege exists, we should be deepening and expanding white privilege, privilege is good, we want to privilege our people first, we want to give them advantages that we don't give others...I want my people winning...Most patriots are white Americans and when they are thinking of America they are thinking of white picket fences, and backyard barbeques, and Sunday schools, and sermons, they are thinking of white America...this comes from white sensibility.

Richard Spencer adopts a philosophical–ideological stance towards the migration-mixing issue. It is not just a pragmatic, policy and constitutional stance, nor is it a step by step culmination of waves of identity politics from civic nationalism to White nationalism to ethno-state. Inspired by Nietzsche, whom Spencer refers to in this podcast (1920, 2018), Evola's 'New man/Spiritual Man' (Hakl 2012; Horowitz 2017) and Benoist's French identarian philosophy (Benoist and Champetier 2012) and the cultural spiritual revival of the West, Spencer wishes that the new White man would rise above the death and despondency caused by Netflix to answer to this utopian call for the re-establishment of White supremacy. This goal, according to Spencer, may be unachievable in one lifetime, and judging by the haunted tone of his voice, he almost wishes that this ideal is not reduced to some version of a White nation state near Alabama. In fact, ethno-state at some level, I argue, in the deepest recess of Spencer's mind, is a conceptualization of White power that is a 'forever struggle' (he calls it an 'endless struggle'), unrealizable, and always aspired for a unicorn that ruptures despondency, satiation by Netflix and 'extreme porn' (Spencer 2017). In fact, at a deep philosophical level, it almost seems that for Spencer, the actualization of the ethno-state would signify the destruction of utopia. It is as if Spencer almost seeks to reinvent himself within the philosophical pantheon of Nietzsche and Evola in exorcising the White man, and therefore the White race from the complacency of consumption, leisure and debauchery by providing a high ideal that goes beyond the pursuit of happiness through an 'objectivist ethics' (Rand 1964, 28) and 'possessive individualism' (Macpherson 1962, 3) of Western liberal democracy. When the interviewer in the afore-mentioned podcast interjected asking what is wrong with an individual that has worked to accumulate enough wealth to allow him/her to spend a day watching Netflix, Spencer says that 'Netflix' is a mere metaphor for life spent in the pursuit of the mundane. For Spencer (2017), 'Happy is not a goal, that is a goal for women and cattle.' White race is supposed to realize itself through 'Wondering, conquering, and building structures,' but if there are no new places to conquer, then life itself should become a struggle for something higher and better, life itself should become an 'endless struggle'.

Nietzsche, Evola and Benoist's inspiration is apparent in Spenser's comments given before. As argued in Chapter 3, for Nietzsche, attaining happiness means accumulation of power, it is the concentration of power that makes an individual 'valuable', not just the accumulation of private property, wealth and emotional nourishment. Happiness is not just contentment or maximization of pleasure and reduction of pain as liberal ethics codifies, but it is the pursuit of power through war and conquest. The happiest individual for Nietzsche is one that is terrifying. Like an aspiring demagogue, therefore, Spencer thirsts to instil a fierceness and create a 'new Whiteman' in the image of Nietzsche and Evola's prescriptions that once again rekindles the passion for colonial conquest that put the White race 'in-charge' of the Brown and the Black people and their resources and territory. Spencer is eager to discursively reinvent White imperialism as a good thing for the White man's soul and civilization because, it will rekindle the West like, it did in the past by sucking resource and labour from the rest of the world ushering the White industrial revolution and White capitalism. Spencer contends that there are places that are still left to be conquered (like 'outer space'). Like Nietzsche (2018), Spencer emphasizes the spirit to strive and conquer and views the liberal ethics of tolerance and empathy towards women, minorities and migrants as weakness. Like Evola and Benoist, Spencer believes not in just a material revolution but a spiritual revival of the 'West' through the creation of a 'new White man' whose spirit is reforged with the zeal and anger to proclaim and reclaim White privilege as not something to be ashamed of, but something to be nourished and deepened because White men constitute a 'people' with unique destiny, history and culture that cannot be separated from race.

When probed, Spencer provides pragmatic prescriptions for achieving the 'ethno-state' as a state carved out of Europe, from Portugal to Vladivostok. The nostalgia for the 'old world', the need to reclaim and preserve 'the White man's history and architecture' is evident when Spencer clarifies that the ethno-state cannot be in the USA, it has to be 'post-USA'. It is unclear whether he means that the USA as it exists must be dissolved and recreated, but it is clear that Spencer is keen on reclaiming history, which, in his mind, seems to be more authentic and abundant in the old world than in the new world. The Alt-right has always equated Whiteness with Europeanness completely glossing over the diversity within European history, languages and culture. Other possibilities for actualizing the ethno-state includes conquest of spaces within the Western hemisphere and investment in Third World countries to which immigrants in the USA who have not struck deep roots could go back. Spencer asserts that just like the creation of the ethno-state of Israel as a safe haven for Jewish identity movement was accomplished by the Zionist movement, the aspiration for reviving the spirit of West through a territorial manifestation of Whiteness is a possibility and necessity. The nostalgia for an 'authentic' White Christian urban/suburban landscape with rows of nice homes, White picket fences, backyard barbecues, Sunday schools is what Spencer's Alt-right evokes as the cultural geography of the ethno-state. When the interviewer interjected that there is no reason to assume that Black and Brown people cannot partake in nice homes and backyard barbecues if they work hard and take advantage of opportunities, Spencer claimed that assimilation into Whiteness only truly happens when the immigrants are of a higher income group and understand the core value of White imagination and willingly surrender their identity to it. But assimilation, according to Spencer, is not happening in proliferating migrant neighbourhoods of Dallas, Houston and El Paso, which look more Mexican than White. While Spencer critiques liberal multiculturalists, it is ironic that his philosophical stance is unconsciously very much a product of liberal individualism. He recognizes that class mobility can enable migrants to become 'White' and backyard barbeques more authentic to White culture, and the 'culture of poverty' on the other hand, makes migrant neighbourhoods more 'deviant' from, and tainting of, the White civilization. It is interesting, however, that the nice neighbourhoods and picket fences are seen as ubiquitously emblematic of White America irrespective of the class position of White folks and a rich history of barbecuing and outdoor cooking among African Americans. What Spencer's Alt-right ideology would not acknowledge is that 'trailer trash', 'mobile home colonies', 'hippie communes', 'redneck hick towns' and 'Hillbilly's honkytonk country side' are as much emblematic of the geography of White America's cultural sensibilities as White middle-class neighbourhoods with picket fences and backyard barbecuing is/can be quintessentially black.

In an effort to explain away assimilation by upper-class immigrants in nice White neighbourhoods by actually avoiding class analysis, Spencer claims that culture and economy are chicken and egg concepts. For Spencer, 'economy is part of society' (meaning culture), in other words, the poor Mexican brings with him his garish culture, offensive music, bright colours, exotic smells because his cultural sensibilities are not 'evolved'; he, therefore, imposes his 'culture of poverty' on America's towns and irreparably taints White man's civilizational expression. The Alt-right never enters into a reverse cultural analysis where Mexico's cultural expression was forcibly converted into Dallas, Houston and El Paso. Spencer never analyses that Sam Huston altered the geography of Texas by overseeing the annexation of Texas from Mexico (Nance 2011; Siegel 2010). The cultural geography that the White man carves through colonization and plunder is not garish, brutish or exotic, they are symbols of refinement, superiority and power. What Greg Johnson omits when he laments that the White man's actions are always dubbed as 'colonialism', 'imperialism', 'genocide' and 'gentrification' is the fact that the superimposition of 'nice White neighbourhoods' on Brown civilizations are blind spots on White memory that conveniently forgets that what looks White was never really White. Therefore, the timeless Whiteness of Houston, Dallas and El Paso, for the Alt-right is tainted by the Brownness of the Mexican migrants, but the fact is, under the White patina of conquest, they were always Brown. Both Johnson and Spencer avoid class analysis of poverty and inequality, understanding black culture and the migrant's culture as absence of refinement rather than as ensemble of relations that manifest through class. But the Nietzschean Alt-right makes the White man a *homo culturalis*, a broad brush stroke imagery of 'White culture' that is not adequately representative of the nuances of White identity, which is often intersected with and mediated by other positions like class. There is a lot of analysis that claim the rise of right-wing populism, Trumpism and even Brexit as economic backlash of the White working class to reclaim the economy from low-income immigrants that pull down the wages, and that these backlashes cannot be simply understood as cultural—racist assertions of exclusion (Davis 2017; Donella 2016; Morgan and Lee 2018; Walley 2017). Therefore, *homo culturalis* and *homo economicus* are more imbricated than Spencer will accept, and the reason he fails to accept this imbrication is because of Alt-right's firm foundations within individual liberalism as a philosophy that negates class as a category.

In the absence of Marxist ideas on value, exploitation and creation of the working class, the Alt- right's understanding of economic position is a superficial analysis of income position and culture expressed as life choices (commodity choices, objectivist ethics, possessive individualism). Although Spencer is quite unconscious of the liberal roots of his cultural-conservatism preferring to philosophize White supremacy within the paradigms of the Nietzschean high ideals of the powerful Man and his quest to strive, to seek, to find, and not to yield, yet these high ideals are in perfect alignment with individual liberalism's apathy for class analysis. Simply put, in Marx's analysis (1963, 1976, 2002), class is not income, or the nature of job, or lack of refinement: it is the condition of specificity (within the factory) and generality (within industrial capitalism) of exploitation produced by wage relations where the owner of the means of production (industrial capitalist/corporations, financial capitalist/Wall street) by virtue of control over the ownership of capital (means of production) can decide wages for those who actually toil and produce—wages that are below the value that the working class produces in the sphere of production and reproduction. Because the wages are never representative of the value produced by the class of workers, value stolen from them in the context of unfair wage relations represents profit, and hence, exploitation of the working class. In Marx's analysis, exploitation happens in the context of wage labour where lowering the wage and increasing the length of the workday entrenches exploitation (other secondary forms of exploitation are imposed by the landlords, banks, retailers). Exploitation is sometimes assumed as an economic condition of surplus value (additional value produced by the working class which is not compensated in the wage they receive) being sucked away with no compensation for the worker (Wright 1982). Low wages and long working days, however, permeate outside the factory to determine the entire domain of social existence. E. P. Thompson (1978) asserts that class cannot be anchored by superficial, static indicators like income because income, GDP, GDP per capita are measures of wealth/private property and do not represent the struggle and exploitation embedded in living and working. Income also does not represent the relative gap between the value accumulated by owners of means of production and the working class, this relative gap is the actual indicator of how, and to what extent, a society is economically exploitative of its own. Class formation, according to Thompson, is spontaneous: People live in societies structured in certain ways and some experience exploitative structures and identify contradictory interests and then struggle against them. In struggle, people discover themselves as classes, and this discovery is their class consciousness. The 'experience' of class, according to Thompson, is not just a case of political organizing. Instead, he explains,

> Class eventuates as men and women live their productive relations, and as they experience their determinate situations, within 'the ensemble of the social relations', with their inherited culture and expectations, and as they handle these experiences in cultural ways. So that, in the end, no model can give us what ought to be the 'true' class formation for a certain 'stage' of process. No actual class formation in history is any truer or more real than any other, and class defines itself as, in fact, it eventuates. (Thompson 1978, 150, emphasis added, quoted in Chatterjee 2016)

For Thompson, therefore, class is a socio-cultural experience of exploitation, it is not an abstract economic category. The beauty of Thompsonian dialectical interpretation is the assertion that there is no a priori, pre-given static conceptual container that can be extracted from a prior model of social totality and provided ahistorically, a-contextually and a-spatially as 'class'. Class emerges out of struggle at a particular historical–geographical moment; the process of struggling in that moment is class consciousness, and therefore, class and class consciousness are always the last, rather than the first stage in historical process. The opposite, argues Thompson, is an undialectical approach rooted in a positivist penchant for a perfect formula: a neat quantitative measurement of this 'pure category', an exercise fraught with 'endless stupidities' (p. 149). For Thompson, it is imperative that we dialectically pry open closed categories in order to understand how class struggle is materialized not only on the factory floor but beyond, in the rioting slums, in the criminal courts, and in the moral machinery of charitable institutions because (p. 150) 'so simple a category as 'theft' may turn out to be, in certain circumstances, evidence of protracted attempts by villagers to defend ancient common right usages or by laborers to defend customary perquisites.' Thompson would agree with Spencer that culture and economy are so dialectically imbricated that they are indeed chicken and egg, but where Thompson's Marxist analysis diverges from Spencer's individual liberalism is that, for Thompson, class eventuates in a historical–geographical moment of living and working through the shared experience of country clubs, polo games or absence of access to housing and education, and these experiences of abundance or struggle are eventuated in cultural ways not as individuals' but within *ensembles of social relations*. In that context, Mexican immigrants, Syrian refugees, 'Africans from shithole countries' are as much class eventuating as 'immigrants from Norway' (Trump 2018) and nice White neighbourhoods with picket fences, backyard barbecues and Sunday schools. Therefore, Thompson will agree with Spencer that economy is part of society—meaning, class is not an abstraction, an a priori category, but where he differs from Spencer is in the latter's belief that culture has an inherent essence that is unique and pure and contained within Whiteness, Americanness and Europeanness and attaches itself to commodities like suburban homes, picket fences, barbecue sauce, French wines and German sausages. Culture eventuates through life experiences of struggle, some of which are struggle over subsistence represented through wages, therefore, nice White middle class neighbourhoods are as much a representation of class culture as are the American inner-cities, the projects, or China town. The history of the White race contained within nation states that Spencer selectively wishes to construct as the European culture represented in nostalgic White neighbourhoods is a pseudo analysis of life that wishes to glorify certain class struggles while diminishing and erasing others. Therefore, White European conquest of the Brown and the Black world is supreme and aesthetic, but an African American person's struggle against police brutality, the Mexican or Latin American migrant's struggle to enter the USA, or Syrian refugee's struggle to escape war induced by the 'West' by coming to a safe space in Europe and America is inferior and akin to culture of poverty, garish and exotic. Commodities that represent 'desired attributes' of White culture such as posh neighbourhoods, picket fences, and by extension, French fashion, and cheese and wine are part of the pantheon of liberal individualism's penchant for accumulation of property (hence happiness). Spencer's Alt-right is happiest when it has ideologically and materially constructed an ethno-state that is a geographical amalgam of these desired commodities individually accumulated by White men—ethno-state is the ultimate spatial representation of White private property. The pioneering and exploitative zeal that brought garish diseases to native Americans in North America and plundered indigenous populations, their art, aesthetics, indigenous knowledge the world over escapes critical evaluation, and is subsumed under 'higher struggles'. The cultural economy of Alt-right's ethno-state and White identity while couched in Evola's 'spiritual racism' (Wolff 2016, 483) and Nietzschean high ideals of endless struggle are, however, reductionist a priori abstract 'pure category', an exercise fraught with 'endless stupidities' (Thompson 1978, 149) because they attach/quantify/categorize 'supremacy' to skin tone, ability to build certain landscapes and accumulate certain commodities as metaphors for conquer, plunder and exclusion. Spencer and Johnson therefore, represent outdated notions of biological racism updated with a heavy dose of White 'spirit' to create an internet based ideology in support of a 'new-world' old-style colonialism not based on corporate profit, neoliberalism, World Bank control through structural adjustment, but through the construction of White geographies where spoils of racism can be relished and consumed through the White male pursuit of happiness. Possessive individualism and racism combine to create an Alt-right culture-class.

Thompson (1978, 150) would disagree with Johnson and Spencer's analysis because, for him, 'no model can give us what ought to be the 'true' class formation for a certain 'stage' of process. No actual class formation in history is any truer or more real than any other...' Similarly, no model can give us what ought to be the 'true' culture of a certain community.

No cultural formation is any truer or superior in history than any other. The settling of Mexican migrants, therefore, create an alternative to picket fences and backyard barbecues, but there is no yard stick of purity/supremacy that can empirically prove that the mosaic of food trucks, taco stands, bright colours and salsa music are any less true or real than the White imagined community that the Alt-right evokes. But indeed, seen from the Marxist context of labouring, theft of surplus value and exploitation, a certain class culture can be more emancipatory than another, in that context, colonialism, imperialism, ethnic cleansing, genocide and gentrification need not be tied to skin tone or national culture—any man (and woman) of any colour is capable of oppression. Pigmentocracy, for example, exists within Latin American countries and is tied to accumulation of land and private property, and dispossession—Whiter colonial descendent usurping surplus value from those that phenotypically resemble native populations (Sidanius et al. 2001; Telles 2014), and within India, higher castes have historically gentrified 'lower' castes (Ghurye 1969; Raheja 1988). Within a dialectical analysis where class eventuates in the context of struggle in a particular historical–geographical moment, White, Brown or Black, West, East or rest, American, European, Mexican and Syrian do not have a priori association to supremacy/imperialism or emancipation/inclusion; a particular class culture (national or otherwise) can be a colonizer, imperialist, genocidal or gentrifier depending on the theft of surplus value. The exploiter/exploited has no a priori colour, culture, gender; she/he emerges in the context of struggle, which she/he experiences within an ensemble of social relations (White, Black, Brown, American, Syrian, Mexican, Christian, Muslim, men, women, queer) to *eventuate* in determinate situations (inner city versus suburbs, middle-class neighbourhoods versus *colonias populares*, gated communities versus sweat shops, the USA versus Mexico) class culture of exploitation or emancipation. In that context, the migrant life-worlds of Houston, Dallas and El Paso are as authentic as the White picket fences in White neighbourhoods; the question is, which endless struggle is to be legitimized: Is it the endless struggle to exploit or the endless struggle to survive?

This is where the 'big dreams' of the Alt-right differs from the 'big dreams' of the left. The Alt-right has, unfortunately, conflated endless struggle for survival as quest for supremacy of the White man when actually, the high ideals of spiritual progress, if we are to follow Marx and Thompson, should be the endless struggle for emancipation of all exploited culture class ('big dream' of communism as Spencer characterizes it). In the Marxian and Thompsonian sense, emancipation is not predicated on the individual's accumulation of picket fences, homes, barbecue grills, smokers and patio paraphernalia (possessive individualism) but on the freedom of a community (class culture) to own the value of their labour as they engage in various productive relations. Liberal ideas of freedom and happiness on which Spencer predicates the White man's superiority is alienating, reductionist and restrictive. Private property accumulated from market competition, imperialism, genocide and gentrification only leads to alienation and estrangement. As discussed in Chapter 2, the cunning of private property is illustrated by Marx as:

> The 'secret' (that private property was the product of alienated labour) was only revealed at 'the culmination of the development of private property'. It could only be uncovered when private property had completed its domain over Man and became a 'world historical power',...Once private property became a 'world-historical power', every new product meant 'a new potential for mutual swindling and mutual plundering'. The need for money became the only need produced by the economic system and the neediness grew as the power of money increased. Everything was reduced to 'quantitative being'. (Marx and Engels 2002, 133–134)

In the Alt-right's analysis, this 'quantitative being', the White man, by virtue of his cultural superiority, masculinity and inherent prowess and spirituality that transcends 'women and cattle' (Spencer 2017), must accumulate 'world-historical power' through the private ownership of 'ethno-state'. Spencer's closet liberalism does not self-consciously recognize his zeal for the

White ethno-state as the individual liberal penchant for the accumulation of private property, he sees it as the ultimate motivating ideal for conservation of a pure cultural breed, the White man and his seed like a pure bred stallion, a specie of red wood or other superior pedigree of animals. This is the ultimate reductionism of the quantitative being, the self-commodification of Whiteness as a pure and valuable commodity. In this self-commodification of White class culture, the Alt-right is invested in the 'conservation' of a cultural economy of the 'ethno-state' where the need for Whiteness is hyped through the production of a selective history and geography, and more the neediness can be enhanced through an internet geography of right-wing populist hysteria, the more the neediness for White supremacist identity would be increased—a 'spiritual' rational for 'a new potential for mutual swindling and mutual plundering' would produce an endless struggle to exploit.

Settler-immigrant and the Melting Pot

The root of much of the White nationalism discussed before is drawn from the guru of conservative American identity politics, Sam Huntington (2004, 40), whose book *Who Are We?* (also discussed in Chapter 3 and 5) has been a source of philosophical inspiration for White supremacist movements. The major assertions that Huntington makes about American identity is the pure essence of a unique White Euro-American culture that Spencer refers to and that Johnson alludes to. This, for Huntington is the 'settler culture', a distinct form of pure identity different from 'migrant culture'. In other words, for Huntington, the 'original' settlers (not native Americans but the English and Dutch colonialists) of America were 'founders, settlers, or planters' not 'immigrants', the term 'immigrant', asserts Huntington, having arrived into America post-1780s to distinguish migrants from 'original settlers'. The settlers created the 'polity', brought their English language, their work ethic, Christian religion, Protestant morality, European art and literature, and 'mental habits to which the immigrants would have to adjust'. Therefore, the soul, or what Huntington refers to as 'core' is that America is a 'colonial society', (p. 41) where the word 'colony' does not refer to its later meaning, which is a group of people ruled by foreign nationals, but rather a settlement created by a cohort of people that left their homes to establish 'a new society on distant turf'. On the other hand, in contrast to Huntington's characterization, Hansen (1927, 500) looked upon the settlers/pioneers of the 17th and the 18th century as 'exiles' or 'fortune hunters' who could not live in their native lands either due to persecution of governments, religion or economic hardships, or were attracted to possibilities of fortune in the new world. But Hansen argues that the distinction (between exiles and fortune hunters) is fundamental. In the one case, the causes are to be found in Europe and in the other, in America. Either the immigrants were 'expelled or they were attracted.' Spickard (2009) argues, on the other hand, that very first fact of American immigration is genocide, it is the displacement and destruction of the Native peoples of North America. This act of genocide is part of the story of immigration and is not just some parallel story. Others like Abu-Laban and Lamont (1997, 25) characterize the pioneering plunder as 'settler colony immigration' fuelling conquer of indigenous people and expropriation of territory. Abu-Laban and Lamont attempt a thorough study of various commissions, immigration policies over the years and indicate how a distinction was created in the 1880s between the immigrant (settler colonialists to use Huntington's term) and the 'new immigrant'. Abu-Laban and Lamont's research deconstruct eugenics inspired 'evidence' that fuelled restrictive, quota-based and exclusionary immigration policy that tied the 'new immigrant's body to a racialized body politic of the melting pot'; where assimilation to the melting pot or exclusion from it was based on a racialized pecking order in which those cast lower in the order were viewed as stable racialized embodiments 'to demonstrate conclusively the social inferiority of the new immigrants' (Handlin 1970, xxxix). Therefore, settler/pioneer and immigrant/new immigrant are distinctions that are embedded within ideo-epistemological positions, while for Huntington, the native American is part of nature, and hence, non-existent, and America is a 'polity' established on a *tabula rasa* by the innovative zeal, work ethic and Christian morality of the founder/settler/planter. For others, like Hansen, these founder/settler/pioneers were exiles, outcasts, opportunists and gold-diggers that were pushed out of their homeland. For Spickard, Abu-Laban and Lamont, racism is the core of America's colonial society founded on genocide, territorial expropriation and eugenic-based gobbledygook that creates false categories such as 'new immigrants' and 'melting pots', with both terminologies produced ingeniously through ideo-epistemological positions masquerading as science.

Ideo-epistemological intellectual work that is based on eugenics has largely been discredited today to the extent that 'eugenics' itself is a taboo concept in all political circles; however, it continues to philosophically influence 'modern' inspirations (e.g., Huntington's work) for White supremacy. Lothrop Stoddard (1923, 165–166), one of Huntington's ideo-epistemological inspirations, writing in the 1920s deconstructs liberal multiculturalism's 'melting pot' in explicit racial ontologies, thus, bringing to the forefront what is latent in the construction of the 'migrant', and the 'new immigrant':

> Above all, there is no more absurd fallacy than the shibboleth of the 'melting-pot.' As a matter of fact, the melting-pot may mix but does not melt. Each race-type, formed ages ago, and 'set' by millenniums of isolation and inbreeding, is a stubbornly persistent entity. Each type possesses a special set of characters: not merely the physical characters visible to the naked eye, but moral intellectual, and spiritual characters as well.

Unlike the multiculturalist's zeal for the melting pot as a site for innovation, creativity and uniqueness, a conservative intellectual lens views the 'melting pot' as an absurd fallacy, because from the conservative stance, human being is an undialectical container of moral (religious values for instance) socio-cultural (work ethics) characteristics that is fundamentally tied to the deeper biological core that essentializes him as a White man with a certain cephalic index. Therefore, the pure essence, the core never melts, it just mixes in awkward ways to produce diluted and inferior essences that is to the detriment of the essentialized pure because the 'mix' between 'a White man and an Indian' is disappointingly an Indian, not White. Environment, education, income, status, ownership of private property, homes with backyard, backyard barbecuing or Sunday schooling will change that. For example, Madison Grant (1918, 17–18), another intellectual inspiration for Huntington, says,

> There exists today a widespread and fatuous belief in the power of environment, as well as of education and opportunity to alter heredity, which arises from the dogma of the brotherhood of man…Recent attempts have been made in the interest of inferior races among our immigrants to show that the shape of the skull does change, not merely in a century, but in a single generation. In 1910, the report of the anthropological expert of the Congressional Immigration Commission gravely declared that a round skull Jew on his way across the Atlantic might and did have a round skull child but a few years later, in response to the subtle elixir of American institutions as exemplified in an East Side tenement, might and did have a child whose skull was appreciably longer whether we like to admit it or not, the result of the mixture of two races, in the long run, gives us a race reverting to the more ancient, generalized and lower type. The cross between a white man and an Indian is an Indian; the cross between a white man and a Negro is a Negro.

Directly contradicting liberal individualism's firm faith on the abstraction called the hardworking, self-interested, profit-seeking rational man whose colour, creed and status do not precondition him for success or failure, and whose acquisition of happiness/good life through the accumulation of private properties and consumer goods confers him the identity 'American', Stoddard and Grant argue that this is the false ideology of the 'brotherhood of men', a liberal's club that does not exist. Human condition is a mechanical cohabitation and competition of group identities based on bio-social characteristics that are resilient to environment and education, and any science that proclaims otherwise is political. There is no subtle elixir that can convert a Mexican or an Iranian to a rational, profit-seeking American consumer. Therefore, Huntington's obvious deduction that the 'settler' is, and will always be, distinct from the 'migrant' because the pure essence of the settler's character is not opportunistic fortune hunting in exile, but a religious–cultural morality tied to his skin colour that allows him to discover new lands and find new societies. A more modern translation of White morality and ethics in direct contrast to migrant ethics is the following comment by Greg Johnson's comment,

> Blacks don't find white civilization comfortable. It is like demanding they wear shoes that are two sizes too small when we impose our standards of punctuality and time preferences, demand that they follow our age-of-consent laws, or foist the bourgeois nuclear family upon them. These things don't come naturally to Africans. White standards like walking on the sidewalk, not down the middle of the street, are oppressive to blacks. Such standards are imposed by the hated 'white supremacy' system. But if we don't impose white standards upon them, we have chaos. We have great cities like Detroit transformed into wastelands. (Johnson 2017)

Based on the 'mechanical' difference, therefore, the White man will always fundamentally differ from the black person and the migrant because the White man's socio-biological essence is always superior, and no amount of education, environmental change, acquiring of private property and accumulation of commodities will denaturalize the immigrant subject allowing him to melt into the White fold, therefore, great White cities and civilization are always on the brink of chaos in 'mixed' societies. President Donald Trump's comment on Mexican gang members should be understood as expressions of similar assumptions of the White man's socio-biological essence. In 2018, US President Donald Trump said immigrant gang members are 'not people' but 'animals' (BBC 2018). It is not uncharacteristic of the leader of the free world to criticize violence unleashed by gangs, but what needs to be deconstructed here is that 'animals' is not just a mere metaphoric rendition for effect, it signifies the easiness with which inferiority, savagery and violence are easily tagged with race in modern policy analysis. It represents the sedimentation of ideo-epistemological discourses from Grant to Stoddard, to Huntington that informs how Whiteness is essentialized vis-à-vis brownness or Blackness.

The Alt-right gaze categorizes the migrant other as a devalued category and no amount of multicultural education or affirmation of diversity will dismantle the deep-seated valuation of the superior essence of Whiteness pitched against Mexcianness. Liberal individualism, on the other hand, hopes that melting the mechanistic bio-social categories created by eugenics-inspired right ideologies into universal abstractions like the 'colourless' rational profit-seeking individual will create a kaleidoscope of celebrated differences. But the celebration of differences ends up becoming ghettoization of differences until prejudice flares through surges of right-wing populism. Neither the Alt-right nor individual liberalism possess the epistemological gumption to admit that humans eventuate as humans when they consciously become aware of systemic oppression and fight against it as a group. In other words, the difference between slavery and slave revolt, between conquistadors and natives, between imperialists and sharecroppers, and between rich and poor are not some essentialized race-based inferiority that distils one group as human and the other as animal, but is essentially a political–economic condition between the oppressor and the oppressed. Being colonized, being slaves, indentured labour or migrants are not a manifestation of weakness, racial inferiority, lack of virility or courage but rather a historical–geographical condition of oppression. The oppressor can become oppressed at moment's notice if provided with the 'correct' systemic conditions (weapons, artillery, war heads, resources). Similarly, the oppressor, at some historical–geographical moment must analyse the political–economic conditions that lead to its emergence as a class of humans that willingly subverted the human condition of another. A dialectical analysis understands historical geography and its present as the eventuation of class of oppressed and oppressor; here, the dialectics lie in the fact that class of oppressed and oppressor are not fixed in skin colour, morality and work ethic, but are eventuated in systemic conditions that allows accumulation of value for some and the devaluation of life and labour for others. In the absence of that dialectical class analysis, devaluation becomes an erratic and unexplainable condition sheathed in paranoia and nihilism; thus, the Alt-right, suddenly waking up to the disappearance of jobs, shrinking of the White middle class, outsourcing of opportunities, vents the angst of its devaluation towards the black other and the migrant other, and the liberal lashes out its angst at the right-wing identity politics of the Alt-right. Neither attempt to correct its epistemological praxis that is deeply flawed: Identity cannot be the site of valuation, nor can the abstract individual unless we have laid out what being human means. If being human really means being White, then how to survive in a world that is constantly destabilizing the White status quo by delegitimizing racism, colonization and policies of apartheid? If being human means rational pursuit of profit, how to survive as an individual whose pursuit of profit will be hindered by visa restriction, contexts of legality and illegality as citizens and declaration of animal status even while being affirmed in Hispanic cultural celebrations in public schools? Class analysis of oppression cannot be avoided, because if being human means emancipation of oppression, economic as well as cultural, then class eventuates dialectically in contexts of oppression and is not tied to skin colour or cephalic indices. Class analysis would mean that right-wing populism must reconceptualize value (as not biosocial), and liberal multiculturalism must reconceptualize value (as not profit accumulation), and both must critique systemic contexts that devalue humans as *classes of oppressed*.

Two Conceptual Fetishes: Diversity and Anti-immigration

Voice of Citizens Together (VCT), more commonly known as American Border Patrol formed by Glenn Spencer, is an anti-immigrant group that criticizes Mexican immigrants as 'cultural cancer'. VCT/American Border Patrol focuses on posting articles and comments that lists and publishes anti-immigrant xenophobia. An example is as follows:

> 'I am somebody! And I demand full equality!' about a dozen of them bellowed last week in the corridors of the Russell Senate Office Building, according to a report in The Washington Post. 'Right here. Right now.' Can we just say it? There's something unseemly—and unsavory—about anyone who is in the country illegally 'demanding' anything. Emboldened by eight years of President Barack Obama's de minimis efforts to stem the tide of illegal immigrants flooding into the country, the estimated 700,000 'Dreamers' in effect are saying,
>
> 'We have a right to stay.'
>
> No, they don't.
>
> Is this any different than shoplifters demanding that they be allowed to keep what they—or, in this case, their illegal-immigrant parents—have stolen?
>
> No, it isn't.
>
> There are laws on the books against being in possession of stolen property, even if you weren't the one who stole that property.
>
> The heartstring-tugging 'they were brought here through no fault of their own as kids' PR campaign by the 'Dreamers' and their megaphones in the liberal media doesn't change that fact. (Parisi 2018)

Demanding stringent immigration policies towards Hispanic immigrants and Muslims is the core characteristic of Alt-right related identity groups. Legality and illegality are evoked to create paradigms of morality where the Deferred Action for Childhood Arrivals (DACA) recipient's identity and existence is wrapped up in illegality for having brought to the country by illegal immigrant parent. For the Alt-right-related groups, no law, no policy and no context can ascribe legitimacy to a DACA recipient. A DACA recipient's illegality is not only tied to the fact that she/he received reprieve under a Black president from the Democratic Party but also because of her/his Hispanic heritage and Brown body. It does not matter that in every other respect, these Brown bodies are American. The DACA recipient bears the burden of ancestral criminality not so much because their parents crossed borders without correct papers, but because their ancestors were Hispanic. Legality, however, is easily ascribed to White bodies on account of their European, Canadian, Australian decent because Whiteness has an exchange value that washes away wrong and makes them right. Therefore, being migrant itself is not wrong, but being Hispanic migrant or a Muslim migrant is a race category, not just a legal position, it is a bio-social attribute that cannot be transmuted to Americanness. The preference for White migrants is often expressed as a demand for highly skilled humans. White nationalist group, Identity Evropa rebranded as American Identity Movement that calls for an immigration policy, which exclusively concentrates on White immigrants, provides a solution to the immigration problem,

> We don't believe America needs to be 100.00 percent white, but we do think that America isn't going to be America if there isn't a European-America super-majority. So when it comes to policies and so forth we're concerned with reversing these trends. We want to end immigration for the time being. And in the future we would like to have immigration policies that favor high-skilled immigrants from, you know, Europe, Canada, Australia and so forth. And we also do want to have programs of re-migration wherein people who feel more of a connection to another part of the world, another race, another culture, even another religion in the case of Islam can return to their native homelands essentially (Casey 2018).

Whether the idealized objective is the creation of a White ethno-state or a super majority, immigration becomes the pivotal issue around which White identity must be crystalized. It is, however, not enough to crystalize an identity around colour lines, what the Alt-right and its affiliate groups must do is affirm value or cultural superiority to Whiteness, and hence, devalue Brownness. The affirmation of value comes in various forms, as discussed before and in the past chapters, it comes in the form of superior IQ enforcing the greatness of European civilization and delegitimizing African, Hispanic, Middle Eastern and South Asian historical–cultural heritage and epistemologically flipping White colonization from a template of plunder to a template of voyaging, dare and conquest, and also, ascribing high-skill status to White migrants. Connection to Latin American heritage or Islamic culture does not bring cultural value' but fetches a return ticket to where the immigrant must return. The Hispanic immigrant's Christianness (Catholic) does not give her/him the porosity to meld with the Alt-right's imaginary of the 'Christian West'; similarly, a Muslim's Whiteness (Muslims come in all skin tones) does not give her/him the entry pass to Americanness, although, since the days of slavery, America has always had a substantial Muslim population (Austin 2012; Gomez 2005). Both Hispanics and Muslims, therefore, within the broad-brush templates used by the Alt-right (Christian, White, West), are arbitrarily destabilized as undesirable and 'new immigrants' that dilute the core characteristics of the super majority. While for Spencer, the ultimate high ideal of the 'ethno-state' is more post-USA–European construct based on reclaiming the idealized Greco-Roman cultural heritage somewhere between Portugal and Vladivostok where all White people would settle; for Identity Evropa, the 'super majority' must re-reclaim America through selective policies of banning immigration and deporting migrants. President Trump, in anticipation of the forthcoming elections, and hence, charging up the base, used coronavirus as a reason to announce temporary pause (60 days) on permanent residency visa and green cards (Kumar 2020).

Lana Lokteff, founder of Red Ice TV, in videos banned from YouTube like 'Go Back to Europe' (Red Ice 2017a), evokes White supremacy and constructs 'White' and Brown as complex categories beyond the popular templates of White-oppressor/ Brown-oppressed and White-monochrome/Brown-diverse dichotomies.

> If you are white and you opposed to massive non-European migration into European countries then you will inevitably hear an antiwhite shout 'Go back to Europe.' The person who shouts this is completely ignorant to European history, but also to European politics, they could not tell the difference between Sweden and Switzerland, they could not tell the difference between Austria and Australia...and they certainly could not tell you the difference in appearance between northern Europeans versus south Europeans, but we are racist if we do not know the difference between Ethiopian for a Somali....every tribe of people on earth have fought for territories and every nation was fought in blood sweat and tear...they do not care who were in America before the native Americans, or that Indians genocided other tribes...antiwhites see all white people the same...millions of white Americans would love to return to Europe because, Europe is an amazing place, ancient land of our ancestors, but Europeans will not take them in because they are white, these days only so called refugees and Third World people get in, I know white Americans in Europe who were deported even though they were employed and paid taxes, a Muslim terrorist has better chances of getting citizenship in Europe than a white American.... (Red Ice 2017a)

The afore-mentioned excerpt is less about establishing the superiority of a White West and more about the construction of White identity as marginalized, othered and oppressed. Interestingly, in the above quote, the colonial legacy of 'White' plunder is not denied, nor is an attempt made to reframe this legacy as 'high ideals' of voyaging and conquest by a virile race to found a civilization that produces a class of settlers. Instead, Lokteff attempts to show how occupation, colonization and plunder is the very foundation on which every nation is built and how the Brown man too 'genocided' and conquered other tribes. Also, is an attempt to demonstrate that while the Brown man and the Muslim always find refuge in the Europe and the USA, the White man cannot find a home in his ancient homeland of Europe because of liberal immigration policies based on demands for diversity. This excerpt is an ideo-epistemological flipping of the immigrant-template from usual rhetoric of savage, uncivilized, un-evolved, culturally backwards, low-skilled to blood-thirsty tribal chiefs, genocidal conquerors and dangerous terrorists. Lokteff's is a brilliant attempt here to destabilize the discourse of the immigrant as a subject that deserves empathy and refuge to one that is violent, maniacal and one that marginalizes Whiteness. In 'Diversity Is a Weapon against White People' (Red Ice 2017b), Lokteff suggests that 'diversity' is a Marxist propaganda term knowing full-well that the easiest way to gain public ire against any discourse is by 'tainting' it with Marxism. In the video, as Lokteff shows pictures of White people, she asks: 'What is diversity? Is it this?' She answers, 'No!' Lokteff then shows a picture of a White girl and asks, 'Is it this?' She answers, 'No!' Lokteff then shows the picture of an Indian girl and answers, 'Yes! We get it. The meaning of diversity used by the establishment is everyone but White people...it is everyone but straight White people.' Lokteff goes on to explain that European civilization is the most diverse in terms of language, architecture and philosophy, yet the Marxists are changing the definition of diversity to mean people of non-European nationalities, colour, religion, economic stratum and sexuality, meaning that Marxist notion of diversity includes non-Whites, Muslims, Jews and anyone non-Christian. The video on diversity argues that Europe was already diverse, but its diversity is rendered invisible under a biased gaze that envisions Whiteness as homogenous and monochromatic. This 'distorted' view of diversity, Lokteff claims, comes out of the Marxist Frankfurt school who were supporters of violent communist dictators, and these Marxists do not see or celebrate diversity within the White race, instead they have taken an innocent term and recast it as politics where diversity arbitrarily includes identities that are non-Christian, non-White, the Third World people and queers (Red Ice 2017b). Lokteff cleverly reassigns liberal multiculturalism's endorsement of diversity as Marxist propaganda, thus drawing a continuum between liberal, left and Marxists. Through an ingenious sleight of hand, Lokteff blends colour, class, race, religion and sexuality into a tapestry of non-Christian migrant essence that is antithetical to everything European. Third World people are inevitably Brown and Black and often represent those immigrants that come from lower economic stratum, so the label 'third world' is meant to imply the unwanted poor and Brown/Black class and race. Lokteff implicitly argues that the 'third world' as a class opens a pandora's box of Blackness/Brownness and non-Christianness. The Marxists, therefore, with their support of the working class consolidate an army of non-White and non-Christian soldiers who, together through electoral politics and intellectual diffusion into civil society, legitimize other kinds of 'aberrations' such as gayness and queerness.

A Marxist-based class analysis understands devaluation as theft of life and labour of a class of people by another, the class being stolen from may reside within the same nation as the oppressor, or a different nation altogether (Third World). What liberal capitalism understands as self-interest, competition and the accumulation of wealth through the accumulation of private property, Marxism critiques as bourgeois political economy, arguing that legitimization of exploitation can only happen when the context of theft is well hidden materially in society through commodity fetish, and I argue, through conceptual fetish. Marx's 'commodity fetish' (Marx 1976) argues that the allure of commodity and the desire to accumulate it hides the struggle that produced it, therefore, sanctifying the entire process through 'objective' conditions of demand, supply and price at the marketplace. Thus, Marx is almost poetic when he claims, 'A commodity appears at first sight an extremely obvious, trivial thing. But its analysis brings out that it is a very strange thing, abounding in metaphysical subtilities and theological niceties' (Marx 1976, 163). Market imparts fairness, price is 'justice' for the labour embedded in goods produced and sold. Bourgeois political economy (liberal and Alt-right) conceptually hides the material contexts of exploitation by discursively shifting analysis of exploitation of people over people by fetishizing Whiteness, Americanness, Europeanness and Christianness. Anti-immigration xenophobia imparts 'fairness' where border walls and immigration pause/ban are justice for essentialized White subjectivities embedded in a class angst over a perceived loss of life and livelihood. Conceptual fetish has the allure of the commodity fetish, it commodifies Whiteness, Americanness and Europeanness through 'metaphysical subtilities' and 'theological niceties' into mythical products that never existed in the first place—a face of White, Christian identity produced through Alt-right plastic surgery, desirable at any cost. Anti-immigrant fetish does for the Alt-right what 'diversity' fetish does for liberal multiculturalism; they accord value to the surface of group identities such as Whiteness for the Alt-right and American pluralism for the multiculturalist, while both fail to excavate that value cannot be added unless one takes stock of what we value as a society, who produces this value, how it is accorded in the society and how it is distributed. Analysis of value is the essence of Marxism and it is founded on a critique of a way of life that realizes value through commodity-conceptual fetishes. Instead, Marxism understands value as the very act of creating life through conscious labouring. In labouring, consciousness is eventuated—consciousness of a class, which is a community of people experiencing similar contexts of oppression. If a community is experiencing contexts of oppression, it must trace its oppression to the theft of value or the theft of life. If a group of internet-based White, middle-class men and women believe that their life is being stolen, then a systemic analysis must excavate what is this value-embedded life that is being devalued, and how is the migrant responsible as an oppressor? If life's value is lost because of the Hispanicization of Houston and El Paso, and the Mexicanization of White middle-class neighbourhoods, and *kebaabification* of backyard barbecues, then the Alt-right must ask itself how it can capture, consolidate, preserve Whiteness in a globalizing world where production and consumption or in other words, the market place that accords justice through demand–supply–price, has gone global? How to depend on Mexican nannies and the El Salvadorian day-caregivers, Honduran maids and Hispanic construction workers while keeping 'Brown culture' out of the ethno-state? If White life is not about the day-to-day mundanity of economic inter-class dependence (on migrant nannies and informal workers), and it is a 'higher' form of cultural ideal based on European cultural consciousness, and if culture is White Western philosophy, architecture, literature and cityscapes, how does this cultural artefact, this antiquated crucible, a European revival to be actualized and maintained without a class that must upkeep and maintain it? If the answer lies in the creation of a White American working class, then how to revert the global political economy of value extraction, whereby the upliftment of the White class has historically been predicated on the devaluation of the Brown and the Black? In Marxist analysis, struggle for existence cannot be sliced into 'higher' and 'lower' struggles, where 'higher' involves 'endless struggle' for the restoration of cultural nostalgia and everything else is lower. The government of the supposed ethno-state will have to eke out a mode of existence the day after the cultural revolution and grapple with questions of disease and hunger, which in the absence of class analysis (which is a non-fetishized analysis of culture as well), will be reduced once again to the celebration of multiculturalist diversity and the chicken and the egg will continue to reproduce each other.

The Ethno-revolution?

This chapter traces Alt-right's anti-immigrant angst and its proposed solution through the actualization of White nation state, or as Spencer calls it, the 'ethno-state'. Although ethno-state is envisioned more as a motivating ideology to shake the vanguards of White culture from their stupor of hypnosis from Netflix, a high ideal to aspire for through a never-ending struggle, rather than a piece of land to be attained, yet both Johnson and Spencer clarify that it would be a geographical territory inhabited by White people. In a modern version of empire building, the Alt-right, through the concept of the ethno-state, hopes to actualize an empire-building project that culminates in the construction of a postmodern identity-based nation state. Such a nation state, according to Johnson, would involve the reclaiming of the USA by deporting recent migrants, and for Spencer, a nostalgic return to the original homeland— Europe. A White nation is inspired by Zionism and the creation of Israel, and therefore, taking a leaf out of that book, ethno-state would be a 'global racial project' to create a 'we', a patriotic amalgam that must be White, set aside from the 'they', the nation's other. This idea of a postmodern identity based nation is inspired by antiquated discourses of America's peopling around the settler–immigrant dichotomy. I have argued that the ideo-epistemological position of the ethno-state is an arbitrarily crafted identity position that fetishizes Whiteness' and therefore, discursively produces anything non-White as a racial body, as a migrant. This chapter indicates how the Alt-right draws inspiration from racist academic works that uses cephalic indices and phenotypes to intellectually legitimize White conquest of native Americans as a settling process that was a harbinger of modernity rather than conquest and migration. If the arrival of the puritans with the pioneering zeal to encroach, loot and plunder can be intellectually established as process of founding a civilization, then it is cast as a unique historical–geographical moment, a civilizing turn of fate that sets it as unique from all future rounds of migration. Hence, whatever is not unique to the cultural core of being American can then be distilled, separated and removed through policy. I have indicated that despite Stoddard and Grant's concerted attempts at using racist socio-biological indicators with no scientific foundations, and Huntington's racist readings of racist immigration policies to establish America as a White-Protestant settler civilization—a template to which all later immigrants must automatically become outcasts—there are alternative interpretations where the 'settler' is seen as plunderer, exile and opportunist. Therefore, the difference between construction of America as a 'nation of immigrants' versus one where the 'founders' were not immigrants, but 'settlers', creates a contrasting template of the same nation, the former, where everyone is an immigrant and everyone is welcome, and the latter, where the ones who established the 'true cultural core' have the right to nationhood and citizenship, and everyone else must fit at the mercy of the settler. The nation of immigrants cast the nation as porous, evolving and fluid. On the other hand, the settler versus migrant template freezes the nation into true, original and static, where the trueness and originality are rendered unstable by the entry of the lesser than true and the un-original migrant. This is an ideological claim, one that is based on the arbitrary affirmation of Whiteness and its ludicrous connection to citizenship built through tenuous linkages like, racist immigration policies of yore. This chapter indicates that the Alt-right movement is influenced by these templates and discourses of nation, citizenship and national culture, which then evoked through imageries of White neighbourhoods, picket fences, backyard barbecues, Sunday schools and the loss of these pure essences that constitute the 'true White community'. These imageries, I argue, are then scaled up to link with Nietzschean and Evolasque ideals of happiness-as-power to reclaim history and engage in endless struggle to realize Western spirituality as manifested through the ethno-state.

This chapter also demonstrates that the Alt-right critiques migration policies that are based on arguments of diversity; they attempt to draw nourishment from ideas that Whiteness does not need diversity as Whites are self-inclusively diverse. Tacit in these arguments are also a deformed criticism of class analysis, particularly Marxist class analysis, because the Alt-right is implicitly aware that class analysis can expose the weakness of White fetishism by providing an inclusive basis to happiness and good life for White, Brown and Black. The Alt-right is also painfully aware that Marxist analysis of imperialism would also systemically expose the hollowness of the high cultures of Western civilization by demonstrating the resource, labour' and value extraction that fuelled the 'building' of such 'high culture'. The Alt-right also understands that culture and class meld to produce neighbourhoods, suburbs, food and picket fences whose demise they so prominently mourn—meaning, poor and the migrant-poor can strut around sheathed in 'high culture', provided they are allowed a fair share of the values that they produce and the values that are stolen from them. Because the Alt-right, its concept of ethno-state, and its critique of diversity, studiously avoids class analysis and critique of oppression that is always already cultural and economic and because liberal multiculturalism also reifies identity (not White but marginal) and ignores the oppressiveness of class by treating humans as individuals who will pull themselves by the boot-straps no matter how unequally precarious her/his position as labour is in the system, I attempt to bring Marxist analysis to the forefront here. Using Marx and Thompson, I indicate how identity, devoid of class analysis, is an ideological–political act of obfuscation that does not recognize the economic poverty of the disappearing White working class, or the contributions of the Black population, and the Brown informal/illegal migrant. In the absence of that class analysis, devaluation becomes a fet-ishized cultural process sheathed in paranoia and nihilism. The Alt-right, in the midst of dire economic conditions, devalues the migrant and hopes to affirm itself through the production of a cultural nation (ethno-state). However, the day after the White revolution, how does the cultural nation propose to deal with a globalizing political economy where capital and labour is transnational? How would the Alt-right re-construct a racist White economy where for some generations now we have depended on Black and Brown, blue- and white-collar labour? How to pursue happiness and accumulate value as an individual, or conduct the business of liberal capitalism within a culturally insulated nation state? While the ethno-nation would want to keep its door closed to the non-White migrant, the capitalist state would want to neoliberalize into a free market based on exploitation of non-White labour within its shores

not elevate White identity, it only dissolves it. The Alt-right is also staunchly opposed to migration and refugee accommodation of non-White and Muslim populations. The Alt-right demands protection, affirmation, and validation for the White man on account of being the stronger and the most intelligent race and sex. The chapters in this book explore the Alt-right's contradictory imbrication with liberal individualism, delve into the ideological underpinnings behind the revival of Alt-right's White male chauvinism and look into the construction of the three Ms—men, migrants and Muslims as sites of acceptable/unacceptable differences.

The broader argument of the book that runs through all the chapters is that while the Alt-right critiques the core principles of modern liberal philosophy (multiculturalism and celebration of diversity), it is actually a product of the same. The Alt-right critiques the race–cultural affirmative aspects of individual liberalism, but plays an inverted multiculturalist identity politics that bases its existence on the affirmation of White identity. While liberal multiculturalism clamours for identity valourization of the identity minority, the Alt-right proclaims identity marginality of the White majority; both seek cultural affirmation without addressing the economic conditions of oppression that produce marginalization. Using Bentham, Mill and Adam Smith's work, I have argued that the central thesis of liberal morality is the self-interested rational man that pursues happiness within capitalism through competitive accumulation of stuff (objects, commodities, private property). Deep seated within the unequal history–geography of capitalism, the self-interested individual derives his/her identity as a productive efficient being by negotiating the inequalities/disadvantages he/she has been placed within. Liberal society does not interrogate political–economic inequality but claims that within universal concepts of freedom of opportunity, a hardworking individual can raise himself/herself in life and identify with success/happiness, and hence, gain affirmation. Therefore, individual liberalism recognizes identity devaluation and creates a mosaic of 'acceptable' identities that need to be valourized, but beyond small diversity quotas, the society system does not accept the onus of rectifying economic injustices that produce gaping inequalities of class, racial, and gendered poverty. Therefore, class–communitarian injustices wreaked by a class-community of oppressors on another class-community of oppressed is not systemically addressed because this would mean setting systemic goals for emancipation, rather than, putting the onus of freedom on the individual. This is a dangerous mistake because without conceptual 'identification' of the oppressor as a class-community that steals, colonizes, displaces, enslaves and exploits, thus laying the template of inequality and oppression within which class–identity devaluation manifests, the distinction between 'acceptable' differences and 'unacceptable' differences disappears. The Alt-right fits very well within the template of liberal multiculturalism because it represents the virulent pursuit of individual self-interest, that is, the maximization of individual's freedom to pursue happiness through the establishment of the 'White male self' as the dominant race/gender that accumulates private property and profit. The Alt-right's aspiration for a glorious White-Western civilization, therefore, includes some bold political polices such as the creation of a White ethno-state, strict immigration policies curtailing the immigration of non-White races and prevention of refugee resettlement.

Liberal Individualism and the Alt-right

The conceptual arguments that I have developed in Chapter 2 are that individual freedom or self-interest has been the core principle of Western liberal capitalism (I concentrated on the USA), and the idea of individual freedom, as argued by critics (both of Marxist and non-Marxist persuasion), is rather narrow. Individual freedom focuses on one-dimensional 'rationality', that is, the idea that freedom includes multiplication of pleasure and minimization of pain, and multiplication of pleasure or happiness is achieved when individuals in society can acquire, accumulate and expand consumption, profit and private property.

In that context, the intersection of the individual within a social matrix or lattice of identity (gender, race, ethnicity, sexuality, linguistics positions, place of origin, migrant-citizen status) creates challenges for liberal philosophy—how to recognize the individual without being subsumed within a group identity? Identity theorists indicate that identity positions emerge out of experiences of exploitation that are situated and particular, that is, individual positions that are also inflected within the identity of other individuals as well. Therefore, identity politics must be interstitial (demonstrating the tapestry of various inflections) and not assimilationist (melting of uniqueness into a 'larger general). This challenge of recognizing the individual and the group identity is achieved within liberalism by the creation of a range of 'acceptable' differences that are spatially and temporally contingent. These acceptable differences are then valourized by equal treatment and through policies of multiculturalism.

This chapter further argues that elements of liberalism allow reactionary identity movements like the Alt-right to germinate and grow root. I indicate that most Alt-right activists denounce core values of liberalism like individual freedom as vacuous and meaningless because they perceive these as being misused by 'weaker' races and the 'weaker' sex through the 'backdoor' of multiculturalism, affirmative action and political correctness. However, it is liberalism's fixation with the individual's self-interest without addressing pre-existing violent tropes of class and cultural oppression that allow reactionary hegemonic identities like, White maleness to claim marginalized positions. Because the violent history of racial and patriarchal suppression is swept under the carpet, oppressive identities (Whiteness, maleness, Christian fundamentalism) go unidentified, and hence, they rear heads in opportune moments (Trump election, refugee crisis, migration crisis) to claim marginalized positions when they have actually always been the master hegemon of White capitalist patriarchy. If the boundaries between acceptable and unacceptable difference are fluid, and if liberal society does not categorically 'identify' what is unacceptable, then the unacceptable can claim inclusion and equality by penetrating the porous boundaries of acceptability. What makes acceptable differences distinct from unacceptable differences (patriarchy, racism, elitism) is the gory history of exploitation, which produced the very tropes of inequality that we contend with in the present. Individual freedom, therefore, provides solid ethical underpinnings to movements like Alt-right based on religious, racial, patriarchal hegemony because it never threatens to dismantle the history–geography of inequality produced by these hegemonic positions. Whether the Alt-right realizes it or not, it is the golden child of liberal individualism.

Philosophy and the Alt-right

In Chapter 3, I look into the works of the philosophical gurus of the Alt-right to understand the ideological underpinnings of the movement. It is my contention that acting and thinking about actions are dialectically conjoined, therefore, philosophy and praxis cannot be synthetically separated. In other words, how we think about our actions, and how our actions produce thoughts cannot be easily distilled. The stance that the Alt-right adopts, that is, how it frames its speeches, interviews, rallies and demands are political acts that are not discreet events in space and time. The racism, misogyny, Islamophobia, Western chauvinism and White supremacy are a carefully selected lattice of identities inspired by thoughts (philosophy) of the group (Alt-right), as well as other groups in different times and spaces. Which lattice of identity makes 'strategic sense' and what constitutes 'racial interests' are things that will be different for different groups (McCulloh 2019a). Certainly, Black Lives Matter will have a completely different racial interest and a completely different lattice of identity that makes strategic sense. The reason for this difference in strategy and interest between the Alt-right and Black Lives Matter are their difference in ideological praxis (philosophy and action). While Black Lives Matter may be influenced by Martin Luther King and civil rights movement, and may fight for justice against police brutality towards Black people (philosophy and action), the Alt-right is influenced by Evola, French Right, Nietzsche, Heidegger and Huntington and 'acts out' against racial equality of people of colour and women. The philosophy that informs praxis and back again is the ideological basis behind why we identify with something, and not others, and where we draw boundaries between us and the other.

Evola laid out the foundations of a class-based feudal society extolling the role of the elite in attaining higher/spiritual status and thus ruling a society of lesser men for their own good. Evola, therefore, endorsed a kind of cultural/spiritual/racial hegemony of the elites and saw it as a panacea from the evils of modernity. Benoist and the French Right influenced by Evola, actually believe that the White French elite must control values, attributes and belief systems, and create a 'cultural hegemony' that will propagate a certain identity, that is, purity of France— France for Frenchmen. Hence, ethnopluralism is the cultural-spatial expression of the 'right' kind of cultural hegemony where dominant identities like French Whiteness are allowed to protect their purity through boundary building. Nietzsche too endorsed the importance of boundaries so that cultures can define their purpose 'wither and wither for', and this purpose, according to Nietzsche, would be fulfilled by powerful genius elites who could contribute a life-affirming destiny to the masses. For Heidegger too, the banality and consumptive mundanity of modernity created an inauthentic existence, which only a biologically and culturally superior group (like the Nazi party) could over-turn to create a meaningful *Dasien*. The cultural supremacy/ elite supremacy is a dominant theme that ran through other biological/cultural determinist theories of Stoddard, Grant and Maddison. The moot point being the celebration of an essential cultural/racial/biological core (Whiteness/Westernness/ maleness), which is superior/separate/distinct, and therefore, possessing the inherent right to preserve itself through boundary making (Benoist and Champetier 2012), conquest, strife, crusade, conquer (Grant 1918; Stoddard 1920; Spencer, 2017) and West's dominance of the rest (Huntington 2000).

Although it might seem that the Alt-right and its philosophical praxis defined by Evola, Benoist, French Identitarian movement, Nietzsche, Heidegger and Huntington et al. is exclusionary, fringe and reactionary, I argue, that the philosophical praxis fits very well within the gamut of liberal individualism. At first, this might seem contradictory because almost all the Alt-right gurus denounce the spirit of enlightenment, as in democracy, equality and modernity, yet when culture is interpreted and understood as decontextualized from the geography/history of its making, it becomes meaningless. In the realm of this decontextualized meaninglessness, it is then possible to create any kind of trauma as the basis for crystallization of identity lattice. Liberal individualism celebrates the freedom to realize oneself as a self-sufficient, competitive individual pursuing happiness through the possessions of property and material good. This notion of a liberal individual is an abstraction, an empty container that does not exist in reality. In the real world, the individual coexists in the context of family, identity and class groups so much so that it is impossible to delineate where the individual ends and the group begins. How to resolve this abstractionist individualism in the context of group existence (identity, class), which is a reality? Multiculturalism becomes an effective solution, the individual lives on to individually create her/his economic success, but in doing so, she/he is allowed to be juxtaposed within diverse identity groups that further her/his individual cultural interests (gender, racial, linguistic groups). The cunning of this philosophical praxis is razor sharp—class interest is ignored because economic gratification must be earned through the rationality of self-interested, competing individuals, but cultural interest is celebrated through the identity lattices validated by multiculturalism. While the Alt-right critiques liberal multiculturalism, and although, Alt-right's praxis goes against the politics of liberal democracy, philosophically, the Alt-right fits very well within this decontextualized container box of multiculturalism. As Trumpism and Alt-right gain momentum, it will be very hard for liberal politics to philosophically exclude unacceptable difference.

While liberal philosophy preserves the economic status quo, Alt-right's philosophical underpinnings preserve the cultural status quo. It will become very hard for liberal philosophical praxis to 'rationalize' why the self-interested man can keep his wealth despite the fact that it has been accrued through generational plunder and elitist tax policies, but it is simultaneously, wrong for the White man to affirm his White superiority even though it has been accrued through cultural–biological plunder of people of colour and women. In essence, liberalism and Alt-rightism is very similar, their praxis is superficially different: Liberal politics practices progressive multiculturalism, Alt-right practices regressive multiculturalism—not only is the dialectics between philosophy and praxis conjoined, liberalism and Alt-right are dialectically conjoined as well!

Women, Neo-masculinity and the Alt-right

In Chapter 4, I take a look at how misogyny and Whiteness intertwine to create a template of perceived trauma, and hence, demand for valourization on the part of Alt-right men. Some scholars argue that the Alt-right's neo-masculinist angst arises out of contemporary contexts of neoliberal free trade, outsourcing, growing unemployment, declining middle class, increasing racial diversity through immigration and an increased fear of disappearance of economic opportunities arising out of competition from women and immigrants. I argue that liberal individualism and multiculturalism provide comfortable breeding ground for neo-masculinist identity angst. Since individual liberalism is the political soul of the body politic of capitalism (the USA and European style), the pursuit of happiness through consumption, accumulation and acquiring private property must remain sacrosanct. In other words, since capitalism is about the persistence of class inequality mediated through classical economic-liberal ideas of self-interest and competition, a political soul (individual liberalism) that enlivens capitalism, must therefore, not disrupt systems of social inequality. Instead, a liberal individual must become competitive through self-interest and hard work to rise to the top of the heap and take advantage of unequal class relations by becoming best in the competition among unequals.

When neoliberal capitalism induced neo-masculinist trauma manifests as Alt-right patriarchy, neoliberal capitalism cannot be cited as the systemic cause for identity annihilation because capitalism is a given good. It then becomes easier for the Alt-right to locate feminists, Muslims and migrants as the site of marginalization. Instead of citing capitalism-induced inequality as the historical–geographical process that marginalizes women, feminism and changing gender roles, women's entry into the work force in offices, colleges and universities become the systemic sites of attack. In the face of this trauma of neglect of the White man, it will not be far-fetched or impossible for neo-masculinist groups to claim acceptability and cultural affirmation. Trump's election victory riding on a neo-masculinist identity wave is ample proof of this fact. It will also not be an aberration to assume that such movements (neo-masculinist) may gain mainstream popularity, transcend their presence in the fringe and clamour for protection under the multicultural agenda.

The Alt-right's anti-women/anti-feminist stance find comfortable breeding conditions rooted in classical liberal ideas such as man as the rational, competitive individual, man as the individual and women as the familial. In these spaces of contradictions, Alt-right views feminism as an antithesis to liberal capitalism where feminists revert the acceptable identity of capitalist geography by leaving home (sphere of the familial) and treading into work/politics/governance (sphere of the individual). It is ironic that liberal feminist agenda is exactly just so, dissolving women from their communitarian ethic and producing the workfare woman-individual that populates the masculine sphere of work—this may seem contradictory to what the Alt-right wants, yet both Alt-right and liberal feminism (as well as liberal multiculturalism) believe in the production of the efficient individual that realizes its life potential through workforce and competition within capitalism. The difference between the Alt-right and liberal feminists being, liberal feminists want more women to become individuals, and Alt-right wants to keep workspaces intact for men.

The 'trad wives" (short form in Alt-right lingo for traditional wives) and what I call in this chapter, 'cad-girls' (Alt-right's YouTube, blogosphere and manosphere star-women that openly critique feminism) are ingeniously crafted. The trad wife is the antithesis of the workfare liberal feminist, she is the apron-clad homemaker and child-bearer—the familial that must support masculine capitalist individualism by grasping the levers of family and community well so as to not disrupt the social order of things. While the trad wife balances the patriarchal economy by valourizing patriarchy as the normal order of work and geopolitics, she must 'gracefully' tread gendered spaces like YouTube, blogosphere and conferences, and hence, commit gender blasphemy by stepping outside the familial, but do so in a way that valourizes the rational man by singing praises of his creative and protective genius. Trad wives claim that women's identity in society is not reduced by patriarchy, but given respectful distinction by pedestalizing motherhood and nurture. At the conference and cyber space, the trad wife is the Madonna of individualism even while she proclaims the feminine virtues of the familial. In turn, the Alt-right man claims that he does not mind women at the work space (they prove it by promoting work-oriented 'cad girls' as internet show hosts that heckle other women and feminists), but why would women not want to take a rest and be a queen at home if her man wants to give her that? The trad wives/cad girls and Alt-right men together cast a gender template where both extoll the importance of women in charge of reproduction and men in charge of production. The 'other', therefore, are women who want to do the opposite, men who support women wanting to do the opposite and feminists who are viewed as symbolic of that opposite. Feminists are the deeper outcasts because not only is their intellectual praxis viewed as destabilizing the place of work, but their philosophical praxis is seen as destabilizing heteronormativity, challenging sexual control and rape culture, and challenging conventional standards of beauty and body. Feminists are, therefore, seen as distorting all aspects of the individual (his self-realization as provider through work, his self-realization as man through his right to demand sex, the self-realization of his masculine gaze through standardization of female beauty as thin, White and blonde). Just as liberal feminism must rethink 'the women as the workfare individual model' and just as, multiculturalism must rethink what cultural valourization means without economic redistribution and analysis of historic exploitation, the Alt-right needs to rethink what it means to be a man.

Islamophobia and the Alt-right

In the post-September 11 world and, more recently, the Syrian refugee crisis, Trump's election, Muslim ban, and wall-building rhetoric have given a new lease of life to the Alt-right and the right-populist movements all over the world. While these movements are not homogenous, yet a common thread is the reliance on the production of fear revolving around this exotic, inhuman and foreign figure of the Muslim. In Chapter 5, I choose 'disembodiment' as the conceptual tool to explicate how contemporary Islamophobia produces the Muslim. Unlike Agamben's (1998) *homo sacer*, a subject position in ancient Rome, whose death did not merit any sacrificial value, the Muslim is disembodied in life, and her/his death is valuable because it is often seen as a true Christian and patriotic act, an act in annihilation of terrorism, a crusade against the savage. The 'Islamic world' is constructed through nebulous orientalist tropes as one that exists outside Western values of freedom, democracy, rationality and the hardworking individual's quest for profit. By framing modernity as civilization, Anglo-America centric and equanimous with individual freedom, the 'Islamic world' is 'placed beyond' and 'outside'. Alt-right and associated right-wing populism's culture talk and cultural framing embodies–disembodies the Muslim as barbaric in her/his cultural habits, gestures, everyday life world, habits of hygiene—she/he is seen irrational in her/his violent disposition, hence, unable to comprehend liberal ideas of freedom and democracy.

I trace the ideology and inspiration behind Alt-right and associated right populist parties to demonstrate how the Muslim is disembodied through White supremacy, anti-immigrant xenophobia and orientalism. Disembodiment as anti-immigrant xenophobia explicates how diverse nationalities of Muslim migrants in Europe and America meld into 'the Muslim' seen as the homogenous alien whose bizarre behaviour in public spaces, manner of praying and using public bathrooms are destroying a sense of home. Disembodiment as orientalism indicates how modernity becomes the solvent by which the Muslim is dissolved into an exotic assemblage of primitive, inward-looking, parochial people produced by her/his 'depraved' religion. For the Alt-right and associated groups, the Muslim, very much like the feminists, only exists in reverse templates of villainy that disrupts the stable order of Western liberalism. According to the Alt-right, liberal media pampers multiculturalism to blatantly disregard universalist principles of Western civilization by unduly favouring the Muslim other. What the supreme settler culture avoids deconstructing is that universalism is actually Judea-Christian particularism, multiculturalism is superficial tokenism, avoiding systemic overhaul of racism, civilization is a mental construct, and the 'West' is an imagination depending on who gets to define what is supreme.

Anti-immigration and the Alt-right

Chapter 6 traces Alt-right's anti-immigrant angst and its proposed solution through the actualization of White nation state, or as Spencer calls it the 'ethno-state'. Although ethno-state is envisioned more as a motivating ideology to shake the vanguards of White culture from their stupor of hypnosis from Netflix, a high ideal to aspire for through a never-ending struggle, rather than, a piece of land to be attained, yet both Johnson and Spencer clarify that it would be a geographical territory inhabited by White people. In a modern version of empire building, the Alt-right, through the concept of the ethno-state, hopes to actualize an empire-building project that culminates in the construction of a postmodern identity-based nation state. Such a nation state, according to Johnson, would involve the reclaiming of the USA by deporting recent migrants, and, for Spencer, a nostalgic return to the original homeland—Europe. A White nation is inspired by Zionism and the creation of Israel, and therefore, taking a leaf out of that book, ethno-state would be a 'global racial project' to create a 'we', that must be White, to be set aside from the 'they', the nation's other (Black, brown, Muslims). This idea of a postmodern identity-based nation is inspired by antiquated discourses of America's peopling around the settler–immigrant dichotomy. I have argued that the ideo-epistemological position of the ethno-state is an arbitrarily crafted identity position that fetishizes Whiteness, and therefore, discursively produces anything non-White as a racial body, as a migrant. This chapter indicates how the Alt-right draws inspiration from racist academic works that uses cephalic indices and phenotypes to intellectually legitimize White conquest of native Americans as a settling process that was a harbinger of modernity, rather than, conquest and migration. If the arrival of the puritans with the pioneering zeal to encroach, loot and plunder, can be intellectually established as process of founding a civilization, then it is cast as a unique historical–geographical moment, a civilizing turn of fate that sets it as unique from all future rounds of migration. Hence, whatever is not unique to the cultural core of being American, can then be distilled, separated and removed through policy.

Therefore, the difference between construction of America as a 'nation of immigrants' versus one where the 'founders' were not immigrants, but 'settlers', creates a contrasting template of the same nation—the former, where everyone is an immigrant and everyone is welcome, and the latter, where the ones who established the 'true cultural core' have the right to nationhood and citizenship, and everyone else must fit at the mercy of the settler. Because the Alt-right, its concept of ethno-state and its critique of diversity, studiously avoids class analysis and critique of oppression that is always already cultural and economic, and because liberal multiculturalism also reifies identity (not White but marginal) and ignores the oppressiveness of class by treating humans as individuals who will pull themselves by the bootstraps no matter how unequally precarious her/his position as labour is in the system, I attempt to bring Marxist analysis to the forefront here. Using Marx and Thompson, I indicate how identity devoid of class analysis is an ideological–political act of obfuscation that does not recognize the economic poverty of the disappearing White working class or the contributions of the Black, Brown informal/illegal migrant. In the absence of that class analysis, devaluation becomes a fetishized cultural process sheathed in paranoia and nihilism. The Alt-right, in the midst of dire economic conditions, devalues the migrant and hopes to affirm itself through the production of a cultural nation (ethno-state). However, the day after the White revolution, how does the cultural nation propose to deal with a globalizing political economy where capital and labour are transnational? How would the Alt-right reconstruct a racist White economy, where for some generations now, we have depended on Black and Brown, blue- and white-collar labour? How to pursue happiness and accumulate value as an individual, or conduct the business of liberal capitalism within a culturally insulated nation state? While the ethno-nation would want to keep its door closed to the non-White migrant, the capitalist state would want to neoliberalize into a free market based on exploitation of non-White labour within its shores and abroad. Conceptual fetish (of Whiteness, anti-immigrant xenophobia) has the same allure as Marx's commodity fetish, it commodifies Whiteness, Americanness and Europeanness into mythical products of 'metaphysical subtilities' that never existed in the first place. Therefore, affirming White identity becomes a system of signification that does not eventuate from material struggles of everyday existence, but has to be artificially evoked through stylized YouTube videos that harnesses the nothingness of Netflix satiation.

The purpose of this book is to demonstrate how individual liberalism provides a favourable ecosystem for differences to be conceptualized and popularized, how then are such differences ideologically nourished, and how they are used to produce 'women', 'migrants' and 'Muslims' as 'unacceptable' identities. In that context, the Alt-right's praxis is not very different from other identity movements that define self versus other, organize and strategize on how to valourize the self, and then, make demands for locating the self through claims for an ethno-space. This book argues that social justice or, at least, desire for human dignity demands a philosophical praxis that is alternative to the Alt-right, but developing such a critical praxis cannot be based on a knee-jerk reaction to everything that is 'right', nor is it enough to base it on affirmation of identity difference; a truly radical praxis that is indeed an 'alt' to the Alt-right must boldly acknowledge the slippery slope of identity politics that can easily use available templates of affirmative and acceptable self–other praxis into unacceptable exclusions where the self is so valourized through racist, misogynist and Christian fundamentalist identifiers, that women, black people, migrants, and Muslims become its automatic other. There is a fundamental difference between racist, misogynistic, and Islamophobic politics, and a social justice praxis that identifies oppression of human beings of whatever colour, gender, ethnicity, and religion, as wrong. Such a social justice perspective must cut through superficial multicultural affirmation where recognition is meant to accord cultural value without fundamentally addressing systemic inequality, geo-historical oppression and class–communal relations. A social justice praxis grounded in a thorough understanding of the Alt-right movement can demystify the fact that the Alt-right's rationality for a White ethno-state is as much based on unjust identity politics as is individual liberalism's penchant for equal opportunity for unequal groups. Both valourize templates of difference that accept pre-exiting discrimination (race for the Alt-right and class for individual liberalism) as a rational order of life. A radical critique of right-populism in general, and Alt-right movement in particular, must intellectually dismantle the very paradigm of rationality that breeds both Alt-right's exclusion and individual liberalism's exclusion—justice is contingent on that act of intellectual overhaul.

Bibliography

ABC News. 2017, 4 December. 'Donald Trump: Billy Bush says infamous Access Hollywood "grab them by the p***y" tape is real."' https://www.abc.net.au/news/2017-12-04/billy-bush-says-infamous-access-hollywood-trump-tape-is-real/9224358 (accessed on March 2020).

Abu-Laban, Y., and V. Lamont. 1997. 'Crossing Borders: Interdisciplinarity, Immigration and the Melting Pot in the American Cultural Imaginary.' *Canadian Review of American Studies* 27 (2): 23–43.

Abu-Lughod, L. 2002. 'Do Muslim Women Really Need Saving? Anthropological Reflections on Cultural Relativism and its Others.' *American Anthropologist* 104 (3): 783–790.

Abu-Lughod, L. 2013. *Do Muslim Women Need Saving?* Cambridge, MA: Harvard University Press.

Agamben, G. 1998. *Homo Sacer: Sovereign Power and Bare Life*. Stanford, CA: Stanford University Press.

Ali, T. 2003. *The Clash of Fundamentalisms: Crusades, Jihads and Modernity*. Brooklyn, NY: Verso.

Almada, J. M. 2017. 'Meet the Hispanic White Supremacist in Southern California's "Alt-right" Movement.' Univision News https://www.univision.com/univision-news/united-states/meet-the-hispanic-white-supremacist-in-southern-californias-alt-right-movement (accessed on March 2020).

Anderson, B. 1983. *Imagined Communities: Reflections on the Origins and Spread of Nationalism*. London: Verso Books.

Anti-Defamation League. 2016. Soldiers of Odin USA. https://www.adl.org/sites/default/files/documents/assets/pdf/combating-hate/Soldiers-of-Odin-USA-Report-web.pdf

Arblaster, A. 1984. *The Rise and Decline of Western Liberalism*. Hoboken, NJ: Wiley-Blackwell.

Atkinson, D. C. 2018. 'Charlottesville and the Alt-right: A Turning Point?' *Politics, Groups, and Identities* 6 (2): 309–315.

Austin, A. D. 2012. *African Muslims in Antebellum America: Transatlantic Stories and Spiritual Struggles*. Abingdon: Routledge.

Bar-On, T. 2014. 'The French New Right: Neither Right, nor Left?' *Journal for the Study of Radicalism* 8 (1): 1–44.

Baskerville, S. 2018, November. 'The Criminalization of Masculinity.' *Occidental Observer*.

BBC. 2017. 'Charlottesville: One Killed in Violence over US Far-right Rally'. https://www.bbc.com/news/world-us-canada-40912509 (accessed on May 2020).

BBC. 2018. 'Trump: Immigrant Gangs "Animals, Not People"' https://www.bbc.com/news/av/world-us-canada-44148697/trump-immigrant-gangs-animals-not-people (accessed on April 2020).

Beauvoir, S. De. 1974. *The Second Sex*. Translated by H. M. Parshley. New York, NY: Vintage.

Beiner, R. 2018. *Dangerous Minds: Nietzsche, Heidegger, and the Return of the Far Right*. Philadelphia, PA: University of Pennsylvania Press.

Beiner, Ronald. 2018, July. Stephen Bannon's World: Dangerous Minds in Dangerous Times. The Conversation. https://theconversation.com/stephen-bannons-world-dangerous-minds-in-dangerous-times-100373 (accessed on October 2019).

Benhabib, S. 1999. 'Sexual Difference and Collective Identities: The New Global Constellation.' *Signs* 24: 1–16.

Benoist, A. D., and Champetier, C. 2012. *Manifesto for a European Renaissance*. Budapest: Arktos.

Bentham, J. 1996. *The Collected Works of Jeremy Bentham: An Introduction to the Principles of Morals and Legislation*. Oxford: Clarendon Press.

Bergman, H. 2018. 'White Men's Fear of Women: Anti-Feminism and the Rise of the Alt-Right'. https://mathias-nilges.com/student-projects-the-new-culture-wars/2018/4/1/White-mensfear-of-women-anti-feminism-and-the-rise-of-the-Alt-Right (accessed on March 2018).

Bernstein, J. 2019. 'YouTube's Newest Far-Right, Foul-Mouthed, Red-Pilling Star Is A 14-Year-Old Girl.' Buzzfeed. https://www.buzzfeednews.com/article/josephbernstein/youtubes-newest-far-right-foul-mouthed-red-pilling-star-is (accessed on March 2020).

Bilge, S. 2010. 'Beyond Subordination vs. Resistance: An Intersectional Approach to the Agency of Veiled Muslim Women.' *Journal of Intercultural Studies* 31 (1): 9–28.

Blackmire, P. 2018. 'If You Hate the Patriarchy, Give Us Back Our Electricity.' Return of Kings. (Accessed on January 2020) http://www.returnofkings.com/195909/if-you-hate-the-patriarchy-give-us-back-our-electricity.

Blaut, J. M. 1992. 'The Theory of Cultural Racism'. *Antipode* 24 (4): 289–299.

Bodissey, B. 2005. 'A Brief History of Transatlantic Counter Jihad Part 1.' Gates of Vienna. http://gatesofvienna.net/2011/11/a-brief-history-of-the-transatlantic-counterjihad-part-i/ (accessed on 18 January 2018).

BombIslam.com. 'BBC films me tearing up a Quaran.' Accessed on February 2021. https://www.bitchute.com/profile/abbMNxzgy6xl/

Bourdieu, P. 1977. *Outline of a Theory of Practice*. Cambridge: Cambridge University Press.

Bourdieu, P. 1989. 'Social Space and Symbolic Power.' *Sociological Theory* 7, no. 1 (Spring): 14–25.

Bourdieu, P., and Wacquant, L. 1999. 'On the Cunning of Imperialist Reason.' *Theory, Culture & Society*, 16 (1): 41–58.

Bourdieu, P. 2013. *Distinction: A Social Critique of the Judgement of Taste*. Abingdon: Routledge.

Braidotti, R. 1993. 'Embodiment, Sexual Difference, and the Nomadic Subject.' *Hypatia* 8 (1): 1–13.

Bray, A., and Colebrook, C. 1998. 'The Haunted Flesh: Corporeal Feminism and the Politics of (Dis) Embodiment.' *Signs: Journal of Women in Culture and Society* 24 (1): 35–67.

Brennan, D. 2018. 'Neo-fascist hustler Yiannopoulos bashes feminism.' *Freedom Socialist Party* (blog). https://socialism.com/fs-article/neo-fascist-hustler-yiannopoulos-bashes-feminism/ (accessed on November 2019).

Buchanan, P. J. 2010. *The Death of the West: How Dying Populations and Immigrant Invasions Imperil Our Country and Civilization*. New York, NY: Macmillan.

Butler, J. 1988. 'Performative Acts and Gender Constitution: An Essay in Phenomenology and Feminist Theory.' *Theatre Journal* 40 (4): 519–531.

Butler, J., E. Laclau, and R. Laddaga. 1997. 'The Uses of Equality.' *Diacritics* 27 (1): 3.

Butler, J. 2011. *Gender Trouble: Feminism and the Subversion of Identity*. Abingdon: Routledge.

Butler, J., and E. Weed, eds. 2011. *The Question of Gender: Joan W. Scott's Critical Feminism*. Vol. 4. Bloomington, IN: Indiana University Press.

Buzzfeed. 2017. 'They Wanted to Be a Better Class of White Nationalists. They Claimed this Man as Their Father.' https://www.buzzfeednews.com/article/lesterfeder/the-man-who-gave-White-nationalism-a-new-life (accessed on October 2019).

Carens, J. H., ed. 1993. 'Possessive Individualism and Democratic Theory: Macpherson's Legacy.' In *Democracy and Possessive Individualism: The Intellectual Legacy of CB Macpherson*, 1–18. Albany, NY: State University of New York Press.

Casey, P. 2018. 'Identity Evropa/American Identity Movement.' https://www.splcenter.org/fighting-hate/extremist-files/group/identity-evropaamerican-identity-movement (accessed on April 2020).

Cassata, F. 1933–1943. Antisemitismo e cospira- zionismo. In Cassata, *A destra del fascismo*, 271–320.

Center for Security Policy. 2010. *Sharia: The Threat to America*.

Chatterjee, I. 2009. 'Deconstructing Vegas: A Class Project?' *Human Geography* 2 (2): 83–85.

Chatterjee, I. 2016. Beyond the Factory: Struggling with Class and Class Struggle in the Post-industrial Context. *Capital & Class* 40 (2): 263–281.

Chatterjee, P. 1993. *The Nation and Its Fragments: Colonial and Postcolonial Histories*. Princeton, NJ: Princeton University Press.

Cohen, C., M. Luttig, and J. Rogowski. 2016. *Understanding the Millennial Vote in 2016: Findings from GenForward*. GenForwardhttps://genforwardsurvey.com/assets/uploads/2016/12/Post-Election-Horse-Race-Report-__-CLEAN.pdf (accessed on March 2020).

Conroy, M. 1984. *The State and Political Theory*. Princeton, NJ: Princeton University Press.

Counter-Current. 2018. 'Germany: Women Are Denouncing the Violence of Migrants.' https://www.counter-currents.com/.../video-of-the-day-german-women- denounce-migrant-violence-and-political-betrayal/ (accessed on April 2020).

Crouch, D. 2014. 'The Rise of the Anti-immigrant Sweden Democrats: 'We don't feel at home any more, and it's their fault.' *The Observer*. https://www.theguardian.com/world/2014/dec/14/sweden-democrats-flex-muscles-anti-immigrant-kristianstad (accessed on January 2018).

Davidson, N. 2012. *Only Muslim: Embodying Islam in Twentieth-century France*. Ithaca: Cornell University Press.

Davis, M. 2017. 'The Great God Trump and the White Working Class.' *Catalyst* 1 (1): 151.

De Lauretis, T. 1990. *Sexual Difference: A Theory of Socio-symbolic Practice*. Bloomington, IN: Indiana University Press.

DeAnna, K. 2012. *Youth for Western Civilization Part 1*. Available at: https://www.youtube.com/watch?v=qWxB_eJ7FsQ (accessed on January 2018).

Dear, M., R. Wilton, S. L. Gaber, and L. Takahashi. 1997. Seeing People Differently: The Sociospatial Construction of Disability. *Environment and Planning D: Society and Space* 15: 455–480.

Donella, L. 2016. 'What's Race Got to Do with it?' *NPR*. https://www.npr.org/sections/codeswitch/2016/06/25/483362200/brexit-whats-race-got-to-do-with-it accessed on April 2020.

E. H. 2017. 'How Immigrantion Is Changing Swedish Welfare State.' *The Economist*. https://www.economist.com/blogs/economist-explains/2017/06/economist-explains (accessed on 7 May).

Eisenstein, H. 2005. 'A Dangerous Liaison? Feminism and Corporate Globalization.' *Science & Society* 69 (3): 487–518.

Elshtain, J. B. 1993. *Public Man, Private Woman: Women in Social and Political Thought*. Princeton, NJ: Princeton University Press.

Evans, Sara M. 2003. *Tidal Wave: How Women Changed America at Century's End*. New York, NY/London: The Free Press.

Eyerman, R. 1984. False Consciousness and Ideology in Marxist Theory. *Acta Sociologica* 24 (1–2): 43–56.

Feder, J. L. 2016. 'This Is How Steve Bannon Sees the Entire World.' *BuzzFeed*. https://www.buzzfeednews.com/article/lesterfeder/this-is-how-steve-bannon-sees-the-entire-world (accessed on October 2019).

Fernandez-Kelly, M. P. 1983. *For We Are Sold, I and My People: Women in Industry in Mexico's Frontier*. Albany, NY: SUNY Press.

Fernando, M. L. 2014. *The Republic Unsettled: Muslim French and the Contradictions of Secularism*. Durham: Duke University Press.

Fershee, J. 2004. 'From Self-Determination to Self-Domination: Native Americans, Western Culture, and the Promise of

Constitutional-Based Reform.' *Valparaiso University Law Review* 39:1.

Fischman, G. E., and McLaren, P. 2005. 'Rethinking Critical Pedagogy and the Gramscian and Freirean Legacies: From Organic to Committed Intellectuals or Critical Pedagogy, Commitment, and Praxis.' *Cultural Studies ↔ Critical Methodologies* 5 (4): 425–446.

Fluri, J. L., 2009. 'The Beautiful 'Other': A Critical Examination of 'Western' Representations of Afghan Feminine Corporeal Modernity.' *Gender, Place & Culture* 16 (3): 241–257.

Foucault, M., 1990. *The History of Sexuality: An Introduction.* New York, NY: Vintage.

Fraser, N. 1995. 'From Redistribution to Recognition? Dilemmas of Justice in a 'Post-socialist' Age.' *New Left Review*: 68–68.

Fraser, N. and A. Honneth. 2003. *Redistribution or Recognition? A Political-philosophical Exchange.* London: Verso.

Freeman, Carla. 2000. *High Tech and High Heels in the Global Economy: Women, Work, and Pink-Collar Identities in the Caribbean.* Durham, NC/London: Duke University Press.

Friedman, M. 2009. *Capitalism and Freedom.* Chicago, IL: University of Chicago Press.

Furedi, J. 2016. 'Burkini Ban: Norway's Right-wing Progress Party Calls for Full-body Swimsuit to Be Outlawed.' *Independent.* http://www.independent.co.uk/news/world/europe/burkini-ban-norway-france-progress-party-right-wing-islam-swimwear-muslims-a7211271.html (accessed on January 2018).

Furlong, P. 2011. 'Riding the Tiger: Crisis and Political Strategy in the Thought of Julius Evola.' *The Italianist* 31 (1): 25–40.

Fuss, D. 1989. *Essentially Speaking: Feminism, Nature and Difference.* London: Routledge.

Gavison, R. 1992. 'Feminism and the public/private distinction.' *Stanford Law Review* 45: 1.

Gee, O. 2015. 'Sweden's Islamophobia is getting stronger.' *The Local.* https://www.thelocal.se/20150102/swedens-islamophobia-is-getting-stronger. (accessed on January 2018).

Geller, P. 2012. *Stop Islamization of America.*(https://www.youtube.com/watch?v=Co05gJM-AD4 (accessed on January 2018).

Gellner, E. 1983. *Nations and Nationalism* Ithaca: Cornell University Press.

Gellner, E. 2008. *Nations and Nationalism.* Ithaca, NY: Cornell University Press.

Ghender, F. 2016. 'Multiculturalism and the European Cultural Diversity.' *Journal of Humanistic and Social Studies* VII (1) 157–168.

Ghurye, G. S. 1969. *Caste and Race in India*. Popular Prakashan.

Gilman, S. 1985. *Difference and Pathology: Stereotypes of Sexuality, Race, and Madness*. Ithaca, NY: Cornell University Press.

Ging, D. 2019. 'Alphas, Betas, and Incels: Theorizing the Masculinities of the Manosphere.' *Men and Masculinities* 22 (4): 638–657.

Glass, A. 2017. 'Bush Announces Launch of Operation Iraqi Freedom, March 19, 2003.' *Politico*. https://www.politico.com/story/2017/03/bush-announces-launch-of-operation-iraqi-freedom-march-19-2003-236134 (accessed on 14 August 2019).

Gökariksel, B., and A. J. Secor. 2010. 'Islamic-ness in the Life of a Commodity: Veiling-fashion in Turkey' *Transactions of the Institute of British Geographers* 35 (New Series): 313–333.

Golshan, T. 2019a. 'Bernie Sanders's free college proposal just got a whole lot bigger.' https://www.vox.com/policy-and-politics/2019/6/23/18714615/bernie-sanders-free-college-for-all-2020-student-loan-debt. (accessed on August 2019).

Golshan, T. 2019b. 'Bernie Sanders's definition of democratic socialism, explained.' https://www.vox.com/policy-and-politics/2019/6/12/18661708/bernie-sanders-definition-democratic-socialism-explained (accessed on August 2019).

Gomez, M. A. 2005. *Black Crescent: The Experience and Legacy of African Muslims in the Americas*. Cambridge: Cambridge University Press.

Gramsci, A. 1992. *Prison Notebooks* (Vol. 2). New York, NY: Columbia University Press.

Grant, M. 1918. *The Passing of the Great Race or the Racial Basis of European History*. New York, NY: Charles Scribner's Sons.

Gregory, D. 2003. 'Defiled Cities.' *Singapore Journal of Tropical Geography* 24 (3): 307–326.

Gregory, D. 2004. 'Palestine and the "War on Terror".' *Comparative Studies of South Asia, Asia, Africa and the Middle East* 24 (1): 183–195.

Guest, S. 2019. '2020 Dems Embrace Abortion Up Until the Moment of Birth.' GOP.com https://www.gop.com/topic/family-values-pro-life/canonical/ (accessed on September 2019).

Hakl, H. T. 2012. 'Julius Evola and the Ur Group.' *Aries* 12 (1):53–90.

Hall, A. 2017. 'The Proud Boys: Drinking Club or Misogynist Movement?' https://www.ttbook.org/interview/proud-boys-drinking-club-or-misogynist-movement (accessed on October 2019).

Handlin, Oscar. 1970. *Introduction to Reports of the Immigration Commission, Volume 1.* New York: Arno and the New York Times.

Hansen, M. L. 1927. The History of American Immigration as a Field for Research. *The American Historical Review* 32 (3):500–518.

Harding, S. 2006. *Science and Social Inequality: Feminist and Postcolonial Issues.* Champaign, IL: University of Illinois Press.

Harding, S. 2009. 'Gaia Theory & Deep Ecology.' *Publicado el* 2 (07): 2009.

Harvey, D. 1978. 'The Urban Process under Capitalism: A Framework for Analysis.' *International Journal of Urban and Regional Research* 2 (1–3): 101–131.

Harvey, D. 2007a. *A Brief History of Neoliberalism.* Oxford, MS: Oxford University Press.

Harvey, D. 2007b. 'Neoliberalism as Creative Destruction.' *The Annals of the American Academy of Political and Social Science* 610 (1): 21–44.

Harvey, D. 2014. *Seventeen Contradictions and the End of Capitalism.* Oxford, MS: Oxford University Press.

Harvey, D. 1989. *The Condition of Postmodernity* (Vol. 14). Oxford: Blackwell.

Hayek, F. A. 2014. *The Road to Serfdom: Text and Documents: The Definitive Edition.* Abingdon: Routledge.

Hazelrigg, N. 2019. 'Sanders vs. Warren on College Debt Relief.' https://www.insidehighered.com/news/2019/06/25/sanders-outflanks-warren-proposal-universal-student-loan-debt-relief (accessed on 19 August 2019).

Heidegger, M. 2003. *The End of Philosophy.* Chicago, IL: University of Chicago Press.

Heidegger, M., J. Macquarrie, and E. Robinson. 1962. *Being and Time.* New York, NY: Harper,

Held, V. 1990. *Mothering Versus Contract.* In *Beyond Self-interest,* edited by J. J. Mansbridge, 287–304. Chicago, IL: University of Chicago Press.

Herald Report. 2018. *Feminism Creates Weak Women—Milo Yiannopoulos.* Herland Report TV. https://www.youtube.com/watch?v=OLusoKVttZE (accessed on September 2019).

Hobbes, T. 1980. *Leviathan (1651). Glasgow 1974.* Oxford: Clarendon Press.

Hobbes, T. 1990. *Behemoth or the Long Parliament.* Chicago, IL: University of Chicago Press.

Hobbes, T. 2013. *Elements of Law, Natural and Political*. Abingdon: Routledge.

Hobsbawm, E. 2008. *On Empire: America, War, and Global Supremacy*. New York, NY: Pantheon.

Hobsbawm, E. J. 2012. *Nations and Nationalism since 1780: Programme, Myth, Reality*. Cambridge: Cambridge University Press.

Hobsbawm, H. 1990. *Nations and Nationalism since 1780*. Cambridge: Cambridge University Press, 1990.

Hooks, B. 1992. *Representing Whiteness in the Black Imagination*, 338–346. New York: Routledge.

Horowitz, J. 2017. 'Steve Bannon Cited Italian Thinker Who Inspired Fascists'. *The New York Times*. https://www.nytimes.com/2017/02/10/world/europe/bannon-vatican-julius-evola-fascism.html (accessed on October 2019).

Horsti, K. 2017. 'Digital Islamophobia: The Swedish Woman as a Figure of Pure and Dangerous Whiteness.' *New Media & Society* 19 (9): 1440–1457.

Hughes, A. and A. Witz. 1997. 'Feminism and the Matter of Bodies: From de Beauvoir to Butler.' *Body & Society* 3 (1): 47–60.

Huntington, S. P. 2000. The Clash of Civilizations? In *Culture and Politics,* edited by L. Crothers, and C. Lockhart, pp. 99–118). New York, NY: Palgrave Macmillan.

Huntington, S. P. 2004. *Who Are We? The Challenges to America's National Identity*. New York, NY: Simon and Schuster.

Ibrahim, R. 2017. 'Oh You Cross-Worshippers, We'll Kill You All—Muslim Persecution of Christians.' https://www.gatestoneinstitute.org/11731/muslim-persecution-of-christians-august (accessed on January 2018).

Illing, S. 2018. 'The Alt-right Is Drunk on Bad Readings of Nietzsche. The Nazis were too.' *Vox*. https://www.vox.com/2017/8/17/16140846/alt-right-nietzsche-richard-spencer-nazism (accessed on October 2019).

Jessee Lee Peterson Show (JLP Show). 2018, July. *Wife with a Purpose on White History Month & Anti-White Hate*. https://www.youtube.com/watch?v=RinV22IIi0Y&list=PL4pSLcFFUtuteXTBg93w-8mTJG4mj_QAT&index=5&t=0s (accessed on January 2020).

Jessop, B. 1991. State Theory: Putting the Capitalist State in Its Place. University Park, PA: Pennsylvania State University Press.

Johnson, G. 2017. 'White Nationalism is Inevitable.' *Crosscurrent Publication*. https://www.counter-currents.com/2017/05/white-nationalism-is-inevitable/? (accessed on April 2020).

Kallis, A. 2015. 'Islamophobia in Europe: The Radical Right and the Mainstream.' *Insight Turkey* 17 (4): 27–37.

Kamat, S., and B. Matthew. 2003. Mapping Political Violence in a Globalized World: The Case of Hindo Nationalism. *Social Justice* 39 (3).

Kaplan Sommer, A. 2017. 'White Nationalist Richard Spencer Gives Israel as Example of Ethno-state He Wants in U.S. Heretz.' https://www.haaretz.com/us-news/richard-spencer-gives-israel-as-example-of-ethno-state-he-wants-in-u-s-1.5459154 (accessed on October 2019).

Kern, S. 2017. 'France Has a Problem with Islam'https://www.gatestoneinstitute.org/9791/france-islamization (accessed on January 2018).

Kobayashi, A., and L. Peake. 1994. 'Unnatural Discourse: 'Race' and Gender in Geography.' *Gender Place and Culture* 1: 225–243.

Kumar, A. 2020. 'Trump's Immigration Pause Falls Well Short of Full Ban.' *Politico*. https://www.politico.com/news/2020/04/21/trump-immigration-green-card-coronavirus-198498 (accessed on April 2020).

Kunzig, R. 2016. 'The New Europeans.' https://www.nationalgeographic.com/magazine/2016/10/europe-immigration-muslim-refugees-portraits/ (accessed on January 2018).

Lokteff, L. 2017. *Go Back to Europe.* Red Ice Radio. https://redice.tv/news/red-ice-videos-banned-from-youtube (accessed on April 2020).

Lokteff, L. 2019. How the Left is Betraying Women—Identitarian Ideas IX Rising from the Ruins. https://www.youtube.com/watch?v=S4fOABAeD14 (accessed on January 2020).

Lombroso, D., and Appelbaum. Y. 2016. 'Hail Trump!': White Nationalists Salute the President-Elect'. *The Atlantic*. Available at: https://www.theatlantic.com/politics/archive/2016/11/richard-spencer-speech-npi/508379/ (accessed on January 2021).

MacLean, N. 2002. 'Postwar Women's History: The 'Second Wave' or the End of the Family Wage?' In *A Companion to Post-1945 America, edited by* J. Agnew, and R. Rosensweig, pp. 235–259. Bognor Regis: Wiley.

Macpherson, C. B. 1962. *The Political Theory of Possessive Individualism: Hobbes to Locke.* Oxford: Clarendon Press.

Malaea, M. 2017, 7 November. 'President Donald Trump attacks "LGBTQ people for 'who they are'," says Human rights campaign head.' *Newsweek*. https://www.newsweek.com/president-donald-trump-attacks-lgbtq-people-who-they-are-says-human-rights-campaign-head-1470538 (accessed on March 2020).

Mamdani, M. 2004. *Good Muslim, Bad Muslim*. New York, NY: Double Day.

Mansbridge, J. J, ed. 1990. 'The Rise and Fall of Self-interest in the Explanation of Political Life.' In *Beyond Self-interest*, pp. 3–24. Chicago, IL: University of Chicago Press.

Marx, K. 1963 (1847). *The Poverty of Philosophy*. New York, NY: International Publishers.

Marx K. 1976 (1867). *Capital Volume 1*. London: Penguin.

Marx, K., and F. Engels. 2002. *The Communist Manifesto*. London: Penguin.

Marx, K. 1844. 'Economic and Philosophical Manuscripts.' *Early writings*. Translated by Rodney Livingstone and Gregor Benton, p. 333. London: Penguin Classics.

Marx, K. 2005. *Grundrisse: Foundations of the Critique of Political Economy*. London: Penguin.

Mattheis, A. 2018/2019. 'Shieldmaidens of Whiteness: (Alt) Maternalism and Women Recruiting for the Far/Alt-Right.' *Journal for Deradicalization* (17): 128–162.

May, R., and M. Feldman. 2019. 'Understanding the Alt-Right: Ideologues, 'Lulz' and Hiding in Plain Sight.' In *Post-Digital Cultures of the Far Right*, edited by Maik Fielitz, and Nick Thurston, pp.25–36. New Rockford, ND: Transcript.

Maza, C. 2017. 'Muslims are the Opposite of Human: Swedish Democrat Says.' *Newsweek*. http://www.newsweek.com/muslims-sweden-martin-strid-muslims-not-human-politician-islam-722921 (accessed on January 2018).

McCarthy, A., H. E. Soyster, and R. J. Woolsey. 2010. *Sharia: The threat to America—Report of team 'B' II*. Center for Policy Security.

McCulloh, R. 2019a, 29 June. 'From Diversity to the "Browning" of the White World: The White Replacement and Destruction Movement Becomes More Explicit.' *Occidental Observer*.

McCulloh, R. 2019b, September 2019. 'Human Pre-History and the Making of the Races, Part 1.' *Occidental Observer*.

McCulloh, R. 2019c, September 2019. 'Human Pre-History and the Making of the Races, Part 2: Genetic Distances.' *Occidental Observer*.

McDowell, L. 2003. *Redundant Masculinities? Employment Change and White Working Class Youth*. Malden, MA: Blackwell.

Middle East Monitor. 2018. 'White Nationalist Richard Spencer Lauds Israel's New Nation-State Law.' https://www.mintpress-news.com/richard-spencer-lauds-israels-national-states-bill-example/246266/ (accessed on October 2019).

Mies, M. 2007. Patriarchy and Accumulation on a World Scale Revisited. (Keynote lecture at the Green Economics Institute, Reading, 29 October 2005). *International Journal of Green Economics* 1 (3–4): 268–275.

Mill, J. S. 1966. 'On Liberty.' In *A Selection of His Works,* edited by J. M. Robson. London: Palgrave.

Mill, J. S. 2010. *The Basic Writings of John Stuart Mill: On Liberty, the Subjection of Women and Utilitarianism.* New York, NY: Modern Library.

Minds.com. 'German Government Now Promoting Islam.' https://www.minds.com/Bombislamdotcom (accessed on January 2018).

Mohdin, A. 2018. 'The Alt-right Are Targeting Disgruntled White Male Lefties to Join Their Movement.' *Quartz.* https://qz.com/1176355/how-richard-spencer-and-the-alt-right-are-adopting-left-wing-language-to-recruit-leftie-men/ (accessed on May 2020).

Molyneux, S. 2019a. *Race, IQ, Income with Stefan Molyneux.* https://www.youtube.com/watch?v=IvvQlhcQ7o0 (accessed on March 2020).

Molyneux, S. 2019b. 'Stefan Molyneux on Orlando Terror: Islam Is Antithetical to Western Civilization. https://www.realclear-politics.com/video/2016/06/15/stefan_molyneux_on_orlando_terror_attacks.html (accessed on March 2020).

Morgan, S. L., and J. Lee. 2018. 'Trump voters and the White working class.' *Sociological Science* 5:234–245.

Morison, T. 1908. *Can Islam be Reformed.* Nineteenth Century, October.

Mouffe, C, ed. 1992. *Dimensions of Radical Democracy: Pluralism, Citizenship, Community.* Brooklyn, NY: Verso.

Mouffe, C. 2013. 'Feminism, Citizenship, and Radical Democratic Politics.' In *Feminists Theorize the Political*, edited by Judith Butler, and Joan W. Scott pp. 387–402). Abingdon: Routledge.

Nance, J. M. 2011. *After San Jacinto: The Texas-Mexican Frontier, 1836-1841.* Austin, TX: University of Texas Press.

Nietzsche, F. W. 1920. *The Antichrist* (Vol. 3). New York, NY: AA Knopf.

Nietzsche, F., 1994. *'Nietzsche On the Genealogy of Morality' and Other Writings*. Cambridge: Cambridge University Press.

Nietzsche, F.W. 2018. *Beyond Good and Evil* (p. 179). New York, NY: Boni & Liveright, Incorporated.

Ohlheiser, A. 2016, 21 July. 'Just How Offensive Did Milo Yiannopoulos Have to Be to Get Banned from Twitter?' *Washington Post*. https://www.washingtonpost.com/news/the-intersect/wp/2016/07/21/what-it-takes-to-get-banned-from-twitter/ (accessed on November 2019).

Ong, A. 2000. 'Gender and Labor Politics of Postmodernity.' In *Globalization and the Challenges of a New Century*, edited by P. O' Meara, H. D. Mehlinger and M. Krain, pp. 253–281). Bloomington, IN: Indiana University Press.

Oza, R. 2006. *The Making of Neoliberal India: Nationalism, Gender, and the Paradoxes of Globalization*. New York, NY: Routledge.

Palgrave, W. G. 1872. *Essays on the Eastern Question*. London: Macmillan.

Parekh, B. 2016. *Bentham's Political Thought*. Abingdon: Routledge.

Parisi, P. 2018. 'The "Dreamers" Have No Right to Demand Anything.' https://www.dailysignal.com/2018/01/03/why-dreamers-have-no-right-to-demand-anything/ (accessed on April 2020).

Parkins, W. (2000) 'Protesting Like a Girl: Embodiment, Dissent, and Feminist Agency.' *Feminist Theory* 1 (1): 59–78.

Pearson, C., E. Gray, and A. Vagianos. 2019. 'A Running List of The Women Who've Accused Donald Trump of Sexual Misconduct.' *Huffington Post*. https://www.huffpost.com/entry/a-running-list-of-the-women-whove-accused-donald-trump-of-sexual-misconduct_n_57ffae1fe4b0162c043a7212 (accessed on March 2020).

Peet, R. 2007. 'Deconstructing Free Trade: From Epistemic Communities to Ideological Communities in Struggle.' *Transactions of the Institute of British Geographers* 32 (4): 576–580.

Peet, R. 2009. *Unholy Trinity: The IMF, World Bank and WTO*. Zed Books Ltd.

Plaut, V. C., K. M. Thomas, and M. J. Goren. 2009. 'Is Multiculturalism or Colour Blindness Better for Minorities?', *Psychological Science* 20 (4): 444–446.

Pociask, S. 2018. 'What Makes Lionesses Better Hunters Than Lions?' https://www.forbes.com/sites/quora/2018/05/16/

what-makes-lionesses-better-hunters-than-lions/#5f2573674a6f (accessed on January 2020).

Poggioli, S. 2017. 'Steve Bannon Aligns with Vatican Hard-Liners Who Oppose Pope Francis. Politics and Policy.' *NPR*. https://www.npr.org/sections/parallels/2017/02/08/514102356/steve-bannon-aligns-with-vatican-hardliners-who-oppose-pope-francis (accessed on October 2019).

Pollard, J., and M. Samers. 2007. 'Islamic Banking and Finance: Postcolonial Political Economy and the Decentering of Economic Geography.' *Transactions of the Institute of British Geographers* 32 (3): 313–330.

Prashad, V. 2001. *Everybody Was Kung Fu Fighting*. Boston, MA: Beacon Press.

Pratt. 2004. *Working Feminism*. Philadelphia, PA: Temple University Press.

Puar, J. 2007. *Terrorist Assemblages: Homonationalism in Queer Times*. Durham, NC: Duke University Press.

Raheja, G. G. 1988. 'India: Caste, Kingship, and Dominance Reconsidered.' *Annual Review of Anthropology* 17 (1): 497–522.

Rana, J. 2007. 'The Story of Islamophobia.' *Souls* 9 (2): 148–161.

Rand, A. 1964. *The Virtue of Selfishness*. London: Penguin.

Rebel News 2015. *Lauren Southern: Slut Walk Revisited (Edmonton)*. https://www.youtube.com/watch?v=lKfdS38aBSk (accessed on January 2020).

Red Ice. 2017a. *Go Back to Europe*. https://redice.tv/news/red-ice-videos-banned-from-youtube (accessed on May 2020).

Red Ice, 2017b. *Diversity Is a Weapon Against White People*. https://redice.tv/news/red-ice-videos-banned-from-youtube (accessed on April 2020).

Reilly, K. 2016. 'Here Are All the Times Donald Trump Insulted Mexico.' https://time.com/4473972/donald-trump-mexico-meeting-insult/ (accessed on March 2020).

Rose, G. 1993. 'A Politics of Paradoxical Space.' In *Feminism and Geography: The Limits of Geographical Knowledge*, edited by G. Rose, pp. 137–160). Cambridge: Polity Press.

Rose, G. 2001. *Visual Methodologies: An Introduction to the Interpretation of Visual Materials*. London: SAGE Publications.

Rosen, Ellen Israel. 2002. *Making Sweatshops: The Globalization of the U. S. Apparel Industry*. Berkeley, CA: University of California Press.

Roth, B. 2015. *Darwinian Evolution revolutionized the natural sciences. The social sciences have been immune for too long*. Available at https://geopol.institute/2015/05/17/the-war-on-human-nature/ (accessed on November 2019)

Safa, H. I. 1981. 'Runaway Shops and Female Employment: The Search for Cheap Labor.' *Signs: Journal of Women in Culture and Society* 7 (2): 418–33.

Said, E. W. 1979. *Orientalism*. New York, NY: Vintage.

Secor, A. J., and B. Gökariksel. 2009. 'New Transnational Geographies of Islamism, Capitalism, and Subjectivity: The Veiling Fashion Industry in Turkey.' *Area* 41: 6–18.

Sedgwick, M, ed. 2019. *Key Thinkers of the Radical Right: Behind the New Threat to Liberal Democracy*. Oxford, MS: Oxford University Press.

Sen, A. K. 1990. 'Rational Fools: A Critique of the Behavioral Foundations of Economic Theory.' In *Beyond Self-interest*, edited by J. J. Mansbridge, pp. 25–43. Chicago, IL: University of Chicago Press.

Sharp, J. 1996. 'Gendering Nationhood: A Feminist Engagement with National Identity.' In *Body Space: Destabilizing Geographies of Gender and Sexuality*, edited by N. Duncan, pp. 91–108. New York, NY: Routledge.

Shaw, D. O. 2018. 'The New Language of Hate: Misogyny and the Alt-Right.' In *Identities in Flux Globalisation, Trauma, and Reconciliation*, edited by Dagmar Kusá, pp.186–198. Bratislava: Kritika & Kontext.

Shiva, V., and M. Mies. 2014. *Ecofeminism*. Zed Books Ltd.

Sidanius, J., Y. Peña, and M. Sawyer. 2001. 'Inclusionary Discrimination: Pigmentocracy and Patriotism in the Dominican Republic.' *Political Psychology* 22 (4): 827–851.

Siegel, S. 2010. *A Political History of the Texas Republic, 1836-1845*. Austin, TX: University of Texas Press.

Smith, A. 1999. 'Three Short Essays on the Division of Labour.' *Policy* (Summer): 62–64.

Smith, A. 2010. *The Wealth of Nations: An Inquiry into the Nature and Causes of the Wealth of Nations*. Hampshire: Harriman House Limited.

Smith, N. 2004. *American Empire: Roosevelt's Geographer and the Prelude to Globalization* (Vol. 9). Berkeley, CA: University of California Press.

Smith, N. 2005. *The Endgame of Globalization*. Abingdon: Routledge.

Southern Poverty Law Center (SPCL). 2019a. 'Fighting Hate.' https://www.splcenter.org/fighting-hate (accessed on June 2019).

Southern Poverty Law Center. 2019b. Mike Cernovich. http://www. splcenter.org/fighting-hate/extremist-files/individual/mike-cernovich (accessed on October 2019).

Spencer, R. 2015a. *Sam's Club and Structural Racism.* https://www. youtube.com/watch?v=oYogiaVskmA (accessed on October 2019).

Spencer, R. 2015b. 'What Is the Alt Right?' Radix Journal. https:// www.youtube.com/watch?v=G74sCg_n9rY (accessed on September 2019).

Spencer, R. 2016. *'Hail Trump!': Richard Spencer Speech Excerpts.* https://www.youtube.com/watch?v=1o6-bi3jlxk (accessed on October 2019).

Spencer, R. 2017. *The Ethno-State with Richard Spencer.*https://www. stitcher.com/podcast/wwwstitchercompodcastdangerous-ideas-2/dangerous-ideas/e/52413822 (accessed on April 2020).

Spencer, R. 2018. 'The Truth About Mohammad.' http://afdi.us/ the-truth-about-muhammad/ (accessed on 23 July 2018).

Spickard, P. 2009. *Almost All Aliens: Immigration, Race, and Colonialism in American History and Identity.* Abingdon: Routledge.

Spivak, G. C. 1999. *A Critique of Postcolonial Reason: Toward a History of the Vanishing Present.* Cambridge, MA: Harvard University Press.

Standing, G. 1989. 'Global Feminization through Flexible Labor.' *World development* 17 (7): 1077–1095.

Steinberg, S. 1992. 'Critical Multiculturalism and Democratic Schooling: An Interview with Peter McLaren and Joe Kincheloe.' *International Journal of Educational Reform* 1 (4, October).

Steinmetz-Jenkins, D. 2017. 'The European Intellectual Origins of the Alt-Right.' *İstanbul Üniversitesi Sosyoloji Dergisi* 38 (2): 255–266.

Stern, A. M. 2019. Salon. 'Alt-right Women and the "White Baby Challenge"' https://www.salon.com/2019/07/14/alt-right-handmaidens-and-the-White-baby-challenge/ (accessed on November 2019).

Stewart, A. 2015. *Explains: Welcome Refugees?? I Blame Feminism, This Is Why.* https://www.youtube.com/watch?v=bTp1Pq6koQs (accessed on January 2020).

Stocker, K. 2012. 'Towards an Embodiment-Disembodiment Taxonomy.' Cognitive Processing 13 (Supplement 1): 347–350.

Stoddard, L. 1923. *The Rising Tide of Color Against White World-supremacy.* New York, NY: Blue Ribbon Books.

Stuart, J., and C. Ward. 2019. 'Exploring Everyday Experiences of Cultural Diversity: The Construction, Validation, and Application of the Normative Multiculturalism Scale.' *European Journal of Social Psychology* 49 (2): 313–332.

Studio 10. 2017. *Milo Yiannopoulos Talks Free Speech, Feminism, Fake News & Australian Tour.* https://www.youtube.com/watch?v=1Ef7Us0zw8Q (accessed on September 2019).

Taylor, R. 2019. 'Why Are White Men Carrying Out More Mass Shootings?' https://news.sky.com/story/why-are-White-men-more-likely-to-carry-out-mass-shootings-11252808 (accessed on March 2020).

Telles, E. 2014. *Pigmentocracies: Ethnicity, Race, and Color in Latin America.* Chapel Hill, NC: UNC Press Books.

Temple, B. 1910. 'The Place of Persia in World-Politics'. *Proceedings of the Central Asian Society.*

The Guardian. 2017a. 'Heather Heyer, Victim of Charlottesville Car Attack, Was Civil Rights Activist.' https://www.theguardian.com/us-news/2017/aug/13/woman-killed-at-White-supremacist-rally-in-charlottesville-named (accessed on October 2019).

The Guardian. 2017b. 'Gary Younge Interviews Richard Spencer: 'Africans Have Benefited from White Supremacy'. https://www.youtube.com/watch?v=puJ-arJgkZU (accessed on September 2019).

Thompson, E. P. (1978). 'Eighteenth-century English Society: Class Struggle Without Class?' *Social History* 3 (2): 133–65.

Tierney, D. 2017, January. 'What Does it Mean That Trump Is "Leader of the Free World?"' *The Atlantic.* https://www.theatlantic.com/international/archive/2017/01/trump-free-world-leader/514232/ (accessed on 14 August 2019).

Tribute to Youth for Western Civilization. 2009. https://www.youtube.com/watch?v=fpPRdssUETY (accessed on January 2018).

Trump, D. 2018. 'Trump Wants Fewer Immigrants from "Shithole Countries" and More from Places Like Norway.' https://www.vox.com/2018/1/11/16880750/trump-immigrants-shithole-countries-norway (accessed on April 2020).

Tulle, E. 2007. 'Running to Run: Embodiment, Structure and Agency among Veteran Elite Runners.' *Sociology* 41 (2): 329–346.

Walley, C. J. 2017. 'Trump's Election and the "White Working Class": What We Missed.' *American Ethnologist* 44 (2): 231–236.

Ward, K. B, ed. 1990. *Women Workers and Global Restructuring* (No. 17). Ithaca, NY: Cornell University Press.

Weber, M. 2013. *The Protestant Ethic and the Spirit of Capitalism*. Abingdon: Routledge.

Wife with a Purpose. 2019. http://wifewithapurpose.com (accessed on January 2020).

Williams, T. C. 2017, December. 'The French Origins of "You Will Not Replace Us."' *The New Yorker*.

Winant, H. 2001. *The World Is a Ghetto: Race and Democracy since World War II*. New York, NY: Basic Books.

Wolff, E. C. 2016. 'Evola's Interpretation of Fascism and Moral Responsibility.' *Patterns of Prejudice* 50 (4–5): 478–494.

Wright, E.O. 1982. 'The Status of the Political in the Concept of Class Structure'. *Politics & Society* 11 (3):321–341.

Yee, V. 2018, 13 January. 'In Trump's Immigration Remarks, Echoes of a Century-Old Racial Ranking.' *New York Times*. https://www.nytimes.com/2018/01/13/us/trump-immigration-history.html (accessed on January 2018).

Yiannopoulos, M. 2017. Milo Yiannopoulos Talks Free Speech, Feminism, Fake News & Australian Tour' *Studio 10*. https://www.youtube.com/watch?v=1Ef7Us0zw8Q (accessed on January 2020).

Yiannopoulos, M. 2018. *Milo Yiannopoulos More Savage Moments!!!* https://www.youtube.com/watch?v=eDOq4Vjtafg (accessed on October 2019).

Young, I. M. 2000. *Inclusion and Democracy*. New York, NY: Oxford University Press.

Zadrozny, B., and C. Siemaszko. 2018. 'The Boys and Girls of White Nationalism: "Proud" Groups Labeled "Extremist" in Newly Revealed FBI Files.' https://www.nbcnews.com/news/us-news/boy-girls-white-nationalism-proud-groups-labeled-extremist-newly-revealed-n938546 (accessed on January 2020).

About the Author

Ipsita Chatterjee is an Associate Professor in the Department of Geography and the Environment, University of North Texas. She completed her PhD in geography at Clark University, Massachusetts, and was an assistant professor at Pennsylvania State University. She was also Assistant Professor at the University of Texas, Austin. Chatterjee focuses on globalization, urban change, class, identity, labour, Marxism and feminism. Ipsita's first book titled: *Displacement, Revolution, and the New Urban Condition* was published by SAGE. It deals with globalization in an Indian city—its gentrification and associated displacement of urban poor, particularly, the Muslim poor. Her second book titled *Spectacular Cities: Religion, Landscape and the Dialectics of Globalization* deals with the disneyization of urban landscapes. In this book, she explores migrant temple landscapes in Dallas and Atlanta in the USA, and their counterparts in India to reveal how landscapes are narratives that ground globalization, citizenship, patriotism, gender, and sexism. Ipsita has also authored numerous articles in academic journals such as *Urban Studies, Transactions of the Institute of British Geographers, Geoforum* and *Gender, Place and Culture* among others.

Index

ideology of individual freedom, 30
immigrant, 119–23, 142–52, 160–64, 172–77, 179–86, 190, 202–04
immoral racial subordination, 156
impediments and friction, 25
individual freedom, 52
individualism, 38–41
Individual self-interest, 36–38, 47–48, 54–57
individualism to liberalism, 33–38
individualist ethic, 47
individual liberalism, 5, 148–52
individual self-love, 41–46
inequality, 122
Islamic colonization, 136
Islamic terrorism, 66
Islamization of Europe critiques, 143
Islamophobia, 128, 148–52
    Alt-right, 201–02
    anti-immigration, 142–48
    orientalism, 133–38
    racism, 138–42

Jews to Christianity, 140
Judea-Christian-Anglo, 82
Judea-Christian civilization, 75

kebaabification of backyard barbecues, 185

lattice of identity, 58
LGBTQ movements, 126
liberal capitalist, 26, 184
liberal feminism, 116, 120
liberal ideas
    freedom and happiness, 171
liberal individualism, 91, 120
    Alt-Right, 193–95

liberalism, 36, 115
liberal morality, central thesis, 4
liberal multiculturalism, 93–94
liberal philosophical, 96
liberal society, 192
liberal theorists, 34
Lokteff, L., 99, 182
    criticized, perversion of gender roles, 100
    diversity, 183
    liberal multiculturalism's endorsement, 184

Madonna of individualism, 125
MGTOW (Men Going Their Own Way), 110
Manifesto for a European Renaissance, 73
manly man, 105
manosphere, 116
marginalization, 98
Marx, 25–30, 33–41, 51–57, 182–86, 188–90
Marxist theory, 26
    individual freedom, 35
melting pot
    multiculturalist's zeal, 174
Mexicanization of White middle-class, 185
minorities, 52
Molyneux, S.
    argument, 132
    philosophy, 129
moral cannibalism. *See* altruism
multiculturalism, 5, 48, 55, 91–95, 114–15, 122–27, 174, 178, 197–204
    critics, 55
Muslim hate groups in Europe, 4
Muslim race, 138
Muslims, 66
Muslims in turbans and beard, 53

neoclassical economic theory, 32
neo-masculinist, 122–23,
     198–201
neo-masculinist movements
     critique, 124
new barbarity, 74
Nietzsche, H.
     characterization of women, 78
Norway's Progress Party's, 143
nouvelle droite (ND—New Right),
     73
nurturing of hatred, 4

objectivist ethics, 27
Occidental Observer, 84
onslaught of diversity, 53
oppressor, 177
orientalism, 133
     antiquated degenerate
          religion, 138
     articles quote, 137
     culture talk, 134
     imperial vagueness, 134
     racist interpretation, 135
ownership, 24
     private property, 25
ownership version of liberal
     democracy, 26

Pan-European Islamophobic
     coalitions, 144
Pat Buchanan's speech, 53
patriarchal gaze, 96–99
Patriotic Europeans Against
     the Islamisation of the West
     (PEGIDA), 143
Persian empire, 138
phallocentricity, 100
philosophical–conceptual
     dimensions, 4
philosophy and praxis, 67
pigmentocracy, 170
pleasure and freedom, 24

political sphere, 102
possessive individualism, 27, 76
post-structural feminists, 40
preachers, 53
private property, 57–60
promotion of equal opportunity,
     40
Protestant ethic, 47
public transport, 24

race, 3
racial/sexual selection, 103
racism, 98
     development, 139
     Mughals, 138
     Muslims, 140
     Western civilization, 140
     Whiteness, 142
Rand, Ayn, 27–33
Rand proclaims, 27
rational self-interest, 30
rational selfishness, 27–29
reactionary identity, 59
red pill, 75
Ricardo's theory, 31
Rising Tide of Color, against
     White World-supremacy
     (1920) claims, 84

sacrifice, 30
self-interest, 24
selfishness, 28
settler, 82–87, 146–48, 156–59,
     172–76, 187–88
sexual revolution, 63
socialist feminists, 40
society, 38–41
species being, 26, 29–30
Spencer, R.
     conference, 79
     migration-mixing issue,
          adoption towards, 161
spiritual payments, 27

Stewart, A.
blames on feminism, 106
subscribers on YouTube, 103
Stop Islamization of America
(SIOA), 137
student, 24
systemic analysis, 122

tax-cutting policy, 51
theory of life, 24
Third World communities, 159
Thompson, E. P.
class formation, 167, 169
Marxist analysis, 168
undialectical approach, 167
traditional family values,
restoration and preservation,
104
trad wives, 107, 117, 119, 125
Trump-era politics, 3

ugly feminist, 102
unacceptable identitarian
movements, 124
unfreedom, 25
upper-class immigrants, 164
utilitarianism, 34

View from the Right (1977), 74
virile men, 103
Voice of Citizens Together
(VCT), 179

Western civilization, 52, 140
Western villainy, 138
White American youth, 191
White babies, 104
White Christian Protestant, 83
White *Dasien*, reclamation, 81
White dispossession, 65
White Euro-American culture,
172
White genocide, 3
white nationalism, 158
immigration/emigration
policy, 158
White supremacy, 152–60, 166,
174–76, 182
Whiteness, 88
White replacement and
destruction movement
(WRDM), 65
women, 198–201
women of Alt-right, 99

Yiannopoulos, M.
feminism criticisim, 111–12
Young European Alliance for
Hope, 144
Youth for Western Civilization
(YWC), 52, 81, 140
You Tube interviews
JLP Show, 104
YouTube interviews
Alt-right conferences, 117